APARTHEID, THOUGHT CRIME AND SOUTH AFRICA'S NEW LEFT

APARTHEID, THOUGHT CRIME AND SOUTH AFRICA'S NEW LEFT

THE POLITICS OF INTELLECTUAL REPRESSION

Allison Drew

JAMES CURREY

First published 2026
James Currey

ISBN 978 1 84701 484 9

James Currey
is an imprint of
Boydell & Brewer Ltd
www.jamescurrey.com
and of
Boydell & Brewer Inc.
www.boydellandbrewer.com

Our Authorised Representative for product safety in the EU is Easy Access System Europe – Mustamäe tee 50, 10621 Tallinn, Estonia, *gpsr.requests@easproject.com*

British Library Cataloguing in Publication Data
A CIP record for this book is available from the British Library

Please note that some of the illustrations in this book have been taken from old newspapers and may include elements that are difficult to discern

'I think, therefore, I am.'
René Descartes, 1637

'the essential crime that contained all others in itself. Thoughtcrime, they called it.'
George Orwell, 1949

CONTENTS

ILLUSTRATIONS

Full credit details are provided in the captions to the images in the text. The author and publisher are grateful to all the institutions and individuals for permission to reproduce the materials in which they hold copyright. Every effort has been made to trace the copyright holders; apologies are offered for any omission, and the publisher will be pleased to add any necessary acknowledgement in subsequent editions.

PREFACE AND ACKNOWLEDGEMENTS

My initial motivation for writing this book was a simple one. I knew and still know some of the people who were in the National Liberation Front, and I have always found it peculiar that the group has been absent in South African historiography when so much has been written about other small political groups. Why spill ink on such a tiny group? In addition to friendship, I have several broader reasons.

First, I seek to highlight the apartheid regime's use of intellectual repression to maintain its power. Unlike most accounts of apartheid, which focus on the economic exploitation and political and physical restrictions of the black majority, I emphasize the regime's intellectual repression of black people, as seen in Bantu Education and university apartheid.[1] Black individuals and organizations were faced with the challenge of overcoming these impediments through self-education. This is crucial to understanding the fate of the National Liberation Front, which was fundamentally intellectual. On the one hand, its experience shows the perennial problem of engaged intellectuals hoping to combine with and influence the direction of political movements. On the other, its trial shows the regime's efforts to make thought a crime and raises important questions about thought crime and conspiracy, issues of continuing and burning salience today: I am all too conscious of the escalating attempts to make thought a crime in my own country.

Secondly, I wish to show that the National Liberation Front was part of an emerging South African New Left, a process cut off by the arrests, imprisonment and massive repression of the early 1960s. South Africa's anti-capitalist socialist movement has existed since the very start of the twentieth century and has always been part of an evolving international socialist movement. The country's first socialist organizations came from Britain, the United States and Eastern Europe, making the local movement particularly porous to international influences. We would expect to find a South African New Left precisely because the country's diverse socialist traditions were enmeshed in the global socialist movement. That this ephemeral New Left was difficult to discern is a problem that needs investigation.

1 The term 'black' refers to all people of colour in South Africa who were subjected to racial oppression. The terms 'African,' 'Coloured' and 'Indian' refer broadly to categories imposed by the South African state.

'Numbers count in history,' notes E. H. Carr in *What is History?*[2] It is crucial to analyse political victors. Years ago, at the 1994 Wits History Workshop in Johannesburg, I was struck by the conference's adulation of the victorious African National Congress (ANC) following the first democratic elections. Euphoria after such a long and valiant struggle is understandable. But the liberation movement extended far beyond the ANC. Is electoral success the main criterion for choosing research topics? In the new South Africa, it has often seemed to be.

In his 1962 preface to *The Making of the English Working Class*, the British historian E. P. Thompson criticizes the approach that 'reads history in the light of subsequent preoccupations, and not as in fact it occurred.' He calls this the 'pilgrim's progress' orthodoxy in history-writing, when historians mine the past to find the forerunners of the present. 'Only the successful … are remembered,' he remarks.[3]

The problem of looking only at the successful is that it makes their success seem inevitable. Of course, successful organizations and movements may deliberately exclude other groups from the political landscape to reinforce their own seeming inevitability and maintain themselves in power. But academics too often skew their research agendas towards those in power to the neglect of others. All of this results in what Neville Alexander, discussing the liberation movement's censorship by omission, called 'white spots' in South African historiography.[4]

There may be much to learn from history's blind alleys, lost causes and losers, as Thompson terms them. Demonstrating the liberation movement's pluralism and diversity challenges the conventional wisdom that the more successful groups were uniquely privileged or succeeded because they were better.

What might we learn from the National Liberation Front? First, it illustrates that the New Left was not confined to Europe, Japan and the Americas but was indeed a global movement, albeit one that was uneven and very weak in Africa. It provides evidence that organizational structure can promote or hinder gender equality. It suggests the importance of political education that is linked to action and foreshadows the Black Consciousness movement's efforts to overturn the impact of inferior and racist education. Moreover, it shows that during the Cold War South African socialism was not limited to

2 E. H. Carr, *What is History?* 2nd ed., London: Penguin, 1987, 1990, p. 50.

3 E. P. Thompson, Preface from *The Making of the English Working Class*, August 1962, in Dorothy Thompson, ed., *The Essential E. P. Thompson*, New York: New Press, 2001, pp. 3–8, 6.

4 Neville Edward Alexander, 'Censorship as Intellectual Terrorism: White Spots in Black South African History, or The Worm Inside the Liberation Struggle,' Second C. Walter and Gerda B. Mortenson Distinguished Lecture, 7 October 1991, University of Illinois Library at Urbana-Champaign, 1991.

communiqués between the Soviets, their satellites and their supporters. Despite the notable bravery of South African communists, some socialists were critical of the South African Communist Party, at the time also a tiny and tenuous group whose ascendency was not inevitable. However, the South African Communist Party survived precisely because it aligned itself with a national liberation movement that included a trade union organization, and it had the support of a superpower. By contrast, the National Liberation Front shows the difficulties facing socialist intellectuals who are isolated from the very workers and peasants they hope to liberate, as well as the virtual impossibility of building a socialist organization from scratch in an authoritarian regime. Its fate raises the painful question – for socialists – of whether socialism can still become a movement rather than remain simply an ideology. Finally, its fate highlights that authoritarian regimes see intellectuals as threats to be silenced and repressed.

***

My thanks first to Mairi MacDonald for suggesting the concept of thought crime when I discussed the National Liberation Front trial with her some years ago. This book has benefited greatly from interviews conducted by the late August Matsemela of Cape Town, who had been a National Liberation Front member and was working on a master's thesis about it before his untimely death. Unfortunately, his draft thesis is missing, but his oral interviews with Kenneth Abrahams, Ottilie Abrahams, Fikile Bam and one unknown person are in the University of Cape Town's Centre for Popular Memory, although they are not attributed to him. His lengthy interview transcript of Neville Alexander is in the Neville Alexander Papers in the university's Manuscript and Archives Department. I also wish to acknowledge the late James Marsh for his early encouragement of this project. My heart-felt appreciation to Lionel Davis for permission to use his etching 'They toll for me' on the cover and my gratitude to Peter van Straten for the photograph. This is especially meaningful since Lionel Davis spent seven years on Robben Island for his National Liberation Front activities, as discussed in this book.

I am very grateful to the British Academy for funding my research trip to South Africa when I was investigating the National Liberation Front from a gendered perspective. I am also indebted to the Stellenbosch Institute for Advanced Study (STIAS) for offering me a fellowship that allowed me to work on the trial in a supportive and intellectually stimulating environment. The staff at STIAS were extremely welcoming and helpful, and the Fellows friendly and encouraging. My thanks and appreciation to the staff at the University of Cape Town Libraries' Manuscripts & Archives Department, the Western Cape Archives, the University of Stellenbosch Library, the National Archives of Namibia and the British Library at Boston Spa.

In addition to work presented at STIAS, I have presented sections of the manuscript at the University of Stellenbosch Department of Sociology and Social Anthropology, University of Cape Town Centre for African Studies, University of Malmo, University of Turin, University of Glasgow Socialist Theory and Movements Research Network and Leeds University Centre for African Studies. I received challenging and helpful comments on all these occasions.

I am very grateful to Kenneth Abrahams, Jr. for assistance in Windhoek, Steve Gordon for news clippings about the trial, Judge Robin Marais for trial documents and insights into the trial, Jan-Bart Gewald, David Howell, David Johnson, Chris Saunders and Shaun Whittaker for commenting on individual chapters, Bettina Drew for meticulous editing, Rachel Goodyear for the index and my colleagues at Writers Together in York for their receptiveness to non-fiction as well as fiction writing. I am especially grateful to Ron Kieve for reading the whole manuscript and asking analytical questions, and for his enduring friendship and moral support. Finally, my sincere thanks to Megan Milan, Commissioning Editor at Boydell & Brewer and to two anonymous readers. Any errors are, of course, my own.

ABBREVIATIONS

African Methodist Episcopal Church (AME)
African National Congress (ANC)
African People's Democratic Union of Southern Africa (APDUSA)
African Resistance Movement (ARM)
All-African Convention (AAC)
Cape African Teachers Association (CATA)
Cape Peninsula Students Union (CPSU)
Coloured Affairs Department (CAD)
Communist Party of South Africa (CPSA)
Federation of South African Women (FEDSAW)
Franchise Action Committee (FRAC)
Front de Libération Nationale (FLN)
International Defence and Aid Fund (IDAF)
Movement for a Democracy of Content (MDC)
National Committee for Liberation (NCL)
National Liberation Front (NLF)
National Party (NP)
National Union of South African Students (NUSAS)
New Era Fellowship (NEF)
Non-European Unity Movement (NEUM, Unity Movement)
Organisation of African Unity (OAU)
Ovamboland People's Congress (OPC)
Ovamboland People's Organisation (OPO)
Pan Africanist Congress (PAC)
Progressive Forum (PF)
Society of Young Africa (SOYA)
South Africa United Front (SAUF)
South African Communist Party (SACP)
South African Students Bursary & Loan Fund (SASBLF)

South West Africa People's Organisation (SWAPO)
South West Africa Student Body (SWASB)
South West Africa National Union (SWANU)
South West Africa Progressive Association (SWAPA)
Sozialdemokratische Partei Deutschlands, the German Social Democratic Party (SPD)
Sozialistische Deutsche Studentenbund, the Socialist German Students' Union (SDS)
Umkhonto we Sizwe (MK, Umkhonto)
United Nations (UN)
Universal Negro Improvement Association and African Communities League (UNIA)
University College of the Western Cape (UCWC)
University of Cape Town (UCT)
University of South Africa (UNISA)
University of the Witwatersrand (Wits)
Yu Chi Chan Club (YCCC)

THE ACCUSED

1 Neville Edward Alexander
2 Don John William Davis
3 Marcus Solomon
4 Elizabeth van der Heyden
5 Fikele Charles Bam
6 Lionel Basil Davis
7 Ian Leslie van der Heyden
8 Dulcie Evon September
9 Dorothy Hazel Alexander
10 Doris van der Heyden
11 Gordon Frederick Hendricks

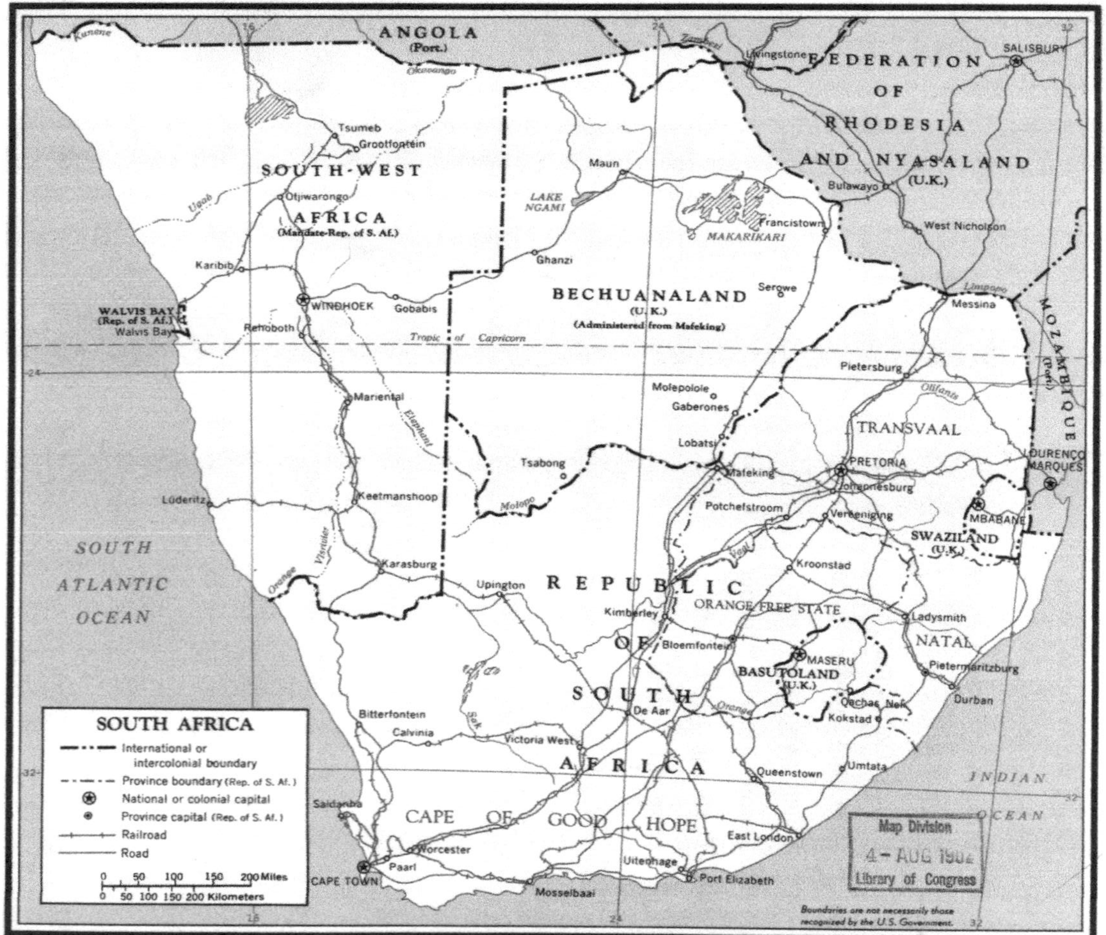

Fig. 0: *South Africa*. US Central Intelligence Agency, Washington, DC, 1962. Source: Library of Congress, https://www.loc.gov/item/96680415/.

Introduction

Intellectual Repression and Thought Crime in Apartheid South Africa

Of all the groups charged in the early 1960s under apartheid security laws, the National Liberation Front (NLF) alone had not used violence. The NLF was a successor to the tiny Yu Chi Chan Club (YCCC), whose name, adopted from Mao Zedong's book *Yu Chi Chan*, meant guerrilla warfare.[1] They were Cape Peninsula breakaways from the Non-European Unity Movement (NEUM, Unity Movement) – an African National Congress (ANC) rival. Although the NLF described itself as a paramilitary organization with political and military aims, it was decidedly intellectual. Its members – mostly young teachers and students – thought, read, discussed, wrote, fundraised to publish articles, distributed articles and formed study groups.

The YCCC and NLF were exceptional among early 1960s underground groups in their concerted attempts to theorize guerrilla struggle and assess its relevance to South Africa and, in the NLF's case, to build a structure of tiny groups – cells – for political education. Despite splintering from the Unity Movement, they nonetheless adapted its educational techniques. The YCCC, formed around April 1962, disbanded in December to organize the NLF. But six months after the NLF's January 1963 launch, its founding members were arrested. While they had produced theoretical analyses and begun setting up study groups, they had not developed a national network nor taken any steps towards armed activities. Yet eleven members received prison sentences ranging from five to ten years. Scholarly literature has neglected – indeed, excluded – these groups. They have virtually been erased from history.

The Rivonia Trial of Nelson Mandela and his comrades in Umkhonto we Sizwe (MK, Spear of the Nation) has been the subject of volumes.[2] Of

1 Mao Tse-tung, *Mao Tse-tung on Guerrilla Warfare (Yu Chi Chan)* [1937] U.S. Marine Corps Reference Publication, Samuel B. Griffith, translator and introduction [1961], 1989, https://archive.org/details/yuchichanenglish00unse/mode/2up?view=theater, accessed 28 January 2025.

2 For example, Awol Allo, ed., *The Courtroom as a Space of Resistance: Reflections on the Legacy of the Rivonia Trial*, London and New York: Routledge, 2015; Jens Meierhenrich and Catherine M. Cole, 'In the Theater of the Rule of Law: Performing the Rivonia Trial in South Africa, 1963–1964,' in Jens Meierhenrich and Devin O. Pendas,

course, their significance is unassailable: Mandela led the first post-apartheid democratic government. The other early 1960s sabotage groups, notably the South African Communist Party (SACP), the National Committee for Liberation/African Resistance Movement (NCL/ARM) and the Pan Africanist Congress (PAC)-aligned Poqo [alone, pure] have been studied in varying degrees.[3]

Yet the NLF has scarcely appeared in the 1960s South African liberation movement historiography, which prioritizes groups engaged in armed struggle.[4]

---

eds, *Political Trials in Theory and History*, Cambridge: Cambridge University Press, 2016, pp. 229–62; Michelle le Roux and Dennis Davis, *Lawfare: Judging Politics in South Africa*, Johannesburg and Cape Town: Jonathan Ball, 2019, pp. 66–95; Joel Joffe, *The State vs. Nelson Mandela: The Trial that Changed South Africa*, Oxford: Oneworld, 2007; Kenneth S. Broun, *Saving Nelson Mandela: The Rivonia Trial and the Fate of South Africa*, Oxford: Oxford University Press, 2012; Paul S. Landau, *Spear: Mandela and the Revolutionaries*, Athens, OH: Ohio University, 2022.

3 On the SACP, Eddy Tshidiso Maloka, *The South African Communist Party in Exile, 1963–1990*, Pretoria: Africa Institute of South Africa, 2001; Stephen Ellis, *External Mission: The ANC in Exile*, Johannesburg: Jonathan Ball, 2012; Irina Filatova and Apollon Davidson, *The Hidden Thread: Russia and South Africa in the Soviet Era*, Johannesburg: Jonathan Ball, 2013; Tom Lodge, *Red Road to Freedom, A History of the South African Communist Party 1921–2021*, Johannesburg: Jacana, 2021; Alan Kirkaldy, *Everyday Communists in South Africa's Liberation Struggle: The Lives of Ivan and Lesley Schermbrucker*, Cham: Palgrave Macmillan, 2022. On the NCL/ARM, Andries du Toit, 'The National Committee for Liberation ("ARM"), 1960–1964: Sabotage and the question of the ideological subject,' MA, University of Cape Town, 1991; Magnus Gunther, 'The National Committee for Liberation (NCL)/African Resistance Movement (ARM), in South African Democracy Education Trust (SADET), *The Road to Democracy in South Africa, vol. 1 (1960–1970)*, Cape Town: Zebra Press, 2004, 209–57; Nadine Gordimer, *The Late Bourgeois World*, London: Bloomsbury, 2013. On the PAC, Tom Geoffrey Lodge, 'Insurrectionism in South Africa: The Pan-Africanist Congress and the Poqo movement, 1959–1965,' PhD, University of York, 1984; Kwandiwe Kondlo, *In the Twilight of the Revolution: The Pan Africanist Congress of Azania (South Africa) 1959–1994*, Basel: Basler Afrika Bibliographien, 2009.

4 SADET, *Road to Democracy*, vol. 1, does not discuss the NLF, although Madeleine Fullard, 'State Repression in the 1960s,' pp. 341–90, p. 367, mentions 'Neville Alexander and 10 others.' Landau, *Spear*, p. 135, writes incorrectly that Neville Alexander 'kept a Maoist study seminar,' and p. 148, that James Marsh and his brother were a '"Coloured" MK unit.' Benjamin Pogrund, *How Can Man Die Better... Sobukwe and Apartheid*, London: Peter Halban, 1990, pp. 212–13 dismisses the YCCC as 'an odd little revolutionary group.' The few scholarly discussions of the YCCC/NLF include H. Strauss, 'South Africa 1960–66: Underground African Politics,' Collected Seminar Papers, London: Institute of Commonwealth Studies, 1973; Na-iem Dollie, "Dialogical Narratives: Reading Neville Alexander's writings," DLitt et Phil, History, University of South Africa, 2015, which highlights Alexander's contributions; Asher Gamedze, 'Ensemble Study and Struggle: A history of the Yu Chi Chan Club

It has been dismissed because of its position to the left of the SACP. It has been overshadowed by the focus on radical whites in the SACP and short-lived NCL/ARM. It has been stigmatized by the label 'Coloured' – as most members were classified – and so, allegedly, as non-African. Indeed, the Unity Movement from which the NLF broke has also been stereotyped as Coloured and marginalized in the historiography. The historian June Bam has discussed the diverse, complex and interwoven histories of the individuals and groups classified Coloured. Many are descended from the indigenous Khoi and San peoples, whom South African whites saw as 'closer to flora, fauna and wildlife than to the human species,' their replicas displayed alongside those of wild animals in Cape Town museums. Others are descended from slaves brought to South Africa during the Indian Ocean slave trade, but whose family histories were wiped out when they were forcibly renamed.[5]

Although the Rivonia Trial has been described as a 'struggle over ideas,'[6] the NLF trial shows more starkly the Orwellian concept of 'thoughtcrime' in apartheid South Africa – when the state criminalized thought. In Orwell's words, 'thoughtcrime' was 'the essential crime that contained all others in itself.'[7] The YCCC and NLF's activities – all revolving around thinking – were

---

and the National Liberation Front,' PhD, University of the Witwatersrand, 2024, which traces the political trajectories of certain members to the 1980s; and Allison Drew, 'A Gendered Approach to the Yu Chi Chan Club and National Liberation Front during South Africa's Transition to Armed Struggle,' *International Review of Social History*, 67, 2022, pp. 179–207.

[5] June Bam, *Ausi Told Me: Why Cape Herstoriographies Matter*, Cape Town: Jacana, 2002, pp. 15–32; Musuva [June Bam], *Peeping through the Reeds: A Story about Living in Apartheid South Africa*, Milton Keynes: AuthorHouse, 2010, pp. 169, 171. See also, *inter alia*, Gavin Lewis, *Between the Wire and the Wall: A History of South African 'Coloured' Politics*, Cape Town and Johannesburg: David Philip, 1987; Courtney Jung, *Then I was Black: South African Political Identities in Transition*, New Haven, CT and London: Yale, 2000; Mohamed Adhikari, *Not White Enough, Not Black Enough: Racial Identity in the South African Coloured Community*, Athens, OH: Ohio University Press, 2005; Mohamed Adhikari, ed., *Burdened by Race: Coloured Identities in Southern Africa*, Cape Town: Juta and UCT, 2009, 2013. On the Unity Movement, see *inter alia*, Lewis, *Between the Wire*; Allison Drew, 'Social Mobilization and Racial Capitalism in South Africa, 1928–1960,' PhD, University of California, Los Angeles, 1991, pp. 423–517; Ciraj Shahid Rassool, 'The Individual, Auto/biography and History in South Africa,' PhD, University of the Western Cape, 2004; Corinne Sandwith, *World of Letters: Reading Communities and Cultural Debates in Early Apartheid South Africa*, Pietermaritzburg: University of KwaZulu-Natal, 2014, pp. 86–172; David Johnson, *Dreaming of Freedom in South Africa: Literature between Critique and Utopia*, Edinburgh: Edinburgh University Press, 2020, pp. 104–32.

[6] Meierhenrich and Cole, 'In the Theater,' p. 230; le Roux and Davis, *Lawfare*, p. 66.

[7] George Orwell, *1984*, I, ch 1.

subversive of both the racial and the capitalist orders. They were explicitly socialist and part of the long 1960s New Left, an international movement of self-consciously intellectual and anti-Stalinist youth – students, socialists and anti-war activists. South Africa's New Left came chiefly out of the Unity Movement. But transnational student and activist networks also carried New Left ideas back and forth between Europe, Japan, the Americas and Africa.[8] This book explores the relationship between this transnational movement and the distinctive conditions producing and then smashing South Africa's New Left. It examines the development of the YCCC and NLF's thinking and practice and why the state came to criminalize their thought.

***

Strikingly, George Orwell's dystopian novel *1984*, published in 1949, anticipated the evolution of South Africa's apartheid regime, launched the year before. The totalitarian state of Oceania provides an illuminating starting point for thinking about apartheid, defined by the United Nations' Apartheid Convention as 'inhuman acts committed for the purpose of establishing and maintaining domination by one racial group of persons over any other racial group of persons and systematically oppressing them.'[9] Both the fictional and the real state were minority regimes that maintained power not only by the threat of force, but by thought control. Orwell's *1984* is often seen as reflecting the Soviet Union's communist regime. Capitalist states such as imperial Japan and post-Second World War America saw communism and socialism as thought crime.[10]

8 For example, Elleni Centime Zeleke, *Ethiopia in Theory: Revolution and Knowledge Production, 1964–2016*, Leiden: Brill; Chicago, IL: Haymarket, 2020; Bahru Zewde, *The Quest for Socialist Utopia: The Ethiopian Student Movement c. 1960–1974*, Addis Ababa: Addis Ababa University Press; Woodbridge: James Currey, 2017; Addis Hiwet, 'Analysing the Ethiopian Revolution,' *Review of African Political Economy*, 30, September 1984, pp. 30, 32–47, 38. Perhaps the Algerian students killed by the FLN during its war were a New Left, Allison Drew, *We are No Longer in France: Communists in Colonial Algeria*, Manchester: Manchester University Press, 2014, pp. 226–7.

9 John Dugard, Introductory Note, Convention on the Suppression and Punishment of the Crime of Apartheid, New York, 30 November 1973, Audiovisual Library of International Law, https://legal.un.org/avl/ha/cspca/cspca.html, accessed 15 March 2025.

10 Max M. Ward, *Thought Crime: Ideology and State Power in Interwar Japan*, Durham, NC: Duke University Press, 2019; Max Ward, 'Thinking Like a State: Policing Dangerous Thought in Imperial Japan, 1900–1945,' *positions*, 30, 1, 2022, pp. 35–60; David M. Oshinsky, *A Conspiracy so Immense: The World of Joe McCarthy*, Oxford: Oxford University Press, 2005 [1983].

1984 depicts a bleak totalitarian future in which people live under surveillance, and human personality and individuality are criminalized. The controlling minority Party consists of an Inner Party comprising about 2 per cent of the population, and an Outer Party comprising about 15 per cent; most people, the proles, are not Party members. The protagonist Winston is a minor civil servant and Outer Party member whose job is to rewrite history, which is continually revised to suit the Party's needs. Winston understands that the Party cannot remain in power solely by brute force; it needs an acquiescent population. Acquiescence is produced by controlling knowledge; critical thought reduced by manipulating language. Newspeak has replaced the old standard English, eliminating subtlety and ambiguity from popular discourse and by extension from people's thinking. The Thought Police are ever vigilant. Doublethink trains people to hold two contradictory opinions simultaneously, exemplified in the Party slogans: 'War is Peace,' 'Freedom is Slavery,' and 'Ignorance is Strength.' The control of thought is essential for totalitarianism, Orwell tells us.[11] Because thought expresses individual will, deviant thinkers are subjected to ruthless punishment, even death.

Unlike Oceania, Western legal systems pride themselves on punishing individuals for criminal actions, not for bad thoughts. This reflects a deeply held belief that human beings have an intrinsic right to mental integrity. As the legal philosopher Gabriel Mendlow argues, that right 'may derive … from the nature and moral significance of personhood … one's mental states, far more than one's actions, determine who one is as a person.'[12] But apartheid South Africa was closer to Oceania's model than to Mendlow's picture of modern criminal jurisprudence. Like Oceania's ruling Party, the apartheid regime had to promote acquiescence, which it did, not through language *per se* – although it imposed language instruction as a means of divide and rule instead of national communication – but through education and censorship. Much of the debate about apartheid has focused on its political economy and state and institutions.[13] But apartheid also strove to control thought, and, in this sense, it aspired to be totalitarian, even if – unlike Oceania – it never

11 This discussion draws on James A. Tyner, 'Self and Space, Resistance and Discipline: A Foucauldian Reading of George Orwell's *1984*,' *Social & Cultural Geography*, 5, 1, March 2004, pp. 129–49.

12 Gabriel Mendlow, 'Why is it Wrong to Punish Thought?' *Yale Law Journal*, 127, 8, 2017–18, pp. 2345–86, 2345–6, 2368, 2376–83, quote p. 2383.

13 On political economy debates, Merle Lipton, *Liberals, Marxists and Nationalists: Competing Interpretations of South African History*, New York and Basingstoke: Palgrave Macmillan, 2007; on state and institutions, Deborah Posel, *The Making of Apartheid, 1948–1961: Conflict and Compromise*, Oxford: Clarendon, 1991, and Mahmood Mamdani, *Citizen and Subject: Contemporary Africa and the legacy of late colonialism*, Princeton, NJ: Princeton University Press, 1996.

achieved its goal. Using censorship, the apartheid regime aimed to control thought through the suppression of texts and ideas, and through the falsification of history. Indeed, contends Christopher Merrett, the regime's very survival depended on intellectual repression.[14]

When the apartheid regime failed to achieve compliance, just like Oceania, it resorted to torture. As Winston learned, the most extreme torture took place in Room 101. In that room the Party set out to break the human mind. Combined with interrogation and various types of torture, the apartheid regime likewise sought to break minds through ever-expanding periods of solitary confinement. After all, the point of solitary confinement is not to contain danger. Even that notorious fictional cannibal Hannibal Lecter, as seen in the film *The Silence of the Lambs*, was not kept in solitary but in an individual cell alongside those of other criminals; the front of their cells consisted of bars enabling them to call out to each other. Rather, solitary confinement aims to break and destroy the human mind.

***

South Africa's thought crime was fundamentally racialized, even if the occasional white was caught in its trap. 'Niggers are not supposed to have any brain here. It is a crime,' wrote the enraged author Peter Abrahams in 1942. 'Nigger with a brain? Nigger thinking? No. I'm sorry to disappoint you. I'm scared to think … I will go mad if I think.'[15] Racism in the country now called South Africa dates from the seventeenth-century European settlement.[16] In 1910 the Union of South Africa consolidated two British colonies and two Afrikaner republics into a repressive state built on colonial conquest, codifying their racism into provincial and national law. Outside a narrow spectrum reserved for whites, the segregationist state did not allow political pluralism, and it soon began criminalizing political speech and thought, especially that of blacks and between blacks and whites. The 1927 Native Administration Act criminalized individuals found guilty of disseminating doctrines 'with intent to promote any feeling of hostility between Natives and Europeans,' targeting activists from the Western Cape ANC and the Industrial and Commercial

[14] Christopher Merrett, *A Culture of Censorship: Secrecy and Intellectual Repression in South Africa*, Cape Town: David Philip; Pietermaritzburg: University of Natal; Macon, GA: Mercer University, 1994, p. 197.

[15] Peter Abrahams, 'Lonesome' [1942] in Stephen Gray, ed., *The Penguin Book of Southern African Stories*, London: Penguin, 1985, pp. 121–5, 122–3.

[16] On nineteenth- and twentieth-century racial ideologies, see, *inter alia*, Shula Marks and Stanley Trapido, 'The Politics of Race, Class and Nationalism,' in Shula Marks and Stanley Trapido, eds, *The Politics of Race, Class and Nationalism in Twentieth-Century South Africa*, London and New York: Longman, 1987, pp. 1–70.

Workers' Union, which the state sought to contain. Intent was crucial. The state arrested British-born white communist Sidney Bunting under the act, but it could not prove Bunting's intent. Soon after, Minister of Justice Oswald Pirow raised the matter in Parliament. To sidestep the difficulties of proving intent, it was decided that whites be excluded from African areas and public meetings controlled.[17]

In the 1948 white general election the *Herenigde* [Reunited] National Party won a slim majority of parliamentary seats with a minority of votes, due to the weighted rural vote. It was an unexpected political victory, but by the 1953 election, the renamed National Party (NP) had increased its share of popular support, even though at 46 per cent it was still less than the combined opposition. White opposition fractured, and in the 1958 election the National Party crushed the United Party.[18] Black people protested with strikes, stay-at-homes and civil disobedience. The best-known protest in apartheid's first decade was the ANC-led Defiance Campaign of 1952–53 in which groups of volunteers courted arrest by defying six unjust laws, generally receiving fines or prison sentences of two to three months.[19]

As a political strategy, apartheid reflected racial ideology, namely, the beliefs that there are distinct human races demarcated by colour, that they must be kept separate and that the supposedly superior European or white race must dominate the others. Of course, racism had permeated South African society long before apartheid. As but one example, the 1945 Blind Persons Act deemed that needy blind whites would receive a £60 per year pension, Indians and Coloureds, £30, urban Africans, £12, rural Africans £9 and Africans in

17 Martin Chanock, *The Making of South African Legal Culture, 1902–1936: Fear, favour and prejudice*, Cambridge: Cambridge University Press, 2001, 147–8; David Johnson and Henry Dee, eds, *'I See You': The Industrial and Commercial Workers' Union of Africa, 1919–1930*, Cape Town: HiPSA, 2022, pp. xxiv, 51–83; '1927 Native Administration Act No 38,' Padraig O'Malley, *The Heart of Hope: South Africa's Transition from Apartheid to Democracy*, https://omalley.nelsonmandela.org/index.php/site/q/03lv01538/04lv01646/05lv01768.htm, accessed 1 August 2024; Allison Drew, *Between Empire and Revolution: A Life of Sidney Bunting, 1873–1936*, London: Pickering & Chatto, 2007, pp. 186–7; Robert A. Hill and Gregory A. Pirio, '"Africa for the Africans": The Garvey movement in South Africa, 1920–1940,' in Shula Marks and Stanley Trapido, eds, *The Politics of Race, Class and Nationalism in Twentieth-Century South Africa*, Harlow: Longman, 1987, pp. 209–53, 234.

18 Gwendolen M. Carter, *The Politics of Inequality: South Africa since 1948*, London: Thames and Hudson, 1958, pp. 32–6, 451; Thula Simpson, *History of South Africa: From 1902 to the Present*, Cape Town: Penguin Random House, 2021, p. 159.

19 Tom Lodge, *Black Politics in South Africa since 1945*, London and New York: Longman, 1983, pp. 40–6.

reserves, £6.[20] But from 1948 the regime began mass social engineering in all areas of life – education, housing, jobs, marriage, movement and transport. These changes occurred alongside the anti-communist Red Scare sweeping the United States. Not surprisingly, social engineering was accompanied by the erosion of basic rights, such as freedom of assembly and association, along with mounting political and intellectual repression, signalled by the Suppression of Communism Act, no. 44 of 1950. This outlawed communists and other socialists, removing communist Members of Parliament who represented Africans in the Cape. It was cast so broadly that any government critic could be prosecuted. Apartheid legitimized, institutionalized and provided authoritative support for racism, writes human rights scholar John Dugard, inhibiting criticism by ostracism and criminal prosecution.[21]

Apartheid split families and compounded the psychological pain caused by racism's stigma. It was a time when blacks, especially girls and women, used skin lightening creams like *Ambi* and *Super Rose*, hoping, praying to become just a bit lighter. It was a time when sadistic white dentists extracted the four healthy front teeth of young, poor and working-class 'Cape Coloureds' – claiming they wanted it. Advocate Gerald Gordon's first novel, *Let the Day Perish*, highlighted apartheid's emotional impact: 'I know what it means to be Coloured. And if they even think you have only a drop of Coloured blood in your veins – you're shunned,' stated one of his characters. So she raised her first-born fair-skinned son to aspire to be white, even though it meant he lived 'on the edge of a volcano, from which his secret might at any moment overflow' – as it finally did.[22]

Education to disempower the black majority was critical to achieve acquiescence. Although the 'Native Education' that preceded apartheid was premised on racial inequality, the few African students who made it to secondary and university levels studied the same syllabi as whites. Proponents of apartheid saw those students – future black professionals – as dangerous. The 1953 Bantu Education Act then prevented them from studying the same syllabi as whites. In the words of Minister of Native Affairs Hendrik Verwoerd, Bantu Education was designed to teach the African that 'there is no place for him [*sic*] in the European community above the level of certain forms

[20] No Sizwe [Neville Alexander], *One Azania, One Nation: The National Question in South Africa*, London: Zed, 1979, pp. 63–4; Freda Troup, *In Face of Fear: Michael Scott's Challenge to South Africa*, London: Faber & Faber, 1950, p. 98.

[21] Le Roux and Davis, *Lawfare*, p. 46; John Dugard, *Human Rights and the South African Legal Order*, Princeton, NJ: Princeton University Press, 1978, p. 106; Oshinsky, *Conspiracy*.

[22] Musuva, *Peeping*, pp. 2–10; Zakes Mda, *The Madonna of Excelsior*, Oxford: Oxford University Press, 2002, pp. 9, 80–2; Gerald Gordon, *Let the Day Perish*, London: Methuen, 1952, pp. 12, 176.

of labour.'[23] As Ezekiel Mphahlele observed, 'inquiry was to become taboo in African education.' The Unity Movement's Isaac Bangani Tabata called it *Education for Barbarism*, the title of a lengthy pamphlet written while he was under banning orders. He traced Bantu Education via Afrikaner Christian Nationalism back to Nazi ideology, noting that Nazism's overwhelming stress on motherhood for females ruled out higher education for girls.[24]

Alongside the state's attempt to instil acquiescence through control of education was its clampdown on the right to engage in non-violent protest. Merrett describes the 1950s as a decade of 'censorship of the individual,' when individuals could be listed, banned and forced from their jobs.[25] Throughout the decade the state squeezed the public space available for peaceful democratic protest and sought to criminalize opposition. The Treason Trial illustrates this transitional legal moment. In pre-dawn raids on 5 December 1956 the police arrested and charged 156 members of the ANC and its allied Congress Alliance with treason under the Suppression of Communism Act. However, charges against many were dropped and, eventually, thirty people went to trial. The state argued that the organizations formed a countrywide conspiracy to undermine the state by violence and replace it with a communist state. Defence lawyers successfully countered that the ANC and Congress Alliance were non-violent and non-communist. The case ended on 29 March 1961 when the judge concluded that the charges had not been proved. Afrikaner nationalism was running high. It was a stunning defeat for the state and a huge embarrassment for the police.[26] As Catherine Albertyn argues, the state failed in the Treason Trial to criminalize anti-apartheid resistance, noting that although 'the judge found that … the accused might have contemplated illegal methods, there was no policy of violence,' nor did they envision a communist state. Thinking about illegal methods was not then deemed to be a criminal act.[27]

The 21 March 1960 police massacres of unarmed demonstrators at Sharpeville Township in the southern Transvaal and Langa and Nyanga

23 Quoted in I. B. Tabata, *Education for Barbarism*, Cumberwood: Apdusa Views, 1979 [September 1958], p. 36, and Lodge, *Black Politics*, p. 116.

24 Ezekiel Mphahlele, 'Censorship in South Africa,' in Ezekiel Mphahlele, *Voices in the Whirlwind and Other Essays*, London: Palgrave Macmillan, 1972, pp. 199–215, 211; Tabata, *Education for Barbarism*, pp. 12–13, 30–2, 38.

25 Merrett, *Culture*, p. 39.

26 Mia Swart, 'The Road to Freedom Passes through Gaol: The Treason Trial and Rivonia Trial as Political Trials,' in Allo, ed., *Courtroom*, pp. 149–70, 161–65.

27 Catherine Albertyn, 'The Rivonia Trial: Domination, Resistance and Transformation, in Allo, ed., *Courtroom as a Space*, pp. 123–47, 132–33; Alan Wieder, *Ruth First and Joe Slovo in the War against Apartheid*, New York: Monthly Review Press, 2013, pp. 93, 98.

Townships in Cape Town – protests organized by the PAC – were a turning point. In Langa, people rioted in fury, setting alight a car, killing its driver and burning buildings, recounted Monica Wilson and Archie Mafeje in their book *Langa*. That Monday evening, wrote Gordon in his novel *Four People*, those in their tiny, crowded homes heard 'bursts of shooting and the other noises of the township's plight – tins of paint exploding here, a building crashing there, the wail of the workshops siren, the shrieks and the shouting.' The smell of fire in their nostrils, they saw 'flames leaping and the red glow streaking across the smoke-filled sky.' Later the army arrived in tanks to help the police. Africans stayed home, refusing to go to work, joined on 28 March by Coloureds who remained home or left work early. The state had suspended pass laws on the 26th – the day of the funeral for the victims – but on the 30th declared a State of Emergency under the 1953 Public Safety Act, the first time that emergency powers were applied to large parts of South Africa outside the rural areas reserved for Africans.[28]

That same day University of Cape Town (UCT) student and PAC leader Philip Kgosana led a peaceful march of some 25,000 from Langa, intending to go to Cape Town's Parliament. But the police persuaded him to stop at Caledon Square Police Station. Advised he could meet the Minister of Justice that afternoon, he was persuaded to call off the crowd. He and his delegation were arrested later that afternoon. Police beatings and mass arrests followed over the months as the police became 'a law unto themselves.' The ANC and PAC were banned. Authorities were empowered to ban any publication deemed subversive and to search and seize proscribed material. The State of Emergency was to last until 31 March 1961 but ended on 30 August 1960.[29] Concurrently, rural people protesting Bantu Authorities launched the Mpondoland uprising at Bizana, eastern Cape, that same March 1960 – the culmination of rural anti-apartheid protest that began in the 1950s. In June, police massacred, wounded and arrested Mpondos assembled at Ngquza to discuss the uprising; at least thirty people were later sentenced to death.[30]

28 Gerald Gordon, *Four People*, Cape Town and Johannesburg: David Philip, 1986 [1964], 210; Richard Rive, *Emergency*, Cape Town and Johannesburg: David Philip, 1988 [1964], pp. 15–18; Monica Wilson and Archie Mafeje, *Langa: A Study of Social Groups in an African Township*, Cape Town and London: Oxford University Press, 1963, pp. 10–11; Tom Lodge, *Sharpeville: An Apartheid Massacre and its Consequences*, New York: Oxford University Press, 2011.

29 Merrett, *Culture*, pp. 41–6; Edward Roux, *Time Longer than Rope: The Black Man's Struggle for Freedom in South Africa*, Madison, WI and London: University of Wisconsin, 1978 [1964], pp. 407–12; Philip Ata Kgosana, *Lest We Forget: An Autobiography*, Johannesburg: Skotaville, 1988, pp. 19–36, esp. 33–5.

30 Thembela Kepe, 'Memorials and Shifting Meanings of Rural Revolts in South Africa: The Mpondo Rural Revolts and Insurgent Scholarship, *Review of African*

The apartheid regime faced a 'crisis of legitimacy,' as Albertyn notes, but also a crisis of control. The flight of foreign capital along with the spectre of mass black resistance compelled the regime to reassert and strengthen its dominance over all opposition. The 1960s brought an expanding security apparatus aiming to control not only movement and protest, but how people develop ideas, censoring the written word and controlling the press, broadcasting and film. Daniel Kunene defines censorship as a 'curtailment or total denial of an individual's freedom to utter his or her ideas either orally or in writing, for any audience, whether actual or potential,' with authoritarian regimes holding a monopoly of propaganda by force.[31] Seeking to prevent the circulation of thoughts and ideas, censorship was crucial to the state's attempts to impose its ideology and will.

The NP's control of the state depended not only on white acquiescence through material privileges but on white unity to replace the divisions between Afrikaners and English-speaking whites that had dominated parliamentary politics since 1910.[32] British Prime Minister Harold Macmillan had already warned the South African Parliament on 3 February 1960 that the 'wind of change' was bringing independence to Africa. Against the communist spectre, argued Macmillan, the West faced 'a struggle for the minds of men. What is now on trial,' he emphasized, 'is much more than our military strength or our diplomatic and administrative skill. It is our way of life.' He urged political liberalization.[33] But most white South Africans disagreed, voting on 5 October for their country to become a republic. The other British Commonwealth states rejected apartheid. South Africa withdrew from the Commonwealth on 15 March 1961, becoming a republic on 31 May 1961. The few whites who dared speak up were persecuted. As Mphahlele points out: 'It won't do for some white moral sensibilities to be outraged; it's bad for "white unity," or the illusion of it.'[34]

Political Economy, 51, 180, 2024, pp. 274–89, 275, 277–8; Allison Drew, 'Govan Mbeki's *The Peasants' Revolt*: A Critical Examination,' in Thembela Kepe and Lungisile Ntsebeza, eds, *Rural Resistance in South Africa: The Mpondo Revolts after Fifty Years*, Leiden: Brill; Cape Town: UCT Press, 2012, pp. 67–89.

31 Albertyn, 'Rivonia Trial,' 124; Daniel P. Kunene, 'Ideas under Arrest: Censorship in South Africa,' *Ufahamu*, 38, 1, 2014 [1981], pp. 219–38, 219.

32 The NP later tried to legitimate its racism by further dividing blacks and reconceptualizing South Africa as a multi-national state, expressed in the Bantustan system. No Sizwe, *One Azania*, pp. 11–12.

33 Harold Macmillan, 'The Wind of Change,' 3 February 1960, *Great Speeches of the 20th Century*, Guardian News and Media, 2007; '1960: Macmillan speaks of "wind of change" in Africa,' http://news.bbc.co.uk/onthisday/hi/dates/stories/february/3/newsid_2714000/2714525.stm, accessed 14 February 2024.

34 Mphahlele, 'Censorship,' p. 199; Janet Robertson, *Liberalism in South Africa, 1948–1963*, Oxford: Clarendon, 1971, p. 208.

However, the state failed to ensure black acquiescence. Concerned that non-violent opposition would no longer be effective or even possible in post-Sharpeville conditions, and with international guerrilla struggles in mind, political activists considered armed struggle. In December 1960 the SACP voted for a campaign of economic sabotage followed by guerrilla struggle. By mid-1961 members of the SACP and ANC were planning armed activity. In September–October 1961 the SACP and the NCL, founded around expelled communist Monty Berman, each launched sabotage actions.[35] In late May 1961 a PAC offshoot formed Poqo, which organized Langa migrant workers who maintained links with their eastern Cape communities of origin – home-boy networks.[36] In December Poqo leaflets in Cape Town's African areas proclaimed: 'Africa will be free on January 1st. The white people shall suffer. The black people will rule. Freedom comes after bloodshed.'[37] Then on 16 December 1961 members of the ANC and SACP launched Umkhonto with sabotage attacks against apartheid structures in Johannesburg, Durban and Port Elizabeth, hoping to 'bring the Government and its supporters to their senses before it is too late, so that the Government and its policies can be changed before matters reach the desperate stage of civil war.'[38]

The government wasted no time responding. Reflecting its double colonial heritage, South Africa's judicial system was based on Roman-Dutch and English common law. Parliament passed statute after statute superseding common law, which was based on custom and legal precedent and allowed elements of

35 Lodge, *Black Politics*, pp. 233–4; Bernard Magubane, Philip Bonner, Jabulani Sithole, Peter Delius, Janet Cherry, Pat Gibbs and Thozama April, 'The Turn to Armed Struggle,' in SADET, *The Road to Democracy in South Africa, vol. 1 (1960–1970)*, Cape Town: Zebra Press, 2004, pp. 53–145, 79–90; Baruch Hirson, *Revolutions in my Life*, Johannesburg: Witwatersrand University Press, 1995, pp. 296–302; Eddie Daniels, *There & Back: Robben Island, 1964–1979*, Cape Town: Mayibuye Books, 1998, p. 105; Allison Drew, ed., *South Africa's Radical Tradition: A Documentary History, vol. 2, 1943–1964*, Cape Town: Buchu, Mayibuye and University of Cape Town Press, 1997, pp. 32–6; Stephen Ellis, 'The Genesis of the ANC's Armed Struggle in South Africa 1948–1961,' *Journal of Southern African Studies*, 37, 4, December 2011, pp. 657–76, 665, 671.

36 Wilson and Mafeje, *Langa*, pp. 14, 47.

37 Lodge, *Sharpeville*, pp. 194–5; Kwandiwe Merriman Kondlo, 'In the Twilight of the Azanian Revolution: The exile history of the Pan Africanist Congress of Azania South Africa, 1960–1990,' DPhil, Rand Afrikaans University, 2004, pp. 284–5, 289–91.

38 Lodge, *Black Politics*, p. 234; Nelson Mandela, *Long Walk to Freedom: The Autobiography of Nelson Mandela*, London: Little, Brown, 1994, p. 326. The date of 16 December, Dingane's Day, was to commemorate the 1838 Battle of Blood River. See 'December 16, the reflection of a changing South African heritage,' *South African History Online*, https://www.sahistory.org.za/article/december-16-reflection-changing-south-african-heritage, accessed 14 April 2021.

due process and individual rights. By contrast, the apartheid system operated through layer upon layer of overlapping statute laws backed up by increasingly severe punishment. The Suppression of Communism, Unlawful Organisations and other Acts were amended year after year with dizzying speed to allow pre-trial detention and solitary confinement for longer and longer periods. People were scooped up and shovelled into prison. The 1961 General Law Amendment Act allowed detention for twelve days. The 1962 General Law Amendment Act no. 76 – the Sabotage Act – defined sabotage extremely broadly and made it a capital crime. The 1963 General Law Amendment Act no. 37 – the Ninety-Day Act – authorized solitary confinement for up to ninety days with the possibility of extension. Penalties for sabotage ranged from five years imprisonment to death. One clause allowed continued detention for renewable twelve-month periods. Robert Sobukwe, teacher, university lecturer and founder of the PAC, was the only person detained under that clause, which became known as the Sobukwe clause. In Mandela's words: 'The law helped to transform the country into a police state.'[39]

The repression of individuals was accompanied by the repression of ideas. 'Banning books is analogous to the imprisonment of persons,' observed Kunene. 'This time, however, it is ideas which are arrested and kept in solitary confinement in the hope that they will somehow wither and die before they contaminate the rest of society.'[40] Banned persons could not be quoted; when the names of 102 banned persons were published in July 1962, the Johannesburg literary magazine *Purple Renoster* [Purple Rhinoceros] called it '102 executions of mind.'[41] The 1963 Publications and Entertainments Act allowed any publication, film or entertainment deemed 'undesirable' to be banned. As Nadine Gordimer remarked: 'We are not to doubt. We are not to question. We are not

39 Merrett, *Culture*, pp. 46–8; Mandela, *Long Walk*, p. 326; David Dyzenhaus, *Hard Cases in Wicked Legal Systems: Pathologies of Legality*, Oxford: Oxford University Press, 2010, p. 42. Chanock, *South African Legal Culture*, pp. 133–51, notes that the Union of South Africa used statutes to control and criminalize political opposition from early days. South African Acts are at https://www.gov.za/documents/acts. On the General Law Amendment Acts see https://www.gov.za/sites/default/files/gcis_document/201505/act-39-1961.pdf; https://www.gov.za/sites/default/files/gcis_document/201505/act-76-1962.pdf, esp. paragraph 21 (2); https://www.gov.za/sites/default/files/gcis_document/201505/act-37-1963.pdf, esp. paragraphs 17 (1), 17 (4) (a); See also Apartheid State at https://omalley.nelsonmandela.org/omalley/index.php/site/q/03lv01538/04lv01828.htm, esp. '1963. General Laws Amendment Act No 37,' https://omalley.nelsonmandela.org/omalley/index.php/site/q/03lv01538/04lv01828/05lv01829/06lv01910.htm; '1962. Sabotage Act General Laws Amendment Act No 76,' https://omalley.nelsonmandela.org/omalley/index.php/site/q/03lv01538/04lv01828/05lv01829/06lv01908.htm.

40 Kunene, 'Ideas under Arrest,' p. 235.

41 Merrett, *Culture*, p. 51.

to inquire. We are not to allow our characters to speak their right thoughts – or yours or mine.'[42] And there was no doubt that the regime feared any attempt to study, research and write about black history. The young communist Sylvia Neame had been working on a thesis about the Industrial and Commercial Workers' Union when she was banned; the police seized her thesis and the historical documents she had collected during her research.[43]

***

The post-Sharpeville clampdown did not only seriously weaken civil society and impede intellectual endeavours. The 1950s had already seen a battle between the judiciary and the executive. Initially the Supreme Court's Appellate Division – the country's highest court – used common law to strike down discriminatory laws, but Parliament passed more statutes to get around this. A key case concerned the government's attempt to strip those Coloureds who still had the franchise from the common voters' roll – the Harris case. The Appellate Division refused to comply. The government persisted. The case continued for five years and led to a constitutional crisis. The government enlarged the Appellate Division, packed it with loyal Afrikaner judges, and insisted that all members be present when determining a statute's validity – the aim being to ensure Parliament's sovereignty over the judiciary. Indeed, judges began deferring to Parliament, interpreting statutes and closing loopholes using facts in the public record to ascertain legislators' intentions and apply the law accordingly. Those judges, in David Dyzenhaus' view, evaded 'political decisions by deferring in matters of doubt or uncertainty … to the actual intentions of those responsible for enacting the legislation.' He calls this the 'plain fact' approach.[44]

The NP's control of the Appellate Division eroded the judiciary's independence and inevitably enhanced police powers. The year 1963 saw 2,169 arrests under the new security laws. Mass arrests of the PAC and Poqo took place in April.[45] July brought the arrests of Umkhonto leaders at Liliesleaf Farm in Rivonia, near Johannesburg, and National Liberation Front leaders

42 Quoted in Mphahlele, 'Censorship,' p. 206.

43 *Cape Times*, 7 October 1963.

44 Dyzenhaus, *Hard Cases*, pp. 38–9, 48–9; David Dyzenhaus, *Judging the Judges, Judging Ourselves: Truth, Reconciliation and the Apartheid Legal Order*, Oxford: Hart, 1998, p. 16; Le Roux and Davis, *Lawfare*, pp. 43–5; Marika Giles Samson, 'Rethinking Judicial Responsibility: The case of judicial persecution,' DCL, McGill University, 2019, pp. 57–60; Jens Meierhenrich, *The Legacies of Law: Long-run Consequences of Legal Development in South Africa, 1652–2000*, Cambridge: Cambridge University Press, 2008, pp. 133–6.

45 Dugard, *Human Rights*, pp. 250–5; Le Roux and Davis, *Lawfare*, pp. 5–6, 21, 32–4, 69.

in the Cape. More arrests followed over the next few years. Members of the ARM, SACP, ANC and South West Africa People's Organisation (SWAPO), among others, were brought to trial.[46] From its own perspective, if not that of most South Africans, the NP succeeded in criminalizing political opposition.

The Rivonia Trial, the most studied 1960s trial, has frequently been assessed using the concepts of 'political trial' and 'performance,' with emphasis on Mandela's oratory. Political trials have been defined variously as those that evaluate a defendant's political views and actions, those that redistribute and consolidate power and those that eliminate enemies of the state. These definitions cover such a broad sweep that a precise meaning of political trials remains elusive.[47]

Scholarly comparisons have focused on the Treason and Rivonia Trials, key trials of the ANC and its allies. Mia Swart argues that while the Treason Trial defence framed its case on legal grounds, successfully showing that the accused used non-violent methods, the Rivonia Trial defence argued on political grounds, assuming that they would lose on legal grounds.[48] This observation highlights the different political and legal contexts. South Africa's law of treason was derived from common law and premised on 'hostile intent' towards the state.[49] By the time of Rivonia, the state had framed new statutory law charges. The shift in the type of law parallels a crucial contextual difference: when the Treason Trial began, the ANC and its allies used peaceful protest to effect political change. By the Rivonia Trial, they had already engaged in numerous sabotage attacks – which no state, authoritarian or democratic, allows.

Michelle le Roux and Dennis Davis see Rivonia as a quintessential political trial, one that 'adopts the form of criminal law to vindicate the existing social and political order by imposing criminal sanctions for the political actions of legitimate political opponents.' Stressing legitimacy, for them Rivonia concerned the political ideas of ANC leaders. Other scholars, similarly, assess Rivonia through 'the verdict of history.'[50] The majority's aspirations were historically democratic, and in 1994 the ANC represented the majority. Yet, the

46 Merrett, *Culture*, p. 54.

47 Jens Meierhenrich and Devin O. Pendas, '"The Justice of My Cause is Clear, But There's Politics to Fear": Political Trials in Theory and History,' in Meierhenrich and Pendas, eds, *Political Trials*, pp. 1–64, 3–9.

48 Swart, 'The Road to Freedom,' pp. 162–5.

49 Thomas G. Karis, 'The South African Treason Trial,' *Political Science Quarterly*, 76, 2, June 1961, pp. 217–40, 221; Dugard, *Human Rights*, pp. 269, 274; Mary Rayner, 'Law, Politics, and Treason in South Africa,' *Human Rights Quarterly*, 8, 3, August 1986, pp. 471–86.

50 Le Roux and Davis, *Lawfare*, pp. 34–5; Awol Allo, 'The Courtroom as a Space of Resistance: Reflections on the Legacy of the Rivonia Trial,' in Allo, ed., *Courtroom*, pp. 1–19, 2.

accused in the other 1960s political trials were also imbued with democratic ideas and aspirations. How then can one begin to differentiate and compare these political trials?

Dugard, stressing procedure, defines a political trial as one aimed 'to eliminate or discredit a political opponent according to established rules.'[51] As he explains, Anglo-American systems use an accusatorial or adversarial system in which pre-trial and trial procedures reflect 'an open and equal confrontation between accuser and accused,' with the judicial officer acting as umpire. By contrast, continental European countries use an inquisitorial system in which the pre-trial procedure and investigation is conducted in private by the judicial officer, and the trial held in public. Until 1960, the South African legal system was accusatorial in both the pre-trial and trial stages. An accused person had the right to counsel, to bail, to hear the prosecutor's case in a preparatory exam before trial and to a timely trial. But the curtailment of procedural rights resulting from solitary confinement without charge and the denial of bail transformed the pre-trial process from an accusatorial system into an inquisitorial system akin to sixteenth-century Holland. However, while the early Roman-Dutch system used judicial interrogation, the post-1960 system authorized police interrogation. Arrests without judicial warrants become common.[52]

Once South Africa became a republic, its new 1961 constitution explicitly entrenched parliamentary supremacy over the courts, ensuring, Marika Giles Samson observes, 'that the courts had no constitutional authority to enquire into the validity of an enactment.'[53] Until 1961, treason cases had been heard in special criminal courts with three judges who needed to reach a majority verdict. But from 1961 they were heard either by a lone judge or a judge with one or two assessors, persons appointed by the judge to give their views on questions of fact but not law – like juries, which were phased out. Although standards of fairness at trial remained, the judiciary's diminished role and the sweeping definitions of political crimes helped the state win convictions. Indeed, after the Treason Trial concluded in 1961, there were no more prosecutions based on common-law treason despite the growing number of political trials. 'Only an over-industrious prosecutor would forego the generous definitions of crime and the easy procedural rules of the new statutory forms of treason for the common law of treason and its more exacting rules of

51 Dugard, *Human Rights*, p. 206.

52 Dugard, *Human Rights*, pp. 267–9.

53 Samson, 'Rethinking Judicial Responsibility,' p. 55.

procedure,' Dugard points out.[54] The impact of these changes is seen in the *State versus Neville Alexander and Ten Others* – the NLF trial.[55]

The concept of 'political trial' may be exceedingly broad, but political trials can be subdivided into narrower categories that illuminate the politics of the societies in which they are embedded. Ronald Christenson divides political trials into those operating within the rule of law – the essence of which entails the protection of the individual from arbitrary state power – and those operating outside it, namely, partisan trials, which 'are fully within the realm of power and completely outside the rule of law.' Within each of these categories he examines trials concerning corruption, dissent, nationalism and regimes.[56]

Early 1960s South Africa was fast becoming a state operating outside the rule of law even while ruling by law. The case of Rossouw versus Sachs is revealing. The lawyer Albie Sachs was arrested under the Ninety-Day Act and held in solitary from October 1963 to March 1964. Sachs' lawyers insisted that he was entitled to the same rights as non-convicted and awaiting-trial prisoners – adequate exercise and reading and writing material – and that the police were not allowed to deprive him of rights and liberties aside from detention in solitary for interrogation. The Cape Provincial Division agreed, contending that it would be surprising that the legislature intended to punish non-convicted or awaiting-trial prisoners. But several months later, on 24 March 1964, the Appellate Division overruled the Provincial Division. It stressed that Parliament 'could not have intended' physical assault or inadequate food or living conditions. However, while accepting that 'for detainees who may broadly be classed as intellectuals, the deprivation of reading matter or writing materials during their detention may approximate to the form of that very "psychological compulsion" so emphatically repudiated by counsel for appellant,' it pointed out that the Ninety-Day Act aimed to induce detainees to speak. Therefore, detainees were not non-convicted or awaiting-trial prisoners and so did not have the same rights to reading and writing material. The Appellate Division clearly saw intellectuals as a distinct

54 Dugard, *Human Rights*, pp. 230–1, 267, 269–73; Le Roux and Davis, *Lawfare*, pp. 19–21, 89–90; Dirk van Zyl Smit and Norma-May Isakow, 'Assessors and Criminal Justice, *South African Journal on Human Rights*, 1, 3, November 1985, pp. 218–35, 220–1. Juries – white and of no benefit to blacks – were forbidden under the Suppression of Communism, Sabotage and Terrorism Acts and abolished in 1969.

55 *State versus Neville Alexander and Ten Others* [hereafter *State vs Alexander*] (Supreme Court of South Africa, Appellate Division). Incomplete copies in the Western Cape Archives, Cape Town and UCT Manuscripts & Archives (UCTMA) BC1538. Sections of Neville Alexander's testimony are missing from both copies. In the UCT copy, a section has been cut out with a knife.

56 Ronald Christenson, 'A Political Theory of Political Trials,' *Journal of Criminal Law & Criminology*, 74, 2, 1983, pp. 547–77, 551–5; Dugard, *Human Rights*, pp. 37–49.

social category. The decision signalled that common-law rights for political prisoners were effectively over.[57]

Yet legal loopholes remained, so the legal onslaught continued. Following the Ninety-Day Act, the 1965 Criminal Procedure Amendment Act doubled detention to 180 days. Applied to potential state witnesses, it allowed the state to hold secret trials in the eastern Cape.[58] The 1967 Terrorism Act gave the police even greater powers of warrantless detention and interrogation: 'the police will now have a free hand to act without legal restraint,' wrote the Afrikaans-language *Die Beeld*. The vagueness of these statutes made prosecution all the easier. As Dugard observed, the courts were reduced to deciphering Parliament's will. By the late 1960s, South African political trials were reduced to a 'visible, discriminatory set of rules of procedure ... rules that seriously undermine the value of the political trial as a process of judicial authentication.'[59] Yet political trials had arguably been reduced to partisan trials several years earlier.

If social movements can encourage ideas, then ruthless social engineering and political repression can smother them. The apartheid regime's increasing use of statutes, which by their nature were arbitrary, overwhelmed the rule of law. The regime produced a culture of conformity, self-repression and self-censorship, stunting people's feelings towards each other. 'A general climate of fear infected the entire society as the regime moved to impose strict censorship and close down any questioning of its ethnic balkanisation,' reflected Dan O'Meara.[60] The NLF's members applied their minds to study and theorize guerrilla struggle, hoping to form a united front with like-minded groups for common action. And, as Orwell anticipated, their imprisonment was 'merely the wiping out of persons who might perhaps commit a crime at some time in the future.'[61]

57 Dyzenhaus, *Hard Cases*, pp. 90–2; *Cape Times*, 2 October, 14 November 1963, Albie Sachs, *Stephanie on Trial*, London: Harvill, 1968, pp. 15–16.

58 Merrett, *Culture*, pp. 48, 55.

59 Dugard, *Human Rights*, pp. 25, 267, 273; Meierhenrich and Cole, 'In the Theater,' pp. 261–2; Dyzenhaus, *Hard Cases*, p. 120.

60 Dan O'Meara, *Forty Lost Years: The Apartheid State and the Politics of the National Party, 1948–1994*, Randburg: Ravan and Athens; OH: Ohio University, 1996, p. 110; Merrett, *Culture of Censorship*, p. 77.

61 Orwell, *1984*, II, ch 9.

Chapter 1

South Africa's 1960s New Left[1]

Sea routes connecting Africa and its diaspora and the syndicalist and socialist world left deep marks on Cape Town, a port city at the intersection of the Atlantic and Indian Oceans that provided fertile soil for an emergent New Left.[2] Sprawled around the flat-topped Table Mountain and adjoining Devil's Peak and Lion's Head Mountains, the city hosted diverse discussion clubs, facilitating the development of autodidact intellectuals who followed world events and produced a vibrant socialist culture with communist, Trotskyist and anti-Stalinist currents. This anti-Stalinism reflected opposition to both the oppressive and exploitative Soviet bureaucracy as well as the local Communist Party's practice and growing influence in the ANC. The speeches and writings of Unity Movement intellectuals in the 1940s–1950s and the Forum Club's 1950s journal *Discussion* provide a few examples of their significant socialist and left-radical theorizing.[3]

The vehemently anti-Stalinist Unity Movement played a crucial role in this 'global thinking' that reflected the interrelationship of international and local dynamics.[4] It was led by the charismatic Isaac Tabata, a Lovedale and

1 This chapter is a revised version of 'Neville Alexander and South Africa's New Left, c. 1957–1964,' *Rethinking Africa Series Occasional Paper*, no. 6, UCT Centre for African Studies, February 2023.

2 Michael R. Hogan, '"Remov[e] Us From the Bondage of South Africa": Transnational resistance strategies and subnational concessions in Namibia's Police Zone, 1919–1962,' PhD, West Virginia University, 2021; Robert Trent Vinson, '"Sea Kaffirs": "American Negroes" and the Gospel of Garveyism in Early Twentieth-Century Cape Town,' *Journal of African History*, 47, 2, 2006, pp. 281–303.

3 I define Stalinism as a political-economic system based on the use of gulag forced labour and psychological terrorism associated with a particular political culture and discourse. In South Africa Stalinism meant consistently uncritical acceptance of Soviet positions. South African communist discourse was shaped by Soviet discourse, but both communists and Trotskyists used stilted language. Sandwith, *World of Letters*, pp. 48–172; Johnson, *Dreaming of Freedom*, pp. 104–32.

4 Christopher Joon-Hai Lee, 'The Uses of the Comparative Imagination: South African History and World History in the Political Consciousness and Strategy of the South African Left, 1943–1959,' *Radical History Review*, 92, 2005, pp. 31–61, 33, 43–4, 49.

Fort Hare College-educated intellectual and isiXhosa-English orator born in 1909 at Bailey, near Queenstown. In 1943 Tabata and other Marxists in the tiny Workers Party of South Africa launched the Unity Movement. A federal organization, the Unity Movement sought to link African, Coloured and Indian organizations through a democratic platform in the hope of undermining the state-imposed sectional divisions. Its two main affiliates were the eastern Cape-based All-African Convention (AAC) and the western Cape-based movement against the Coloured Affairs Department (CAD) – the Anti-CAD movement. Tabata and other Unity Movement leaders were inspired by the exiled Soviet dissident Leon Trotsky, creatively adapting his thinking to South African conditions. Nonetheless, factionalism culminated in a split in December 1958.[5]

Denied equal access to education, black South Africans revered teachers, and the Unity Movement had a particularly strong teacher base: the Teachers' League of South Africa was affiliated to the Anti-CAD movement, and the Cape African Teachers Association (CATA) to the AAC. All Unity Movement affiliates subscribed to its Ten Point Programme of minimum democratic rights to be achieved through non-collaboration with racial institutions. The Ten Point Programme was an attempt to fight class collaboration and apply Trotsky's notion of working-class independence to South African conditions. In 1922 the Communist International proposed the notion of a united front – an alliance of working-class organizations to fight for their common interests against the capitalist class. The aim was to build working-class solidarity as opposed to class collaboration with the bourgeoisie. But in racially divided South Africa white workers opposed alliances with blacks. So black South Africans developed a conception of united fronts for joint action across the state-imposed sectional identities, organizing tactical fronts for both specific goals and broader strategic fronts. The political basis for black unity lay in the common lack of democratic rights. The Unity Movement argued that since state authority assumed a racial form, a united front based on non-collaboration through a boycott of racial institutions raised the possibility that the black working class could establish its own institutions and challenge the state through dual power.[6]

Unity Movement intellectuals argued for the multiple origins of human civilization worldwide and compared South Africa's developing authoritarianism

5 Lewis, *Between the Wire*; Drew, 'Social Mobilization,' pp. 423–517; Sandwith, *World of Letters*, pp. 86–172; Johnson, *Dreaming of Freedom*, pp. 104–32.

6 Leon Trotsky, 'On the United Front,' 2 March 1922, in *The First Five Years of the Communist International*, vol. 2, https://www.marxists.org/archive/trotsky/1924/ffyci-2/08.htm, accessed 9 June 2025; Drew, 'Social Mobilization,' pp. 431–2; Allison Drew, *Discordant Comrades: Identities and Loyalties on the South African Left*, Aldershot: Ashgate, 2000, pp. 149–50, 207.

and racism with European fascism. In short, the Unity Movement used world history to make sense of South African developments and to overcome the isolation felt by black intellectuals in a white supremacist society. Against the state's use of racial ideology, they argued for non-racialism. Not only did they reject a biological notion of race, but they also argued that the very concept of race was used to subjugate people deemed non-white, training them to think of themselves in racial ways. Alongside this they rejected the notion of white or Western civilization, arguing instead for a world civilization.[7]

Signalling the importance of education to Cape Town's black elite, the extraordinary political leader Dr Abdullah Abdurahman, the grandchild of Muslim Malay slaves who earned his medical degree from the University of Glasgow, launched Cape Town's first two high schools for children of colour: Trafalgar High in District Six in 1912 and Livingstone High in Claremont in 1926. Most black intellectuals were schoolteachers, generally excluded from the University of Cape Town (UCT) looming above the city against the backdrop of Devil's Peak. Underlining the exclusion, in 1934 the university erected a bronze statue of arch-British imperialist mining magnate Cecil Rhodes, seated chin on hand, pensively gazing at the city. The University of the Witwatersrand (Wits), UCT's rival, was up north in Johannesburg, whose location, like that of other Witwatersrand towns, was determined not by a source of water but by a supply of gold. Wits began as the South African School of Mines and, like UCT, revolved around racial, class and gender exclusion. Ironically, however, most studies of South African socialist theorizing focus on university-based scholarship, especially that of the 1970s. This emphasis on academic scholarship overlooks intellectual work produced by blacks – and by white communists like Sidney Bunting, excluded from Wits because of his politics.[8] Indeed, the country's structured racism meant that despite the left's commitment to non-racialism, it was nonetheless fractured across racial and regional lines.

Academics examining 1970s socialist theorizing generally stress the impact of European Marxist currents on white South African academics. Andrew Nash, Kirk Helliker and Peter Vale discuss Western Marxism in South Africa. Tom Lodge's *Red Road to Freedom* presents South African communism as a continuous century-old national organization, stressing white male communist intellectuals such as Harold Wolpe. There are exceptions, however. C. R. D.

7 B. M. Kies, *The Contribution of the Non-European Peoples to World Civilization*, Cape Town: Teachers' League of South Africa, 1953; 'Benjamin Magson Kies,' *South African History Online*, https://www.sahistory.org.za/people/benjamin-magson-kies, 2020, accessed 13 August 2024; Crain Soudien, 'A Re-reading of Ben Kies's "The Contribution of the Non European Peoples to World Civilisation",' *Social Dynamics*, 48, 2, 2022, pp. 191–206.

8 Drew, *Between Empire and Revolution*, pp. 59, 215–16.

Halisi suggests that the early Black Consciousness movement was influenced by the transnational New Left. In turn, Ian Macqueen and Alex Lichtenstein point to New Left influence on the socialist intellectual Rick Turner while he studied in Paris, and Turner's subsequent interactions with Black Consciousness proponents when back in South Africa.[9] Nonetheless, if one takes the late 1960s and 1970s as the point of departure in studying South African socialist theorizing, it appears largely as the product of white academics.[10]

Yet, looking back just a decade, the tiny and ephemeral Yu Chi Chan Club (YCCC) and National Liberation Front (NLF) of 1962–63 appear as the germ of a South African New Left – heretofore virtually unseen and unsearched for, the roots of which go back to the late 1950s, especially to critical youth in the Unity Movement and the Western Cape and Wits student movements. The NLF was crushed by the apartheid regime. But, before their arrests, its members produced a small body of writing and a practice reflecting the group's position in a transnational New Left movement.

'Just as the ANC is at the center of things, so the center of things is increasingly within the ANC,' wrote John Saul and Stephen Gelb in 1981.[11] Although that centre embraced the South African Communist Party (SACP), which cultivated an extremely close relationship with the ANC, the ANC's dominance was not then assured: throughout the 1980s the liberation movement engaged in a fierce internal power struggle. The theoretical problem implicit in Saul and Gelb's claim concerns the relationship of the centre and the margins: can the shifting political centre really be understood in isolation from the margins, which are also in a state of flux as individuals and groups move to and from the centre? Viewing the YCCC and NLF not only as part of the

9 C. R. D. Halisi, 'From Liberation to Citizenship: Identity and Innovation in Black South African Political Thought,' *Comparative Studies in Society and History*, 39, 1, January 1997, pp. 61–85, 74–5; C. R. D. Halisi, *Black Political Thought in the Making of South African Democracy*, Bloomington and Indianapolis: Indiana University, 1999, p. 9; Ian Martin Macqueen, 'Re-imagining South Africa: Black Consciousness, radical Christianity and the New Left, 1967–1977,' University of Sussex, PhD, 2011, pp. 10, 13–15, 44, 51, 71, 74–6, 146; Alex Lichtenstein, 'Rick Turner and South Africa's "Sixties",' *Working USA: Journal of Labor & Society*, 19, 4, January 2016, pp. 447–66.

10 Andrew Nash, 'The Moment of Western Marxism in South Africa,' *Comparative Studies of South Asia, Africa and the Middle East*, 19, 1, 1999, pp. 66–82; see also Nash, 'Clearing a Path to Academia: A Tribute to Lungisile Ntsebeza,' *Review of African Political Economy*, 51, 180, 2024 pp. 191–200; Peter Alexander, 'History, Internationalism and Intellectuals: The Case of Harold Wolpe,' *Transformation*, 62, 2007, pp. 109–26; Kirk Helliker and Peter Vale, 'Marxisms Past and Present,' *Thesis Eleven*, 115, 1, 2013, pp. 25–42.

11 John S. Saul and Stephen Gelb, *The Crisis in South Africa*, Monthly Review Press, 1986 [1981], p. 146.

longer-term South African socialist movement but as part of a transnational generational movement, one avoids both the overwhelmingly national focus that overshadows studies of South African communism and the inherent white bias of studies of apartheid-era university Marxists.[12] Paradoxically, a transnational perspective illuminates small groups by seeing them as part of a diffused global movement, whereas a national perspective leads to their being overshadowed by larger and formal political parties.

What was the New Left?

Known for its presence in Europe, the Americas and Japan, the youth movement called the New Left was concerned with finding new non-hierarchical organizational forms to avoid the bureaucracy of both Soviet communism and social democratic organizations, such as the West German *Sozialdemokratische Partei Deutschlands* (SPD, the German Social Democratic Party) and British Labour Party. The year 1956 was pivotal. In Europe, Soviet leader Nikita Khrushchev's February revelations of Stalin's terror, the June crushing of Polish working-class protests and the November Soviet invasion of Hungary led to disillusionment with the Soviet Union and resignations from communist parties. As Ellen Meiksins Wood suggests, 'what made the New Left "new" was above all its dissociation from the traditional forms of "old" left politics, both Stalinist Communism and social democracy.'[13] Indeed, the New Left was very much concerned with the organizational ossification predicted fifty years earlier by the German-born Italian sociologist and theorist Robert Michels.[14]

While not forgetting class struggle, the New Left gave greater recognition to struggles against oppression, especially anti-colonial, national liberation and civil rights movements. The European New Left saw anti-colonialism as a new antifascism, argues Andrea Brazzoduro. In March 1956 when the *Parti communiste français* voted to give the government Special Powers to do everything possible to maintain order in Algeria, young French leftists linked their anger to a critique of the Soviet system, and supported Algeria's Front de

12 Drew, 'Social Mobilization,' pp. 519–46; Drew, *Discordant Comrades*, pp. 275–81.

13 Ellen Meiksins Wood, 'A Chronology of the New Left and its Successors, or: Who's Old-Fashioned Now?' *Socialist Register*, 31, 1995, pp. 22–49, 24; Terence Renaud, *New Lefts: The Making of a Radical Tradition*, Princeton, NJ: Princeton University Press, 2021; Gerd-Rainer Horn, 'The New Left as a Global Current since the Late 1950s, in Marcel van der Linden, ed., *The Cambridge History of Socialism*, Cambridge University Press, 2022, pp. 584–614; Zewde, *Quest*, pp. 22–4.

14 Robert Michels, *Political Parties: A Sociological Study of the Emergence of Leadership, the Psychology of Power and the Oligarchic Tendencies of Organisation*, trans. Eden and Cedar Paul, 1915, New York: The Free Press, 1962 [1911].

Libération Nationale (FLN).[15] Egyptian President Gamal Abdel Nasser's July 1956 nationalization of the Suez Canal, Israel's retaliatory invasion backed by Britain and France, and the year-long Battle of Algiers intensified the youth revolt. Henri Alleg's *La Question*, published in February 1958, showed that France's use of torture during the Algerian war was routine; it made 'quite an impact' on the young South African socialist Neville Alexander when he read it as a doctoral student at the University of Tübingen in the Federal Republic of Germany – West Germany.[16] In autumn 1959 Frantz Fanon published his analysis of the Algerian Revolution, *L'An V de la révolution algérienne* [*Year Five of the Algerian Revolution*], which intensified antagonism to France's occupation of Algeria.[17] The Algerian liberation struggle profoundly affected Alexander and many others across the South African left.[18]

The historian Quinn Slobodian remarks that 'Alexander's biography reads like a précis of the trajectories leading to the emergence of an international New Left in the 1960s … show[ing] how individual education migrations knit together transnational networks of opposition.'[19] Born in the eastern Cape town of Cradock in 1936, Alexander was the eldest of six children of primary schoolteacher Dimbiti Bisho Alexander and carpenter David James Alexander. His Ethiopian-born maternal grandmother Bisho Jarsa, one of a group of captured Oromo children en route to a Jeddah slave market, was freed by a British warship near Yemen and settled at South Africa's Lovedale mission in August 1890. After training as a teacher, she obtained a post in Cradock and married a local minister. As a child Alexander was mesmerized by his grandmother dancing and chanting in Oromo.[20]

15 Jane Jenson and George Ross, '1956: French Communists Turning a Corner,' *French Politics and Society*, 5, 1–2, February 1987, pp. 30–6; Drew, *No Longer in France*, pp. 195–6, 242; Horn, 'New Left,' pp. 584–6.

16 Andrea Brazzoduro, 'Algeria, Antifascism, and Third Worldism: An Anticolonial Genealogy of the Western European New Left (Algeria, France, Italy, 1957–1975), *Journal of Imperial and Commonwealth History*, 48, 5, 2020, pp. 958–78, 960–1; August Matsemela, interview with Neville Alexander, University of Cape Town Manuscripts & Archives (UCTMA) BC1538 A2.1, p. 27; Henri Alleg, *La Question*, Paris: Les Editions de Minuit, 1958.

17 Drew, *No Longer in France*, pp. 237, 241; Frantz Fanon, *L'An V de la révolution algérienne*, Paris: François Maspero [1959], trans. as *A Dying Colonialism*, New York: Grove, 1967.

18 Brazzoduro, 'Algeria, Antifascism,' pp. 960–1; Allison Drew, 'Visions of Liberation: The Algerian War of Independence and its South African Reverberations,' *Review of African Political Economy*, 42, 143, March 2015, pp. 22–43.

19 Quinn Slobodian, *Foreign Front: Third World Politics in Sixties West Germany*, Durham, NC and London: Duke University Press, 2012, pp. 23–4. Slobodian mistakenly claims Alexander was an ANC member.

20 Sandra Rowoldt Shell, 'Bisho Jara,' 27 October 2015, updated 6 November 2020, https://www.sahistory.org.za/people/bisho-jarsa, accessed 6 May 2025.

Alexander had an extraordinary ability to block out distractions and focus precisely on an intellectual task. Although his mother was a Congregational Protestant and his father technically a Methodist, he was educated by German nuns at the Holy Rosary Convent in Cradock. As a result, he developed a deep affinity for Catholicism and was active in the Cradock Catholic Church. His later concern with social justice and politics flowed from his early religious beliefs and developed at UCT, which he entered in 1953 and finished with honours in record time. By the early 1960s he was already a transnational intellectual-activist, having received an Alexander von Humboldt Foundation fellowship for doctoral studies in West Germany and completed a magna cum laude doctorate on style change in the work of German Nobel Prize winner Gerhart Hauptmann at the University of Tübingen in 1961.[21]

Charismatic, with a wonderful smile, Alexander made friends easily. The emerging West German New Left that he encountered consisted of dissident socialists in and around the well-established Social Democratic Party (SPD); the tiny Communist Party of Germany had been banned on 17 August 1956 but functioned underground. In November 1959 the historically socialist SPD eliminated class struggle from its programme, agreeing to reform rather than overthrow capitalism.[22] The *Sozialistische Deutsche Studentenbund* (SDS, Socialist German Students' Union) had been founded in 1946 as the SPD's student wing, but over the 1950s tensions between them mounted. In November 1961, the SPD leadership declared that membership in both the SPD and SDS was irreconcilable. Those remaining in the SDS were expelled, to become the New Left.[23]

Germany had lost its colonies after the First World War, and West German New Leftists supported anti-colonial struggles. The 1950s and 1960s saw a rapid influx of African and Asian students into West German universities – from 200 in 1951 to 12,000 in 1962. African and Asian students formed the Afro-Asian Students Union and introduced their West German counterparts to new ways of thinking about colonialism, pushing them to support national liberation struggles. Indeed, argues Slobodian, they – including Alexander – were essential to the development of a West German New Left. The relationship was reciprocal as these foreign students applied and reinterpreted ideas encountered in Europe to their own countries.[24]

21 *State vs Alexander*, p. 1654. Brigitta Busch, Lucijan Busch and Karen Press, eds, *Interviews with Neville Alexander: The Power of Languages against the Language of Power*, Scottsville: University of KwaZulu-Natal, 2014, pp. 29–30; Neville Alexander, *Studien zum Stilwandel im dramatischen Werk Gerhart Hauptmann*, Stuttgart: J. B. Metzlersche, 1964.

22 Renaud, *New Lefts*, p. 210.

23 Renaud, *New Lefts*, pp. 226–8.

24 Slobodian, *Foreign Front*, pp. 8, 17, 28.

Figure 1: Neville Alexander as a student at the University of Tübingen, West Germany. Courtesy Freie Universität Berlin, Universitätsarchiv, Sig. Lieck. Sig. 1.

The European New Left had an intellectual and cultural impact precisely because of the open political space – the environment available for political activity – afforded by democracy.[25] By contrast, New Leftists in colonized regions were concerned with the conquest of power. The key example is the Cuban Revolution, where Latin American New Leftists – although they did not label themselves as such – had a momentous albeit brief success before the revolution was subsumed under the influence of Soviet communism.[26]

On 1 January 1959 Fidel Castro and Ernesto 'Che' Guevara proclaimed the victory of the Cuban revolution over Fulgencio Batista's military dictatorship – under the nose of US imperialism. Guevara became Latin America's New Left spokesperson. He argued that Cuba's revolution showed that popular forces could defeat a regular military force, that insurrection could create revolutionary conditions and that, by promising agrarian reform to win over the peasants, the countryside could be the locale for revolution. Indeed, echoed Cuban commentator Luis E. Aguilar, 'Castro's victory shows that extremism

25 Distinguished from public space, political space exists within and across institutions and expands or shrinks horizontally and vertically, above and underground. David Howell, *British Workers and the Independent Labour Party, 1886–1906* (Manchester: Manchester University Press, 1983), pp. 129–32, 277–82, discusses expanding political space in a democratizing society.

26 Horn, 'New Left,' p. 608, notes that the term was not used in 1960s Latin America, but that the chronology was very similar to that of Europe and debate subsequently focused on Latin American specificities of the New Left and the term's limitations.

is no longer an infantile disease … that a small band of fighters is capable of creating the subjective conditions for revolutionary victory.'[27] The Soviet Union was pursuing Peaceful Coexistence – negotiation rather than war to settle international disputes – along with the refusal to export revolution or counter-revolution.[28] The Latin American New Left insisted on ideological independence from international communism and stressed broad movements rather than political parties.

European New Leftists saw the small guerrilla unit as a new organizational form applicable to the 'asymmetrical power that they experienced under heavily policed capitalist democracies.'[29] Studying in West Germany, Alexander recalled that Jean-Paul Sartre and other French intellectuals went to Cuba and returned 'speaking in the loftiest tones about this Cuban revolution … that really captured the imagination of the intelligentsia … and in some ways helped to popularize the Cuban revolution in Germany as well.' Imagining Castro and Guevara as 'epic heroes,' he reminisced, the revolution 'reinforced the whole guerillarist [*sic*] tendency inside me … All it needed … was Sharpville [*sic*] to make me realise that this was the road we had to go … out of these different strands there was almost some inevitability about where I eventually landed.'[30] In turn, the Cuban experience influenced the YCCC and NLF's thinking and writing about guerrilla struggle, as did Mao Zedong's book *Yu Chi Chan*. But this incipient South African New Left was smashed by the apartheid regime almost as soon as it emerged, underlining the New Left's dramatic regional diversity across the First, Second and Third Worlds.

The roots of a South African New Left

Coming to power in 1948, the apartheid regime rejected the anti-colonial wave sweeping Africa, repressing dissent throughout the 1950s and 1960s. The Cold War provided a convenient rationale for apartheid. The Suppression of Communism Act was passed on 26 June 1950. In anticipation, the Communist Party of South Africa (CPSA) – the precursor of the SACP – had dissolved itself on 20 June, the earlier Trotskyist groups having already collapsed. Nonetheless, the common threat posed by the act facilitated short-lived

27 John D. Martz, 'Doctrine and Dilemmas of the Latin American "New Left",' *World Politics*, 22, 2, January 1970, pp. 171–96, 176–7; quote p. 196; Ernesto Che Guevara, *Guerrilla Warfare: A Method*, Peking: Foreign Languages Press, 1964.

28 Victor P. Karpov, 'The Soviet Concept of Peaceful Coexistence and its Implications for International Law,' *Law and Contemporary Problems*, Fall 1964, pp. 858–64, 863.

29 Renaud, *New Lefts*, p. 245.

30 Matsemela, interview with Alexander, A2.1, pp. 36–8.

discussions between Communists and Trotskyists about the way forward, seen in Cape Town's Forum Club and Africa Club debates.[31]

The new underground SACP formed in 1953 represented a demographic break with its predecessor: only an estimated fifth of CPSA members were recruited into the new party, numbering some several hundred.[32] Although several Wits University students spearheaded the SACP, like its predecessor it was very much Old Left, retaining its pro-Soviet stance and hierarchical structure. It experienced some internal disquiet over Khrushchev's Stalin revelations and the Soviet Union's Hungarian invasion, but most members accepted them. As one communist admitted, many SACP members were 'very, very rigid' when it came to Soviet communism.[33] Despite the Hungarian invasion, very few communists left the party – a marked contrast with the exodus from European communist parties, notably the British. Even in the 1960s exile period, Lodge notes, 'the party's senior leadership in London remained well insulated from any wider intellectual currents generated by the emergence of the New Left.'[34]

SACP members worked clandestinely in the still legal ANC and its allied Congress organizations. The Congress Alliance mirrored the Unity Movement's attempt to erode the state-imposed sectional divisions. But the presence of white communists in Congress Alliance structures caused discord within the ANC that culminated in a split over internal democracy and the national question, and the launch of the Pan Africanist Congress (PAC) in April 1959.[35]

Notwithstanding the Unity Movement's intellectual accomplishments, its hesitancy about mass action was already apparent in the Train Apartheid Resistance Campaign, formed in late 1948 as a group of organizations to fight the government's segregation of Cape Peninsula trains – an apartheid test case. Many Capetonians wanted to board the newly segregated trains in protest at the racist policy, but the campaign's leadership, most of whom were Unity Movement members, claimed that the masses were not ready. As a result, the

31 Drew, 'Social Mobilization,' pp. 429–30; Drew, *Discordant Comrades*, pp. 266, 280.

32 Lodge, *Red Road*, p. 291; Sheridan Johns. 'Invisible Resurrection: The Recreation of a Communist Party in South Africa in the 1950's [*sic*],' *African Studies Quarterly*, 9, 4, Fall 2007, pp. 7–24, 10, http://web.africa.ufl.edu/asq/v9/v9i4a2.htm, accessed 26 June 2022.

33 Kirkaldy, *Everyday Communists*, pp. 61–3; Lodge, *Red Road*, pp. 314–77; Hirson, *Revolutions*, pp. 255, 279–80, 302.

34 Lodge, *Red Road*, p. 376.

35 Launched in 1955, the Congress Alliance included the ANC, Indian Congress, Coloured People's Congress, white Congress of Democrats and South African Congress of Trade Unions. Lodge, *Red Road*, pp. 302, 314; Johnson, *Dreaming of Freedom*, pp. 133–57.

campaign fizzled within six months. Several months later, after the communists had dropped out, the Train Apartheid Resistance Campaign affiliated to the Unity Movement. The Unity Movement consistently maintained that mass action was not possible until the masses were sufficiently politically educated, and the revolutionary moment arrived.[36]

The Unity Movement's refusal to support popular action was soon seen again in the Franchise Action Committee (FRAC), formed to fight the Separate Representation of Voters Bill, which became law in June 1951. Just as Africans had been placed on a separate voters' roll in 1936, so Coloureds were removed from the common voters' roll and placed on a separate roll. The FRAC included communists; however, the Unity Movement chose not to fight the bill but to boycott the law once it was enacted. The FRAC quickly collapsed, but the Congress Alliance emerged from joint meetings of the ANC, FRAC and South African Indian Congress. The South African Coloured People's Organization (from December 1959, Coloured People's Congress) was formed from FRAC members.[37]

The 1950s marked the last major wave of youth to join Unity Movement affiliates. As Ezekiel Mphahlele acknowledged, the ANC 'never really interested itself in educational and cultural matters as an important front of our activities.'[38] This left the intellectual arena open to the Unity Movement, whose youth found its theoretical discussions far more compelling than those of the Congress movement. '[U]nlike the ANC,' recalled young Alexandra Township resident Roseinnes Phahle, the Unity Movement 'had developed a political literature of its own in the writings of IB Tabata, Benny Kies, Hosea Jaffe, Dora Taylor (alias Nosipho Majeke) and by other members; and the organisation also had a programme of demands – the Freedom Charter was yet to come.'[39]

Youth entering the Unity Movement in the 1950s thought the ANC outflanked it in townships because it responded to popular pressure over working-class issues. They hoped to give the Unity Movement a more activist profile. There was no shortage of issues. In June 1952 the ANC and its allies spearheaded the Defiance Campaign against six unjust laws: the pass laws, the Group Areas Act, the Separate Representation of Voters Act, the Bantu Authorities Act, the

[36] K. A. Jordaan, 'The T.A.R.C. Debacle,' *Discussion*, 1, 1, [June 1950?], pp. 8–15; Fred Carneson, 'Short History of Betrayal,' *Freedom*, New Series, 1, 5, 1 November 1948, pp. 1–2.

[37] Drew, 'Social Mobilization,' pp. 449–54.

[38] Tom Lodge, 'Charters from the Past: the African National Congress and its Historiographical Traditions,' *Radical History Review*, 46/7, 1990, pp. 161–88, p. 168.

[39] Roseinnes Phahle, 'The 1957 Alexandra Bus Boycott and its unsung heroes,' June 2019, https://www.sahistory.org.za/archive/1957-alexandra-bus-boycott-and-its-unsung-heroes-roseinnes-phahle-june-2019, accessed 14 November 2022.

Rehabilitation Scheme and the Suppression of Communism Act. The campaign was based on non-violent passive resistance, and while it failed to repeal the acts, it put the ANC on the national and international map. But the Unity Movement leaders too often castigated the ANC's efforts as piecemeal 'stunts.'[40]

Despite the legal impediments, Africans flocked to the cities. Tabata sought to address their political education. In Cape Town the New Era Fellowship (NEF) and other fellowships fell under the Anti-CAD umbrella and were led by Ben Kies and Hosea Jaffe. The fellowships were geared to educating an intelligentsia rather than training young cadres to promote working-class political education; the reading lists reflected a liberal and Western-centric approach to literature, culture and politics. They attracted a predominantly Coloured and often middle-class audience, with educated men the prominent speakers.[41] For this reason and to counter the ANC Youth League, in 1951 Tabata launched the Society of Young Africa (SOYA), whose formation as an AAC affiliate increased his organizational base within the Unity Movement.

The Society ran discussion sections and soon acquired national momentum with branches in the Cape Province, Transvaal, Natal and Orange Free State and contacts in Lesotho and Botswana. In 1953, for example, when Archie Mafeje enrolled at Healdtown College in Fort Beaufort, he joined the local SOYA and met the teacher and AAC activist Livingstone Mqotsi; he had already been influenced by Unity Movement teachers in CATA while at Nqabara Secondary School in Willowvale. Cape Town's SOYA branch organized in Langa and Nyanga. By 1954 the branch's active membership had risen to fifty and included migrant workers, clerks, teachers and a few students; 'being a Soyan carrie[d] prestige,' it reported, while the Western Province SOYA made 'desperate efforts' to attract women members. Under pressure from Coloured and Indian youth, SOYA became non-racial, although some members wished it to remain African only. In 1957, when Mafeje enrolled at UCT, he joined Cape Town SOYA, meeting Alexander and student Fikile Bam.[42]

Once Alexander arrived in Cape Town, he quickly joined the Unity Movement, deeply impressed by Tabata. 'I stopped short of hero worshipping Tabbie, the way in which most other people did,' he asserted. Nonetheless, he acknowledged, 'there's no doubt, as far as my own style, even my writing,

40 Lodge, *Black Politics*, pp. 42–5; Drew, 'Social Mobilization,' pp. 359–63.

41 Author interview with Kenneth Jordaan, Harare, 14 December 1987; hereafter, the author is the interviewer when unnamed; Soudien, *Cape Radicals*, pp. 77–112.

42 All African Convention, 'Minutes of the All African Convention Conference,' Queenstown, December 1954, pp. 34–5; Drew, 'Social Mobilization,' pp. 484–6; Bongani Nyoka, 'Archie Mafeje: An intellectual biography, DLitt et Phil, University of South Africa, 2017, pp. 27–30.

and … politics in general is [*sic*] concerned, that … politically Tabbie was the greatest influence on my life. Politically we all grew up at his feet.'[43]

Alexander became romantically involved with Gwendolyn Wilcox, a member of the NEF and SOYA, who was about eight years older. From Wilcox he learned about political activism. As he recollected, 'she was the driving force … the one who had ideas, had initiative and also experience.' She edited *The Soyan*, he assisted, and they read, discussed and wrote together until he left for West Germany.[44] SOYA became the most important political organization in Alexander's life before his departure. Under Tabata's guidance, he recalled, the 'Chinese road out of colonial oppression was put as the alternative to the Indian road … in the sense of methodology, method of liberation as well as the goals of liberation and the process of liberation.' They read Joseph Needham, Edward Snow and Mao Zedong, especially his philosophical works. They even read some of Mao's writings on guerrilla struggle but were mainly concerned with how China was promoting development: 'Nobody at the time even thought of guerrilla warfare as a revolutionary method,' Alexander observed. Later, though, when he seriously studied guerrilla strategy, the background on China would be important.[45]

From Cape Town to Johannesburg and back again

On the Witwatersrand, SOYA was involved in Alexandra Township and Western Native Township [later Soweto]. Activists like Sefton Vutela were CATA teachers dismissed for their opposition to Bantu Education. But in contrast to Alexander's glowing recollections of the Cape Town SOYA, the experience of Witwatersrand Soyans foreshadowed the Unity Movement's growing generational conflict, which resulted in splits and expulsions in the late 1950s and 1960s.[46]

Pressure on the Unity Movement was greatest on the Witwatersrand because of the social protest movements and strong ANC presence. Led by Vutela, Wits Soyans became convinced that the AAC president W. M. Tsotsi and general secretary Leo Sihlale were leading the organization down a bourgeois democratic path by interpreting the Ten Point Programme – conceived as a minimum, transitional programme – as a set of maximum demands. That meant that working-class needs were side-lined to those of an aspirant African bourgeoisie that followed continental nationalist leaders who compromised with imperialism. The Wits Soyans insisted that the Ten Point Programme be openly recognized

43 Matsemela, interview with Alexander, A.2.2, p. 50.

44 Matsemela, interview with Alexander, A. 2.2, p. 49; Deirdre Levinson, *Five Years: An Experience of South Africa*, London, 1966, pp. 58–9.

45 Matsemela, interview with Alexander, A2.2, pp. 54–7.

46 Drew, 'Social Mobilization,' pp. 487–88.

as a transitional programme to socialism – even though the Suppression of Communism Act raised serious safety concerns. Ideologically, the Wits Soyans were closest to the Unity Movement's Western Cape Kies-Jaffe faction. [47]

The history of the Progressive Forum (PF), another Johannesburg-based Unity Movement affiliate, also illustrates township youth pressure. It began as a Wits-based intellectual circle that examined international events. In the early 1950s it had about twenty-five members and attracted township youth to its discussions. Its members, Phahle, Andrew Lukele, Baruch Hirson and Seymour Papert, among others, espoused a range of views. It was more overtly socialist than the Unity Movement, with probably a third of members identifying as Marxist or Trotskyist. Yet Hirson felt pressure to conform, remembering how difficult it was to critique Tabata's 1950 book, *The All African Convention*.[48] Indeed, wrote Phahle, they pointed out that Tabata's book 'began by noting that South Africa's problem was both political and social,' but never addressed the social question. Nevertheless, since 'Tabata was seen as a leading NEUM theoretician … his faction treated the book as a bible.' So PF meetings never discussed the social question.[49]

However, there was debate. Some members stressed the primacy of the national struggle, arguing that organizing for socialism was premature. They claimed that since white workers would not support the small black proletariat, black workers needed to align with black peasants and intellectuals. Such an alliance necessarily raised the problem of how to keep the movement from being co-opted by an aspirant bourgeoisie. Others, like the Wits Soyans and western Cape Kies-Jaffe faction, believed that the Unity Movement should organize directly for socialism, although few dared to espouse this position openly.[50]

The need for activism was acute. The young mathematician Ismail Mohamed recalled becoming theoretically equipped from the PF discussions but simultaneously seeing the ANC leading the townships struggles. He sold the English-language newspaper, *The Torch*, which was aligned with the Unity Movement, but most Coloured working-class people spoke Afrikaans. The language difference symbolized the Unity Movement's distance from workers,

47 Drew, 'Social Mobilization,' pp. 488–92; Society of Young Africa National Executive Committee, 31 May 1959, 'The Maritzburg Conferences and the Tasks of the Immediate Future,' *The Soyan*, Durban, December 1959, p. 22.

48 Drew, 'Social Mobilization,' p. 500; interviews with Baruch Hirson, London, April 1987, Ismail Mohamed, Johannesburg, May 1988, Seymour Papert, Cambridge, Massachusetts, December 1988; All African Convention, 'Minutes of the All African Convention Conference,' pp. 30–3; I. B. Tabata, *The All African Convention: The Awakening of a People*, Johannesburg: People's Press, 1950.

49 Phahle, '1957 Alexandra Bus Boycott.'

50 Hirson, *Revolutions*, p. 258; Drew, 'Social Mobilization,' pp. 498–90; interviews with Hirson, Papert and Alexander.

he felt. Indeed, the Unity Movement underestimated the urban working class, instead stressing the need to organize migrant labour in the reserves.[51]

These ideological and political differences came to a head with the 1957 Alexandra bus boycott, which precipitated the breakaway of Unity Movement youth. Alexandra Township was unusual because blacks could own freehold land. Organized around three open squares, densely populated, class stratified and politically pluralist, its residents did not need permits. It was a 'haven,' Dan Mokonyane recollected, compared to the closed townships surrounded by fences. Its residents supported the ANC and Congress Youth League, the Communists, Africanists and, in the mid-1940s, the African Democratic Party led by the iconoclastic radical lawyer Hyman Basner. The township also had a tradition of bus boycotts.[52]

Born in 1936, Roseinnes Phahle and his brothers George and Livingstone grew up in Alexandra. Their parents were keen educationists. His father was a director of St Hubert's Catholic Mission School, his mother Hilda, a teacher and later principal at Jabulani School [later M. C. Weiler School], who also founded Pholosho School. From 1950–52 Roseinnes Phahle boarded at the prestigious St Peter's School in Rosettenville [now St Martin's].[53] Apart from state-funded education, African education was provided by missionary societies. St Peter's was run by the Anglican Community of the Resurrection and led by Trevor Huddleston but folded in 1956 under the pressure of apartheid.[54] After St Peter's, Phahle attended Johannesburg Bantu High School [now Madibane]. At Bantu High he joined the ANC Youth League in Sophiatown, and under the leadership of the ANC's Robert Resha, he and other students organized the Sunday public meetings at Sophiatown's Freedom Square against the government's proposed forced removals. He also arranged meetings with high school students in Johannesburg and Pretoria so that Ahmed Kathrada could inform them about the Youth Congresses held periodically in Soviet Bloc countries. But in 1953–54 he left the Youth League and joined the Unity Movement,

51 Drew, 'Social Mobilization,' pp. 500–1; Curtley Solomons, 'Reading the Voices of a Fractured Coloured Elite: Coloured intellectuals and newspapers in the Cape, c. 1959–1966,' MA, University of Stellenbosch, 2022, pp. 41–73.

52 Dan Mokonyane, *Lessons of Azikwelwa*, 2nd ed., 1994 [1979], pp. 19–22; Lodge, *Black Politics*, pp. 14–15, 156; Philip Bonner and Noor Nieftagodien, *Alexandra: A History*, Johannesburg: Wits University Press, 2008, pp. 125–53.

53 Dawne Y. Curry, *Apartheid on a Black Isle: Removal and Resistance in Alexandra, South Africa*, New York: Palgrave Macmillan, 2012, pp. 9, 125, n. 32; South African Union for Progressive Judaism, SAUPJ Support, 'A Pioneering School that Survived Against the Odds,' 2 April 2013, https://saupj.org.za/a-pioneering-school-that-survived-against-the-odds, accessed 23 January 2025.

54 Catherine Anne Woeber, '"A Good Education Sets up a Divine Discontent": The contribution of St Peter's School to Black South African autobiography,' DPhil, University of the Witwatersrand, 2000, pp. 280–4.

attracted by its Ten Point Programme. In 1956 he enrolled at Wits, obtaining a degree in Pure Maths and Applied Maths in 1959.

In mid-1953 Phahle had looked up the Alexandra SOYA but found that all its members except Lukele had left and joined the local branch of the Movement for a Democracy of Content (MDC). The antifascist MDC bore the hallmarks of an incipient New Left. A transnational group launched in London in 1947 with the German-language journal *Dinge der Zeit* [*Contemporary Issues*], the MDC distinguished itself from Soviet communism and European social democracy, opposed Leninist party structure, and was seen by many as anarchist. The hard-drinking dissident Afrikaner poet-activist Vincent Swart and his wife Lilian Swart introduced it to South Africa in 1951 after returning from several years overseas. The MDC attracted activists such as Dan Mokanyane, Arthur Magerman, and Martin and Deborah Machake Mabiletsa. The daughter of a washerwoman, Deborah Mabiletsa was a petite woman and forceful speaker who trained as a teacher, attended Wits University and became a staunch women's rights advocate.[55]

The Alexandra bus boycott was launched on 7 January 1957 in response to a proposed fare increase, and continued for several months.[56] 'Nights before the boycott was due, the location's fast-beating heart increased its pace,' wrote James Matthews in a short story.

> Wherever a man raised his voice, a group formed around him … until the location throbbed one great meeting place. There were the wild ones whose … cry was 'Burn the buses!' Then there were those few who whispered, 'Accept the terms.' But there were also the many who defiantly said, 'Azikwelwa! We will not ride!'[57]

Once the SOYA and PF refused to join the Alexandra People's Transport Action Committee, their Alexandra regulars pulled out of the groups, scoffing that the Unity Movement was boycotting the boycott. By contrast, the MDC

55 Allison Drew, 'Roseinnes Daniel Phahle,' https://www.sahistory.org.za/archive/roseinnes-daniel-phahle-allison-drew; Phahle, '1957 Alexandra Bus Boycott,' 'An Extraordinary Life,' *Sowetan Live*, 2 November 2011, https://www.sowetanlive.co.za/news/2007-11-02-an-extraordinary-life, accessed 15 January 2024; Marcel van der Linden, 'The Prehistory of Post-Scarcity Anarchism: Josef Weber and the Movement for a Democracy of Content (1947–1964),' *Anarchist Studies*, 9, 2001, pp. 127–46, 137; Jean Meiring, '"Do you remember still?" – Some Unknown Juvenilia of Vincent Swart,' *Litnet*, 13 April 2022, https://www.litnet.co.za/do-you-remember-still-some-unknown-juvenilia-of-vincent-swart, accessed 27 December 2022.

56 *Star*, 7, 8, 10, 11,18, 22, 22, 23, 24, 25, January 1957; *Star*, 26 February 1957; *Star*, 1, 2, 5, 6, 7, 8, 9, 18, 19, 21, 22 March 1957.

57 James Matthews, 'Azikwelwa,' in Richard Rive, ed., *Quartet: New Voices from South Africa*, New York: Crown, 1963, pp. 35–44, 35–6.

was extremely active. Its members Simon Noge, Mokonyane, Swart and Magerman were a minority on the committee. But, learning from the evolving struggle, they successfully insisted on public meetings. 'We were not scared of our oppressors. We felt we needed to stick to our guns. We were still young and fired up by the feeling of resentment,' reminisced Noge.[58] Some whites gave lifts to the residents, but others became irritated as the strike dragged on. 'Meetings like the recent ones designed for mass shouting of "Azikwelwa" [We will not ride] serve only to keep public opinion inflamed,' reported the *Star* of 7 March. Nonetheless, the boycott carried on. The people won; the Public Utility Transport Corporation backed down and kept the old fare.

As the Unity Movement affiliates splintered, the MDC's members were harassed by the police; it later disintegrated, both in South Africa and overseas.[59] From 1957 on, Phahle recollected, his 'group was in search of a political home or a guiding ideology.' All were intellectual-activists and, with one exception, Wits graduates. They even had their own authority on Marxism – Isaiah Lepolesa, an economics graduate who died young. Some formed the short-lived Transvaal Indian and Coloured Teachers Association, hoping to link up with the Teachers' League and CATA. Vutela's group and others campaigned to boycott Soweto Advisory Boards. Phahle and Derrick de Jager went to Cape Town in December 1958 in search of the Marxist historian and teacher Kenneth Jordaan, admired on the left for his critical analyses and whose articles Phahle had read in an Alexandra library. Jordaan had been in the Fourth International Organisation of South Africa and after its collapse helped launch the Forum Club.[60] The following December Phahle returned to Cape Town to meet up with Jordaan and his political circle, radicals associated with the by-then-defunct Forum Club, including the brothers Enver and Cardiff Marney. From then on Jordaan began visiting Johannesburg annually, and in 1962 he brought along Neville Alexander and Cardiff Marney. That Christmas 1962

58 Isaac Mangena, 'The bus boycott that forced an apartheid U-turn,' *Mail & Guardian*, 1 November 2007, https://mg.co.za/article/2007-11-01-the-bus-boycott-that-forced-an-apartheid-uturn, accessed 4 November 2024; Phahle, '1957 Alexandra Bus Boycott'; '"Azikwelwa!" Leaflet on the bus boycott issued by the Alexandra Peoples Transport Action Committee' [n.d.], in Karis and Gerhart, eds, *From Protest to Challenge*, vol. 3, Stanford: Hoover Institution, 1977, pp. 394–6.

59 Phahle, '1957 Alexandra Bus Boycott'; Mokonyane, *Lessons*, p. 36; Lodge, *Black Politics*, pp. 155–71; Interview with Hirson; Swart's influence in SOYA and his criticism of the Ten Point Programme is discussed in All African Convention, 'Minutes of the All African Convention Conference,' December 1954, p. 32.

60 For example, K. A. Jordaan, 'The Land Question in South Africa,' *Points of View*, 1, 1, October 1959, in Drew, ed., *Radical Tradition*, vol. 2, pp. 325–39; Baruch Hirson, 'A Question of Class: The Writings of Kenneth A. Jordaan,' *Searchlight South Africa*, 1, 2, February 1989, pp. 21–35.

Martin and Deborah Mabiletsa went to Cape Town with Phahle's introduction to Jordaan, and hit it off.[61]

The government, meanwhile, continued to attack black education. The Bantu Education Act had imposed separate and unequal education on Africans, aiming, in Tabata's words, 'to wrench the African from the progress of the civilization of mankind [and] condition him for life in a backward, tribalized community.'[62] In 1956 the Extension of University Education Bill (university apartheid) was introduced in Parliament. As one example, Fort Hare College, then part of Rhodes University, had heretofore admitted all non-Europeans but was now to be restricted to Africans only, then to Xhosa people only. It was not simply a matter of separating the so-called races, Tabata explained, but 'the logical completion of turning a whole population back to barbarism … stifling the development of their minds.'[63]

The Unity Movement had campaigned against Bantu Education, but this new bill hit its Cape Town leadership particularly hard, Alexander suggested, because of its stress on higher education and UCT's mystique for the western Cape's Coloured intelligentsia.[64] Heretofore, tiny numbers of black students had enrolled at UCT and Wits, which together had less than 100 African students in the late 1940s. By 1958, out of 12,019 students at all English-speaking universities, 269 were African, 350 were Coloured, and 606, Indian. In 1959 university apartheid became law, prohibiting black students from registering at formerly open universities without written permission from the Minister of Internal Affairs – an attempt to stifle the development of black intellectuals and professionals.[65]

The attack on black education enraged and energized students. The overwhelmingly white university students were organized into the National Union of South African Students (NUSAS), which campaigned against academic segregation, although many members accepted social apartheid. At Fort Hare the ANC overshadowed the AAC, but the Universities of Cape Town and Natal were Unity Movement strongholds among the tiny numbers

61 Roseinnes Phahle, 'Reminiscences of the Arrest of Fikile Bam & Marcus Solomon in 1963,' *South African History Online*, August 2019, https://www.sahistory.org.za/archive/reminiscences-arrest-fikile-bam-marcus-solomon-1963-roseinnes-phahle-august-2019, accessed 15 November 2022.

62 Tabata, *Education for Barbarism*, p. 16.

63 I. B. Tabata, *University Apartheid in South Africa*, April 1957, p. 8.

64 Matsemela, interview, Alexander, A2.2, pp. 57–8.

65 M. A. Beale, "The Evolution of the Policy of University Apartheid", 1992, p. 82, https://sas-space.sas.ac.uk/4228/1/M_A_Beale_-_The_evolution_of_the_policy_of_university_apartheid.pdf, accessed 27 May 2020; John A. Marcum, *Education, Race, and Social Change in South Africa*, Berkeley, CA, Los Angeles, CA and London: University of California, 1982, pp. 3–5.

of black students. Alexander, UCT medical student Kenneth Abrahams and other students decided to form 'a progressive national students union' to counterbalance NUSAS. They wanted 'a mass type of organization where they could resist and protest … without in a sense becoming revolutionaries.' As Alexander explained, it was to be a 'mass organization that was not sectarian, that was not tied to the Unity Movement or to the Congress movement [and] which would concentrate on educational questions and not on politics.'[66]

The Unity Movement's Kies-Jaffe faction opposed the idea of a student organization as a potential rival to the fellowships.[67] Nonetheless, Alexander, Abrahams and others organized at Coloured high schools, at Langa High and at Hewat Training College, writing articles and forming study groups on South African history and education. Although Alexander had organized for SOYA, this was his first experience building an autonomous organization from scratch. In March 1957 the Cape Peninsula Students Union (CPSU) was launched at Woodstock Town Hall. In contrast to NUSAS, the CPSU countered that academic non-segregation would still allow social apartheid rather than full democracy. Precisely to prevent the CPSU from being drawn into the Unity Movement's internal disputes, Alexander pushed for it to remain politically non-aligned. Most members were 'just students. But a few people became activists and eventually joined Soya.'[68] The next year Alexander left for Tübingen.

Neville Alexander in Germany

If the Movement for a Democracy of Content was a nascent New Left influence in Alexandra Township, then West Germany, where Alexander studied from October 1958 to February 1961, was a point of departure for later New Left influence into Cape Town. Through Alexander's Unity Movement background, he knew 'that Stalin was a monster who had caused the deaths of millions of people.' Otherwise, his knowledge of Stalinism was 'abstract and theoretical … The concreteness of Stalinism in South Africa for us was always linked to the ANC.'[69] His politics evolved rapidly in Europe. Before Tübingen, he spent a week or so with Jesse Eichman and Bernard Berman, two Johannesburg SOYA members studying in London. They introduced him to the fragmented Trotskyist left, and he learned about the broader Fourth

66 Matsemela, interview with Alexander, A2.2, pp. 62, 67.

67 Matsemela, interview with Alexander, A2.2, pp. 62, 67, 77.

68 'Calling All Students to the Inaugural Meeting of the 'Cape Peninsula Students Union,' Mowbray Town Hall, 10 March [1957], author's possession; Matsemela, interview with Alexander, A2.2, pp. 64, 68, 78–9; *State vs Neville* Alexander, p. 1657. The CPSU produced *News Bulletin*, *The Student*, *Students Primer*, and *Students Journal*.

69 Matsemela, interview with Alexander, A2.1, pp. 7–8.

International movement formed around Trotsky. He met Irish-born Gerry Healey's 'Newsletter group,' South African-born Ted Grant, leader of the Labour Party's Militant Tendency, and people who had broken with the British Communist Party after the Hungarian invasion. He 'knew very little of those things at the time. But of course very quickly learned a lot about it.' It was his first encounter with socialist groups, he remembered, and 'very different from what we had been used to in the Unity movement where everything was codified.'[70] He quickly realized that British-based Trotskyists like Healey saw Britain and Europe as the centre of the world revolution, believing that socialism would have to come to power in Europe before the colonies. Alexander was sceptical of this view: 'I had come to believe, not because of Mao, but because of what we in the Unity Movement had grown up to believe, that the centre of gravity of world revolution had shifted to the colonies … the metropolitan areas were in a sense caught up in the cold war.'[71]

From London, Alexander proceeded to medieval Tübingen, a small but cosmopolitan university town built along the Neckar River. After the Second World War the Allies had divided Germany into four zones under American, British, French and Soviet control; Tübingen was in the French zone. The Soviet-aligned German Democratic Republic was proclaimed in the east in October 1949, and the Allied administration of what became West Germany ended on 5 May 1955. Tübingen still showed signs of the war, and people were hungry for contact with foreigners, which Alexander enjoyed. The rapid influx of African and Asian students into the university kept the spirit of the April 1955 Bandung Conference of African and Asian states alive. Alexander joined the Afro-Asian Student Union and in autumn 1960 formed the first SDS working group on Africa; influenced by Third World students, the SDS formed several such working groups.[72]

For the first time in his life, Alexander was free to do whatever and go wherever he wanted. He threw himself into academic studies and student politics, recalling 'a real genuine warmth and cameraderie [*sic*] such as I never had experienced before … I was really secure in a social and emotional sense.' His involvement with the SDS began with the Algerian solidarity movement, strong in Tübingen due to its past location in the French zone. The SDS embraced a mix of socialists, and Alexander met Trotskyists who strengthened his links with the movement in Europe. But in contrast to Healey's Trotskyism, he found that 'SDS participation in [the] Algerian solidarity movement

70 Matsemela, interview with Alexander, A2.1, pp. 6–8, 13.

71 Matsemela, interview with Alexander, A2.1, p. 10.

72 Slobodian, *Foreign Front*, pp. 23–5.

mark[ed] the opening of solidarity action with revolutionary … movements.' He felt that the SDS started radicalizing from 1959–60 on.[73]

Alexander and other SDS students made a two-day trip to Tunis to meet Algerian student leaders of the Union générale des étudiants musulmans algériens [General union of Muslim Algerian students] to explore possibilities for solidarity. Learning about the refugee camps in Morocco and Tunisia, the SDS began mobilizing medical students to collect supplies and work as doctors for the FLN during their university breaks.[74] This youthful support for the Algerian struggle illustrates the stark contrast between New Leftists and Soviet Communists. In September 1958 the FLN established its provisional government. While the clandestine Algerian Communist Party recognized it two months later, the USSR only did so in late 1960.[75]

For Alexander, the March 1960 Sharpeville-Langa massacres of unarmed demonstrators provoked a major psychological shift. He felt acutely that non-violence and non-collaboration would be a waste without preparing for armed struggle. He travelled around West Germany lecturing on apartheid. He participated in SDS debates in Tübingen and Frankfurt on party democracy and factions, believing that factionalism should be tolerated even in one-party systems. He helped to organize foreign seasonal workers in the metal workers union, producing special issues of the metal workers newsletter and a report of trade unions in Africa.[76] He had several girlfriends but fell in love with Irmgard Bolle, a German doctoral student and SDS comrade who later worked in the SDS Office for International Affairs with responsibility for Africa.[77]

Once more in Cape Town

Alexander could have remained in West Germany, teaching and organizing a European anti-apartheid movement. Instead, obtaining his DPhil in February 1961, he returned home. On his way back he visited Trotsky's widow Natalia

[73] Busch, Busch and Press, eds, *Interviews*, pp. 57–60; Matsemela, interview with Alexander, A2.1, pp. 28, 30–1.

[74] Matsemela, interview with Alexander, A2.1, pp. 24–5; 'Fourth International Practical Internationalism: Solidarity in Germany with the Algerian Anti-colonial Liberation Struggle,' Manuel Kellner interview with Hans Peiffer, *Europe Solidaire Sans Frontières*, 11 April 2018, http://www.europe-solidaire.org/spip.php?article46818, accessed 28 July 2022.

[75] Henri Alleg, ed., *La Guerre d'Algérie*, vol. 3, Paris: Messidor, 1981, p. 468.

[76] Matsemela, interview with Alexander, A2.1, pp. 31–3.

[77] Martin Klimke, *The Other Alliance: Student Protest in West Germany and the United States in the Global Sixties*, Princeton, NJ: Princeton University Press, 2010, pp. 31, 255, n. 77; Svenja Kunze, Hamburger Institut für Sozialforschung, to author, 3 February 2020; Levinson, *Five Years*, p. 62.

Sedova in Paris and met with representatives of Michel Pablo's Fourth International, which stressed anti-colonial and guerrilla struggles. He pushed the idea of armed struggle; they advised him that if the Unity Movement sent two representatives to Paris, the Fourth International would assist with preparations for armed struggle. He arrived home in July 1961 convinced of the need to build international solidarity networks to enable black South Africans to study abroad.[78]

Political conditions had deteriorated significantly during Alexander's two-and-a-half-year absence. University apartheid was now law. The University College of the Western Cape (UCWC), founded for students classified as Coloured, enrolled its first class in 1960. It provided training in an empty primary school near Bellville South for low to mid-level school and civil service jobs – light years from UCT.[79] Alexander had received teaching offers in Europe, but he could not obtain a post at UCT – even though very few South African academics had a doctorate. A former UCT professor evidently advised him to apply to UCWC, but he categorically rejected teaching at a 'bush' college, as the separate racial colleges were derisively called. He blotted out the pain with alcohol. After a weekend drinking spree, he applied for a job at Livingstone High School, where he began teaching in September 1961. Livingstone's politicized staff represented the full spectrum of the liberation movement. The school was routinely under security police surveillance. A number of teachers had been dismissed and banned in the 1950s, including Ben Kies; Richard Dudley, George Abrahams, Victor Wessels and Alie Fataar were banned in 1961. The school had outstanding intellectuals such as Kenneth Jordaan, with whom Alexander became close friends. Nonetheless, he had lost the freedom and equality he had discovered in West Germany.[80]

78 Matsemela, interview with Alexander, A2.3, p. 36; Busch, Busch and Press, eds, *Interviews*, pp. 59–62, 66–67; Alex de Jong, 'The Revolutionary Life and Times of Michel Pablo,' *Jacobin*, 23 March 2024, https://jacobin.com/2024/03/michel-pablo-greece-algeria-revolution, accessed 4 July 2025; Marcio Lauria Monteiro, 'The International Trotskyist Movement and the Postwar Revolutions: An Analysis of its Theoretical and Programmatic (Re)interpretations (1944–1963),' *Critique*, 44, 4, 2016, pp. 329–49.

79 Cornelius C. Thomas, 'Disaffection, Identity, Black Consciousness and a New Rector: An Exploratory Take on Student Activism at the University of the Western Cape 1966–1976,' *South African Historical Journal*, 54 (2005), pp. 72–90, 73; Cornelius Thomas, 'Finding the Durban Moment in Cape Town: New Directions in Student Activism in the Western Cape, 1972–1976,' https://www.sahistory.org.za/sites/default/files/Paper_Cornelius_Thomas.pdf, accessed 31 August 2022.

80 Alan Wieder, *Teacher and Comrade: Richard Dudley and the Fight for Democracy in South Africa*, Albany, NY: SUNY Press, 2008, pp. 90–1; Shadley Fataar to author, 5 April 2024; https://www.shadleyfataar.com/blog, accessed 5 April 2004; Levinson, *Five Years*, pp. 139–40, 150; Busch, Busch and Press, eds, *Interviews*, p. 67; discussion with Alexander, September 1987.

Figure 2: Livingstone High School teachers, c. 1960–61. Reginald Francke and Leslie van der Heyden would join the NLF. Front row: Messrs Bok (facing right), Gorvalla, Richard Dudley, Ms XXX, Mr Alie Fataar, Ms Francis?, Ms Daphne Jordaan. Second row: Messrs Murison, Ascher, XXX, Esterhuizen, Butler, Wessels (facing left), XXX, Reginald Francke (facing left), XXX, Samuels, Arendse?, Ward. Third row: Messrs Williams, Reed, Abrahams, Gentles?, Ms Carlier, Mr Leslie Van der Heyden. Fourth row: Messrs Classen, Kenneth Jordaan, Fowler?, XXX. Courtesy Shadley Fataar and Livingstone High School.

Repression was increasingly intense, political space squeezed. The 1960 Unlawful Organizations Act No 34 had outlawed organizations seen as threatening public order and safety. Certain political leaders had already been banned – Tabata in 1956, for his oratory successes, for instance. Now, the ANC and the PAC were banned. The ANC-aligned Coloured People's Congress could still operate, although many of its leaders went into exile. The Unity Movement had already split, largely along Anti-CAD and AAC lines, following the AAC's December 1958 conference and the expulsion of the Wits SOYA and the Cape Peninsula fellowships; SOYA became mired in these disputes.[81] The CPSU had withered and affiliated to the AAC, a move that prevented it from attracting students from different political tendencies. Similarly, a Durban

[81] Lewis, *Between the Wire*, pp. 270–1; for different perspectives see 'Presidential Address to the All-African Convention Conference,' Edendale, 14–16 December 1958, Lady Frere: SOYA, which criticizes the left-wing tendencies, and the Witwatersrand SOYA's description of the 1958 conferences in Society of Young Africa, 'The Maritzburg Conferences,' *The Soyan*, Durban, December 1959.

Students Union had been formed, but it too sought to mobilize students to follow the Unity Movement.[82]

Divided, the Unity Movement was squeezed by the Congress movement's expansion and marginalized by its own reluctance to engage in mass protests. As with the Alexandra bus boycott, its leaders tried to mask their reticence with the concept of the indivisibility of all struggles: that people must accept the Ten Point Programme before it would support popular struggles. Following the March 1960 shootings, the police had cordoned off Langa and Nyanga and brutalized their residents, who needed food. Phyllis Ntantala Jordan and others organized food donations. But Unity Movement leaders derided their efforts as 'liberal.' Tabata's pamphlet on the March events reiterated the Unity Movement's position: people do not develop ideas on their own through struggle; rather, 'those sections of the population who have learned to handle ideas' teach them national consciousness. When UCT academic and isiXhosa scholar A. C. Jordan refused to translate the supercilious pamphlet into isiXhosa, he and his wife Phyllis were isolated in Unity Movement circles, and Jordan suspended in 1961.[83] The Unity Movement had outstanding intellectuals, but many of its younger members saw their refusal to engage in popular struggles as arrogant.

After the Langa shootings Tabata visited the township as an elder statesman to address a PAC meeting. The township was in an uproar. Tabata called for no further bloodshed. A PAC representative asked him what his policy was. But the master orator had no policy for post-Sharpeville conditions. At that moment, reported one observer, Tabata looked like an old man. He was escorted to his car.[84] His response about what to do came later. In December 1960 he, Jane Gool and Alie Fataar launched the African People's Democratic Union – from January 1961 the African People's Democratic Union of Southern Africa (APDUSA). Affiliated to the AAC, it was a unitary organization that

82 Matsemela, interview with Alexander, A2.3, pp. 33–4; interview with John Samuels, Cape Town, 11 February 1987; Robin Kayser and Mohamed Adhikari, 'Land and Liberty! The African People's Democratic Union of Southern Africa during the 1960s,' in SADET, ed., *Road to Democracy*, pp. 319–39, 322–4.

83 On the events, Lodge *Black Politics*, pp. 221–4; on NEUM debates, Levinson, *Five Years*, pp. 105–11, and August Matsemela, interview with anonymous, UCT Centre for Popular Memory, https://ibali.uct.ac.za/s/center-for-popular-memory/item/104261, accessed 3 September 2025. Rassool, 'The individual, auto/biography,' pp. 382–3, 463–4; I. B. Tabata, *The Pan-African [sic] Congress Venture in Retrospect*, NEUM, September 1960, pp. 27–8; Phyllis P. Jordan, *A Life's Mosaic: The Autobiography of Phyllis Ntantala*, Claremont: David Philip and Bellville: Mayibuye, 1992, pp. 171–80; she does not mention the NEUM's treatment. Johnson, *Dreaming*, pp. 125–6 on Tabata and Jordan's intellectual differences.

84 Interview, Kenneth Jordaan, Harare, 14 December 1987. Jordaan's sources, a man named Jako and his wife in Birmingham, UK, said Tabata 'could not reply,' when asked.

individuals joined directly. It prioritized the demands of black workers and peasants, attracting a younger and more militant membership that was not occupationally restricted mainly to teaching.[85]

Conclusion

South Africa became a republic on 31 May 1961. Anti-apartheid politics receded further underground as public meetings were banned and sabotage began.[86] Convinced that the Unity Movement would be further diminished if it did not plan for armed struggle, Alexander conveyed the Fourth International message to the Unity Movement executive. His friend Deirdre Levinson witnessed some of the exchanges. British, from a devout Jewish family, she attended Oxford on a scholarship, then taught at UCT for five years until 1962. A participant-observer in Unity Movement discussions, she captured the tensions in her fictionalized memoir. Propaganda and theory were not enough to sway peasants, Alexander tried to convince Tabata and Gool. They needed material help. The Unity Movement had been applying non-collaboration mechanically, not simply boycotting government initiatives, but also popular organizations, he said.[87] However, Tabata and Gool forbade him to speak about these issues, worried the Unity Movement would be banned if it came out for armed struggle. Alexander was invited to a secret leadership caucus, but at the meeting he 'crossed swords with Jane [Gool]' and decided not to attend any further caucus meetings.[88]

Whatever the concerns of Tabata and Gool, sabotage against an unyielding state was inspiring, wrote Dennis Brutus – poet, English and Afrikaans teacher and well-known bodybuilder – when a blown-up pylon fell and blacked out large parts of Johannesburg:

> Here, thunderheads rear in the night
> dominating the awed quiet sky;
> On the quiet-breathing plains
> fractured metals shriek abandoned wails;
> My country, an ignorantly timid bride,
> winces, tenses for the shattering releasing tide.[89]

85 Matsemela, interview with Alexander, A2.3, pp. 33–4; Kayser and Adhikari, 'Land and Liberty!,' pp. 322–4.

86 Lodge, *Black Politics*, pp. 231–44; Robertson, *Liberalism*, p. 208.

87 Levinson, *Five Years*, pp. 144–5; Ralph Levinson, 'In Memoriam: Deirdre Bergson (Levinson) (English, 1951) 1931–2023,' *St Annes College Ship Magazine*, 2023, p. 89, st-annes.ox.ac.uk, accessed 3 January 2025.

88 Matsemela, interview with Alexander, A2.3, p. 38.

89 Dennis Brutus, 'Sabotage, 1962,' in Dennis Brutus, *Stubborn Hope*, Three Continents, 1978, p. 83, quoted in William E. Thompson, 'Dennis Brutus: An Interview,'

The preconditions for a New Left among Unity Movement and former Unity Movement youth were present in the rejection of Stalinism and the NEUM's rigid bureaucracy. While an incipient New Left emerged first in Alexandra Township, Alexander's return from Germany accelerated its development around Cape Town. From these radicalized strands emerged South Africa's tiny and ephemeral New Left. Profoundly intellectual, they would develop the Unity Movement's educational approach through small underground reading and discussion groups but break with it in their support for armed struggle, thus challenging both bureaucratic hierarchy and state power. The following chapters trace their formation, thinking and efforts to expand.

Ufahamu, 12, 2, 1983, pp. 69–77, 76, https://escholarship.org/uc/item/6tc554rb, accessed 1 April 2024. Courtesy Justina Robertson.

Chapter 2

Gender and Education in the National Liberation Front[1]

The groups comprising Cape Town's New Left – the Yu Chi Chan Club (YCCC) and its successor, the National Liberation Front (NLF) – consisted almost entirely of young students and teachers in their twenties. Intriguingly, the NLF's Cape Town cells had a greater proportion of women than the other early 1960s underground groups considering armed struggle. Four of the eleven NLF members imprisoned for conspiracy to overthrow the state were women – Elizabeth van der Heyden, Doris van der Heyden, Dorothy Alexander, and Dulcie September. Dorothy Adams, who led an NLF cell in the wine-producing town of Wellington in the Berg River valley, was detained, released and banned. The Namibian activist Ottilie Abrahams (née Schimming) chaired local and regional NLF meetings and edited its organ *Liberation* but returned to South West Africa [now Namibia] before the arrests. These women were intellectuals motivated by a desire to learn and to fight apartheid. They helped write and produce the YCCC's pamphlets and the NLF's *Liberation*, all of which the state would see as examples of thought crime. Nonetheless, they have been overshadowed by their male comrades, especially the trial's accused number one, Neville Alexander.[2]

Indeed, when Elizabeth van der Heyden was released from prison in 1974 after ten years for conspiracy, veteran anti-apartheid campaigner Helen Suzman asked her what Robben Island Prison had been like. There were no women prisoners on Robben Island, replied van der Heyden.[3] The exchange reflects a common misconception about anti-apartheid politics. Male experiences have been universalized, with those of Robben Island's black political prisoners overshadowing all others. The anti-apartheid struggle was based on an ideal of heroic masculinity that marginalized women's experiences and depreciated them as active political agents. Most studies of the South African

1 This is a revised version of Drew, 'Gendered Approach.'

2 Dollie, 'Dialogical Narratives,' p. 90.

3 Helen Scanlon, *Representation & Reality: Portraits of Women's Lives in the Western Cape, 1948–1976*, Pretoria: Human Sciences Research Council, 2007, p. 210; *State vs Alexander*, p. 1966.

left during the early armed struggle years have focused on the ANC and its allies and have neglected gender.[4]

By contrast, the underground South African Communist Party (SACP) formed in 1953 was arranged hierarchically into area, district and central committees. When ANC leader Nelson Mandela launched Umkhonto we Sizwe in December 1961, he recruited SACP and ANC men, although ANC women's leader Dorothy Nyembe states she was recruited that year, and communist journalist Ruth First was involved in Umkhonto's discussions.[5] 'You can count your lucky stars that we still have respect for women in our country,' First's interrogator told her when she was detained in August 1963 – referring obviously to white women. 'You could have been charged in the Rivonia case. But we didn't want a woman in that case.'[6] However, the state's attitude to incarcerating women activists, especially black women, was hardening. While First spent 117 days in prison, Nyembe, arrested the same year, was sentenced to three years. Moreover, the number of women in underground structures was also increasing. When communist lawyer Bram Fischer was arrested in September 1964, six of the twelve white detainees charged with him were women. By the decade's end, the detention and torture of Winnie Mandela's network showed the state's utter viciousness towards all women and men seen as threats.[7]

4 Some exceptions using life story approaches are Scanlon, *Representation*, see esp. pp. 12–14; Arianna Lissoni and Maria Suriano, 'Married to the ANC: Tanzanian Women's Entanglement in South Africa's Liberation Struggle,' *Journal of Southern African Studies*, 40, 1, 2014, pp. 129–50; N. Z. Mbatha, 'Narratives of Women Detained in the Kroonstad Prison during the Apartheid Era: A Socio-Political Exploration, 1960–1990,' *Journal for Contemporary History*, 43, 1, 2018, pp. 91–110; Emma Elinor Lundin, '"Now is the Time!" The Importance of International Spaces for Women's Activism within the ANC, 1960–1976,' *Journal of Southern African Studies*, 45, 2, 2019, pp. 323–40; Shanthini Naidoo, *Women Surviving Apartheid's Prisons*, Washington, DC: Just World Books, 2021.

5 Nelson Mandela, *Long Walk to Freedom: The Autobiography of Nelson Mandela*, London, 1994, pp. 259–62; 'Dorothy Nomzansi Nyembe,' *South African History Online*, https://www.sahistory.org.za/people/dorothy-nomzansi-nyembe, accessed 3 February 2021; Ruth First, *117 Days: An Account of Confinement and Interrogation under the South African 90-Day Detention Law*, London, 2010 [1965], pp. 7, 53–7, 138–9; Paul S. Landau, 'Gendered Silences in Nelson Mandela's and Ruth First's Struggle Auto/biographies,' *African Studies*, 78, 2, 2019, pp. 290–306.

6 First, *117 Days*, p. 139.

7 Mbatha, 'Narratives,' p. 105; Stephen Clingman, *Bram Fischer: Afrikaner Revolutionary*, Cape Town: David Philip; Bellville: Mayibuye; Amherst: University of Massachusetts, 1998, p. 337; Jonny Steinberg, *Winnie and Nelson: Portrait of a Marriage*, London: William Collins, 2023, pp. 226–34, 238–41; Joyce Sikakane, *A Window on Soweto*, London: International Defence and Aid, June 1977, pp. 59–70.

Political space had expanded during the early 1950s as masses of people – especially women – openly protested apartheid's imposition. But as state repression increased, political space contracted and moved underground. As M. Bahati Kuumba observes, the shift from public to underground politics has generally facilitated the dominance of military factions, skewing 'the gendered participation in the movement toward men.' This was certainly so for Umkhonto: by the mid-1960s Umkhonto recruits sent abroad for military training were predominantly men.[8] However, the NLF's focus on learning and its small horizontally organized cells facilitated women's participation, although their brief experience of gender equality in these groups was cut off by their arrests. This chapter discusses the NLF's development, arguing that the group's relatively flat organizational structure and non-gendered activities facilitated women's participation.[9]

The gendered antecedents of the Yu Chi Chan Club and the National Liberation Front

Members of YCCC and NLF came from Unity Movement affiliates, especially the Cape Peninsula Students Union (CPSU) and the African People's Democratic Union of Southern Africa (APDUSA).[10] South Africa was home to the early socialist feminist Olive Schreiner, and the Unity Movement accepted the idea of gender equality. Yet its conception of political activism assumed an abstract individual with traits then associated mainly with men – active, public, political and vocal, in contrast to the traits then linked to women – passive, private, domestic and silent.[11] Point One of the Unity Movement's Ten Point Programme declared: 'the right of every man and woman over the age of 21 to elect, and be elected to Parliament, Provincial Councils and all other Divisional and Municipal Councils.' Point One's explanatory remarks called for 'the end of all political tutelage, of all communal or indirect representation, and the granting to all Non-Europeans of the same … ballot as at present enjoyed by Europeans.' But those demands would not be sufficient to

8 M. Bahati Kuumba, *Gender and Social Movements*, Walnut Creek, CA: AltaMira, 2001, pp. 83–4; Simon Stevens, 'Violence, Political Strategy and the Turn to Guerrilla Warfare by the Congress Movement in South Africa,' *Journal of Southern African Studies*, 47, 6, 2021, pp. 1011–28, 1027.

9 Joan Acker, 'Hierarchies, Jobs, Bodies: A Theory of Gendered Organizations,' *Gender and Society*, 4, 2, June 1990, pp. 139–58; Rosabeth Moss Kanter, 'The Impact of Hierarchical Structures on the Work Behavior of Women and Men,' *Social Problems*, 23, 4, April 1976, pp. 415–30.

10 Interview, Kenneth Abrahams, Windhoek, February 1988.

11 Joan Wallach Scott, 'French Feminists and the Rights of "Man": Olympe de Gouges's Declarations,' *History Workshop*, 28, Autumn 1989, pp. 1–21, 4.

end gender inequality, as white women were also subjected to sexism. Point Six called for: 'Full equality of rights for all citizens without distinction of race, colour and sex.' Yet its explanatory remarks stated only: 'this means the abolition of all discriminatory Colour Bar Laws.'[12]

The Unity Movement's ambiguity towards gender was hardly unique. Unlike the Unity Movement, the ANC had a Women's League, founded in 1918 as the Bantu Women's League by the feminist activist Charlotte Maxeke. But only in 1943 did it accept women as full rather than auxiliary members. Its June 1955 Freedom Charter called for gender equality, albeit confusedly. Describing South Africans as a 'brotherhood' and as 'countrymen and brothers,' it nonetheless added that 'only a democratic state ... can secure to all their birthright without distinction of colour, race, sex or belief ... The rights of the people shall be the same, regardless of race, colour or sex.' However, it concluded: 'All laws which discriminate on grounds of race, colour or belief shall be repealed.'[13]

The liberation movement was aware of gender inequality. The 1950s had opened with mass demonstrations of African women pushing open political space by protesting the state's efforts to impose passes on them. The Congress-aligned Federation of South African Women (FEDSAW) adopted a detailed *Women's Charter* at its April 1954 inaugural conference. The charter called for social provision for mothers and children and 'the removal of all laws, regulations, conventions and customs that discriminate against us as women, and that deprive us in any way of our inherent right to the advantages, responsibilities and opportunities that society offers to any one section of the population.'[14]

The communist members of FEDSAW facilitated its membership in the Soviet-aligned Women's International Democratic Federation, whose overseas conferences offered FEDSAW access to international political space. The Federation's Helen Joseph, Lillian Ngoyi, and Dora Tamana attended the July 1955 World Congress of Mothers in Lausanne, Switzerland. On their return, FEDSAW convened its own Congress of Mothers in August 1955.[15]

[12] 'The Ten-Point Programme' [1943], in Allison Drew, ed., *South Africa's Radical Tradition: A Documentary History, vol. 2, 1943–1964*, Cape Town: Buchu, Mayibuye and UCT, 1997, pp. 62–3.

[13] 'The Freedom Charter adopted at the Congress of the People at Kliptown, Johannesburg on 25 and 26 June 1955,' in Drew, ed., *Radical Tradition*, vol. 2, pp. 121–4, 121–2.

[14] 'Report of the First National Conference of Women held in the Trades Hall, Johannesburg, South Africa, 17 April 1954, in Drew, ed., *Radical Tradition*, vol. 2, pp. 115–21, 118; Bahati Kuumba, *Gender*, pp. 40, 81; Cherryl Walker, *Women and Resistance in South Africa* 2nd ed., Cape Town: New Africa Books, 1991 [1982], part three.

[15] Meghan Healy-Clancy, 'The Family Politics of the Federation of South African Women: A History of Public Motherhood in Women's Antiracist Activism,' *Signs*, 42, 4, 2017, pp. 843–66, 857–9.

But FEDSAW was denied formal membership in the ANC-led Congress Alliance, thus limiting its national political space. Nonetheless, the *Women's Charter* and the earlier Ten Point Programme were pressures for the Freedom Charter's adoption. The rigid sectarianism dividing the Unity Movement and the Congress movement made it unlikely that FEDSAW influenced Unity Movement women, although they could not have missed some 20,000 women coming from across the country and marching on Pretoria's Union Buildings on 9 August 1956. Soon after, in 1957–58, women from Zeerust in the north-west region launched their own campaign against the government's attempt to impose passes on them.[16]

The Unity Movement's leaders had no comparable international links, although they had contacts with the small, fragmented Fourth International. But they encouraged radical education through lectures and discussions outside formal teaching institutions. In 1937 they launched the New Era Fellowship (NEF) to provide an intellectual space for black UCT students excluded from the university's non-academic spaces – clubs, sports and social events, for example. It held meetings at the Art Deco-style Stakesby-Lewis Hostel and the Fidelity Hall in multicultural District Six, a potpourri of Eastern European Jewish exiles, freed slaves from Africa and Malaysia and former indentured workers from India and China.[17] In marked contrast, white supremacy permeated UCT's atmosphere, penetrating the psyches of its tiny numbers of black students who, with rare exceptions, sat together at the back of lecture theatres and congregated outside at a campus spot cynically called Blackies' Corner or, optimistically, Freedom Square.[18]

Unity Movement-affiliated educational fellowships mushroomed around the Cape Peninsula in the 1940s and 1950s. Cape Town's laws impeded the influx of Africans, and fellowship audiences were generally people classified as Coloured with some higher education – many were teachers – so Tabata had launched the Society of Young Africa (SOYA) to promote the political education of African youth. Benita Parry attended NEF lectures and estimated that women constituted some 35–55 per cent of its audiences. Nonetheless, men dominated the discussions as they often had higher educational qualifications

16 Healy-Clancy, 'Family,' pp. 861–2; Lundin, 'Now,' pp. 327–8. The Congress Alliance included the ANC, South African Indian Congress, Coloured People's Organization (from December 1959, Coloured People's Congress), Congress of Democrats and Congress of Trade Unions; Charles Hooper, *Brief Authority*, London: Collins, 1960.

17 Lionel Davis, 'Telling My Story: Memories of District Six and Robben Island,' in Mario Pissarra, ed., *Awakenings: The Art of Lionel Davis*, Cape Town: Africa South Art Initiative, 2017, pp. 29–38, 29; Sandwith, *World*, pp. 157–8; Crain Soudien, *The Cape Radicals: Intellectual and Political Thought of the New Era Fellowship, 1930s-1960s*, Johannesburg: Wits University Press, 2019.

18 Levinson, *Five Years*, p. 68.

than women, making participation less intimidating. The 'woman question' was rarely if ever discussed – an interesting silence given that the Russian Marxists on whom Unity Movement leaders drew their inspiration had often discussed and written about the topic.[19]

Jane Gool was a significant exception to the male-dominated leadership. Born in 1902, as a young woman she joined the Lenin Club and helped launch the tiny Spartacist Club and Workers Party of South Africa, and then the larger Anti-CAD and Unity Movement. An organizer, newspaper contributor, pamphleteer and public speaker, she nonetheless 'had no time for other women,' remembered Ursula Fataar (née Wolhuter). 'They saw her as strange and quirky. She would speak at their [Unity Movement] conferences and was part of the inner group that organized the Unity Movement.'[20]

By contrast, Benita Parry stressed Gool's courage. The daughter of an elite conservative Muslim family, she broke racial and religious barriers by attending the South African Native College (Fort Hare) and marrying an African – Isaac Tabata. But Gool never promoted herself as a spokesperson for women or pushed the woman question. 'It seems to me that she was positioned as a figure-head which confirmed the movement's commitment to a gender equality that never was,' Parry recalled. She was 'on all the important committees,' Parry explained, and 'well-versed in Marxist literature and in Trotskyites [*sic*] debates both national and international. She invariably contributed to internal theoretical discussion, and was also a practiced and effective public speaker.'[21] Yet an experienced public speaker well versed in Marxist theory was certainly not a figurehead. Neville Alexander described her as 'almost my political mother … who, behind the scenes, played a very, very important role.' Her niece Nina Hassim, who once caught her reading a book as she cooked, saw her as an aunt, mentor and comrade who encouraged her to read whatever she liked. She 'could speak well and had a good presence … and saw herself as a revolutionary, devoted to politics.'[22]

In contrast to Jane Gool's influential public role and behind-the-scenes power, the Scottish immigrant, author and Marxist literary critic Dora Taylor played an extremely important behind-the-scenes intellectual role – refraining,

19 Benita Parry to author, 26 July 1996; *cf.* Sandwith, *World*, 167; Soudien, *Cape Radicals*, pp. 8, 128; Richard Stites, *The Women's Liberation Movement in Russia: Feminism, Nihilism, and Bolshevism, 1860–1930*, Princeton, NJ: Princeton University Press, 1978, pp. 233–77, 317–422.

20 Interview, Ursula Wolhuter Fataar, 24 June 2018, Wynberg, Cape Town; 'Jane Gool – A Tribute,' African People's Democratic Union of Southern Africa, 16 January 2020, http://www.apdusa.org.za/jane-gool-a-tribute, accessed 21 August 2025.

21 Parry to author.

22 Matsemela, interview, Neville Alexander, A2.3, pp. 39–41; interview, Nina Hassim, Cape Town, 10 May 2019.

as a white person, from overshadowing the Unity Movement's public proceedings. She worked closely with Tabata, and her breadth of intellect profoundly influenced Alexander. Similarly, Joyce Meissenheimer edited *The Torch* from 1948 until her banning in September 1961, but she too remained hidden behind better-known men.[23]

Yet Tabata encouraged individual women. When the Unity Movement organized a boycott of the April 1952 Jan van Riebeeck Tercentenary Festival commemorating the arrival of Dutch colonizers, he insisted that Phyllis Ntantala Jordan – evidently disliked by Jane Gool – speak on a public podium. She was reticent. 'But when I took up the theme of "We have Nothing to Celebrate" and related it to the position of African women, the exploited workers in the cities and the widows of the reserves,' she realized, 'I was not at a loss of what to say.'[24] However few in numbers, the Unity Movement had important women intellectuals, despite their apparent lack of feminist sisterhood. Nonetheless, they seemingly had less involvement in popular organizations than their communist and Congress movement counterparts.

Student politics and political families

With Unity Movement organizations largely silent on gender, young socialist women of those years did not directly challenge the gender hierarchy in which they had been socialized and politicized. Instead, they became activists in issue-oriented student movement politics, feeling more comfortable speaking in the small study circles popping up across the western Cape, rather than in large, hierarchically organized meetings.

Cape Town political circles were small, and politics was very much a 'family business,' according to activist James Marsh. One knew who the politically engaged families were, the van der Heydens being a case in point.[25] Elizabeth van der Heyden credits growing up in a 'free-thinking family … a big rowdy family' as crucial to her intellectual and political development. Born in December 1935, her father was a carpenter, and her mother, a housewife who cleaned for a white family. They lived in Gleemoor, a working-class area of Athlone, which was classified Coloured during apartheid. Their council house carried a stigma, but the children were fortunate in being allowed to

23 Matsemela, interview, Alexander, A2.2, pp. 52–53; Sandwith, *World*, pp. 66–128; cf. 167; Johnson, *Dreaming*, pp. 107, 119–30; Solomons, 'Reading,' pp. 47–9; Rassool, 'The Individual, Auto/biography.

24 Jordan, *Life's* Mosaic, pp. 151–2; Levinson, *Five Years*, p. 81.

25 Interview, James Marsh, Kenwyn, Cape Town, 30 June 2018.

talk and ask questions, and in this way, she learned to speak in small groups. They spoke English at home and listened to BBC radio.[26]

Although her mother warned her that men did not like smart women, van der Heyden was a good student and voracious reader. With her father's support she reached standard 10 – the end of high school. She attended Wynberg and Athlone High, and at both schools was strongly influenced by her Unity Movement teachers. Thus politicized, she began attending the Cape Flats Educational Fellowship. The sandy Cape Flats sprawled south-east of central Cape Town. Africans had been forcibly relocated from the city centre to the flats from the start of the century. They were moved first to Ndabeni Location, comprising military tents, dormitories and corrugated iron huts, then Langa, a supposed garden city with surveillance, then Nyanga and Gugulethu, to accommodate the growth of squatter camps. Nonetheless, when Group Areas became law in 1950, the flats were still relatively unpopulated. But from 1957 on, Coloureds and Africans were pushed further away from the city centre and into the flats. In addition to breaking up established communities and causing mass social disruption, Group Areas made life more difficult for girls and women. They had to travel longer distances to school and work, meaning numerous transfers between buses and trains, so they hesitated about attending evening social events and political meetings. Athlone, Bonteheuwel, Elsies River, Grassy Park, Langa, Lansdowne and Nyanga were just some of the Cape Flats townships.[27]

Nursing and teaching were generally the only professions open to black women. Van der Heyden's younger brother Leslie was groomed for university, but she was expected to go to teacher training college, although later their younger sister Doris attended university. Elizabeth took a two-year teacher training course at Hewat Training College, where the NEF held joint meetings with the college debating society. In 1956 she began teaching at Grassy Park High. There Elizabeth met Ursula Wolhuter, politicized through her Livingstone High teachers, who had also attended Hewat and who found van der Heyden 'very revolutionary.' Wolhuter had taught Domestic Science at Alexander Sinton High in Athlone before transferring to Grassy Park, whose students, she felt, were less vocal than those in Athlone, perhaps because the Athlone parents

26 Interview, Elizabeth van der Heyden, Elfindale, Cape Town, 8 June 2018; Scanlon, *Representation,* p. 202.

27 John Western, *Outcast Cape Town*, Cape Town, Pretoria and Johannesburg: Human & Rousseau, 1981, pp. 31–58, 70–81, 99, 103–12; Christopher Saunders, 'The Creation of Ndabeni,' and 'From Ndabeni to Langa,' in Christopher Saunders, ed., *Studies in the History of Cape Town*, vol. 1, Cape Town: History Department, UCT, 1979, pp. 132–66 and 167–204; 'Athlone – or Cape Flats, Cape Town,' *South African History Online*, 14 July 2011, https://www.sahistory.org.za/place/athlone-or-cape-flats-cape-town, accessed 15 July 2024; Shadley Fataar to author, 14 July 2024.

were more middle class and intellectual. Indeed, despite the efforts of Grassy Park's politically conscious teachers, certain male teachers brazenly chased female students, giving the school a poor reputation amongs the locals.[28] The next year van der Heyden joined the Teachers' League of South Africa, but it was male dominated and consumed by the Unity Movement's factionalism. Although many teachers were women, most Teachers' League leaders were men with the higher qualifications prized for the top posts.[29]

The university apartheid bill had catalysed the CPSU's March 1957 launch – despite opposition from the Anti-CAD, which saw it as a potential rival to the educational fellowships. Already teaching, van der Heyden became an associate CPSU member. Previously, in her words, an 'observer rather than participant,' in the CPSU she became an activist. The office-bearers were all male except for Nasheba Jardine from Livingstone High, who was the treasurer. Kenneth Abrahams was president, and Alexander editor of its organ *The Student*; in van der Heyden's recollection, they were the main speakers and movers. [30]

At the CPSU, van der Heyden met Fikile Bam, Marcus Solomon and Ottilie Schimming. Van der Heyden and Bam became romantically involved. Tall, attractive and self-confident, Bam came from a renowned educated Christian African family that, very unusually, owned property – Grasslands Farm, some 1,058.5 acres near Tsolo in the Transkei. In the nineteenth century the British had granted quitrent farms to certain Mpondomise people, including the Bams, who were considered local gentry. Fikile, born in 1937, had three older sisters – his name meant 'he has arrived.' As the oldest son, he was due to inherit the family farm, although by the 1960s, it was heavily in debt.[31] His parents were teachers, but since married women could not teach, his mother stopped work, although she later retrained as a nurse, eventually becoming a community health educator. His father, an advisor to the Pondoland paramount chief and a member of the Transkei's *Bunga* [council], joined the army during the Second World War and was based in the Transvaal, where he remained after the war. Raised mainly by his mother, Bam attended mission school in Pondoland, where the ANC's Oliver Tambo taught. When his family moved to Sophiatown, Johannesburg, he studied at St Cyprian's and at St Peter's, where he again met Tambo, who profoundly influenced him. He entered UCT

28 Interview, van der Heyden; interview, Fataar; Musuva, *Peeping*, p. 134.

29 Interview, van der Heyden; *State vs Alexander*, pp. 1517–18; Scanlon, *Representation,* pp. 204–5.

30 *State vs Alexander*, pp. 1517–18, 1657; *The Student*, n.d. [1957], UCT BC1538 D3.5; interview, van der Heyden; Scanlon, *Representation,* pp. 204–5; Nina Hassim to author, 16 April 2020.

31 Seán Morrow, *The Bams of Grasslands Farm: A Family History*, Auckland Park: Staging Post, 2024, pp. 13–18, 21, 29–31.

in 1957, recalling that there were 'six black African students and no more than about 26 coloureds and Indians.' An African nationalist when he arrived, he soon fell under the Unity Movement's sway, becoming best friends with Archie Mafeje and lodging with Unity Movement stalwarts A. C. and Phyllis Jordan, the Nobles, the Abrahamses and the Kobuses. After completing his BA in 1960, he began a law degree.[32]

Bam's family heritage weighed heavily on him, and he was expected to marry a woman of appropriate social standing. Nonetheless, he 'courted women with determination and success,' wooing them with poetry. At UCT, when his English girlfriend committed suicide, he was very distressed, Seán Morrow recounts. Deirdre Levinson, close friends with the young woman, thought otherwise. Sceptical about Neville Alexander's girlfriends, she was scathing about Bam. In her telling, Bam refused to marry the woman after she became pregnant, despite his earlier professions of love, and quickly recovered to pursue other women, including van der Heyden.[33]

Marcus Solomon came from a very different background. Born in Grahamstown in 1939, he spent much of his childhood in Port Alfred. His father, a waiter, was a Hindu born of Tamil parents; his mother was of Scottish and Khoi descent and belonged to the mixed Xhosa and Coloured Protestant Congregational Church. After his mother died, his younger sister and brother were sent to an Mthata orphanage, but he was raised by his religious aunt in Grahamstown and briefly became a teenaged street preacher. He received his junior certificate from Rhodes University College Coloured Practising School and started working as a train bedding boy. But keen to continue his studies, in 1957 he moved to Cape Town, where he went to Trafalgar High and Hewat College, attended NEF lectures and joined the CPSU, meeting the Schimming siblings.[34]

Like van der Heyden, Ottilie Schimming came from a political family. Born in 1937, she grew up in the multi-ethnic Old Location at Windhoek, where she attended St Barnabas Anglican Mission School, whose teachers were mainly English-speaking South Africans. When apartheid was introduced, the Schimming children were classified as Coloured and compelled to change schools. So her parents sent Ottilie, her sisters Nora, Charlotte and Isabella

32 UCT Legal Resource Centre Oral History Project, interview, Fikile Bam, 29 November 2007, p. 3; Len Morris, interview with Fikile C. Bam, Cape Town, 2 August 1999, pp. 1–2, www.columbia.edu/cu/lweb/digital/collections/oral_hist/carnegie/pdfs/fikile-bam.pdf, accessed 3 September 2025; Seán Morrow, *Saturday Star*, 11 June 2016; Morrow, *Bams*, pp. 83–5; *State vs Alexander*, p. 2015; Nyoka, 'Mafeje,' p. 29.

33 Morrow, *Bams*, pp. 85, 98, 168–70; Levinson, *Five Years*, pp. 10–13, 113–19; discussion with Neville Alexander, Cape Town, June 1987.

34 Allison Drew, 'Marcus Solomon,' 13 May 2019, *South African History Online*, https://www.sahistory.org.za/people/marcus-solomon, accessed 30 January 2021.

and their brother Harold to study in Cape Town, despite local people insisting that the girls would return with 'a big stomach.'

Ottilie was vivacious and driven. In Cape Town she attended Zonnebloem College and Trafalgar High – which like Livingstone had a left-wing teaching staff with strong Trotskyist and Unity Movement influence.[35] Impressed by her teachers, she 'made sure [she] met the right kind of people.' Active in the CPSU and SOYA and in Namibian circles, in 1960 she joined the South West Africa People's Organisation (SWAPO). Graduating from UCT in 1961 with a Bachelor of Arts and a Higher Primary Teachers' Certificate, she began teaching at Livingstone, 'already clear that the man [she] was going to marry … would have to come to Namibia.' She found that man in Kenneth Abrahams.[36] Born in 1936 in Cape Town, Abrahams was one of eight siblings in a working-class family – his mother more politically conscious than his apolitical father. He attended Upper Ashley Street Primary whose headmaster was George Golding, dubbed 'collaborator' because he supported the government's plan to form a Coloured Affairs Department (CAD). But Golding helped him get bursaries so he could attend Trafalgar High, where, influenced by his Unity Movement teachers, he sold *The Torch* and distributed Anti-CAD flyers. At Trafalgar he became good friends with Harold Schimming, Ottilie's brother; they enrolled at UCT's medical school together. Through Harold he met Ottilie and other Namibians and became engaged in their struggle.[37]

Van der Heyden launched the CPSU's South Peninsula Branch in Grassy Park and urged her good friend Dulcie September to join. Born in August 1935, September's parents were apolitical, her father a primary school principal, and her mother a housewife. The Septembers and van der Heydens lived around the corner from each other in Athlone, although the Septembers had a higher social standing.[38] Dulcie's father treated her brutally, favouring

35 Allison Drew, Interview with Ottilie Abrahams, Windhoek, February 1988; Basel Africa Library, TAA18_9_A, TAA18_9_B.

36 August Matsemela, interviews, Ottilie Abrahams, Windhoek, 31 October, 3 November 1988, UCT Centre for Popular Memory [hereafter UCTCPM] BC1223; interview, Ottilie Abrahams, Windhoek, February 1988; interview, Kenneth Abrahams; Yvette Abrahams, 'Tribute to "Mother of Education",' *The Namibian*, 4 July 2018, https://www.namibian.com.na/179164/archive-read/Tribute-to-Mother-of-Education, accessed 3 August 2020; *State vs Alexander*, pp. 1930–54; Curriculum Vitae, Ottilie Grete Abrahams (née Schimming).

37 'Kenneth Abrahams: A Doctor in the Struggle at Home and in Exile,' in Colin Leys and Susan Brown, eds, *Histories of Namibia: Living through the Liberation Struggle – Life Histories*, London: Merlin: 2005, pp. 139–57, 139–41; photo of UCT's graduating medical class and discussion with Kenneth Abrahams, Jr., Windhoek, 16 October 2022.

38 [Michael Arendse?], 'Dulcie September Biography,' n.d., courtesy Michael Arendse; *State vs Alexander*, p. 1583.

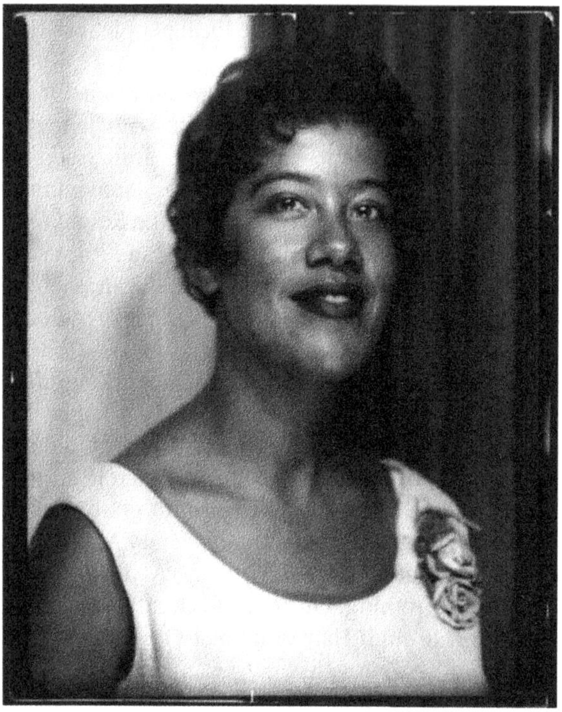

Figure 3: A young Dulcie September, no date. Source: Unknown.

his younger daughter. To avoid his beatings, Dulcie frequented the van der Heyden home, and she and Elizabeth became good friends. Not academically inclined as a child – perhaps because of the beatings – September was twice held back, so that she was in the same class as her younger sister. Like van der Heyden, she attended Athlone High, where she was similarly politicized by her Unity Movement teachers. But in standard 8 – normally 13 or 14 years, but she may have been older – her father removed her from school. He threw her out of the house when she was still a teenager, so she slept on the front stoep until she found new accommodation – learning early the price of speaking back to power.[39]

Nonetheless, she persevered, attending evening classes while working days, and passing standard 8. She began but did not finish a teacher training course at Wesley Training College in Salt River. However, her mother appealed to Dr Richard van der Ross, principal of Battswood Teacher Training College in Wynberg. Determined, September enrolled and completed the course. In July 1956 she began teaching at Bridgetown Primary, Athlone's first primary school, where the entering students were already nine or ten years old. Struck

39 Interview, van der Heyden.

by the local poverty and the overcrowded classes, she 'became aware of the struggle people were facing.' She joined the Teachers' League and attended CPSU meetings but never joined, despite van der Heyden's urgings.[40] Van der Heyden and September resigned from the Teachers' League because of its endless squabbles and joined APDUSA.[41]

The move to underground politics

With the prohibition of open-air gatherings that the government deemed a danger to public peace, political space receded underground. Activists met secretly in their homes. Using a methodology of reading and discussion, study groups sprang up to assess the rapidly evolving conditions, especially after sabotage began. Once Alexander returned from Europe, he broached the subject of armed struggle to the Unity Movement leadership, but they insisted he not discuss it. Resenting their stricture, he began addressing different study groups about the Algerian war.

Alexander's CPSU friends Ottilie Schimming and Kenneth Abrahams, now married, were both in SWAPO, which in 1961 'resolved to prepare for the eventual armed struggle.'[42] Kenneth Abrahams pushed the SWAPO line. At SOYA's January 1962 conference he was suspended on the grounds that he was in SWAPO; by extension he was suspended from all Unity Movement affiliates. Abrahams was not present, but Alexander was, and he was suspended for defending Abrahams.[43] Ottilie had loved the Unity Movement's intellectual stimulation but dropped out once her husband and Alexander were suspended.[44]

The two men had supporters. Like the van der Heydens and Schimmings, the Alexanders were a political family. Neville and his younger sister Dorothy were both live-wires.[45] Born in August 1938, Dorothy attended Holy Rosary

40 September Biography; *State vs Alexander*, pp. 1560–61, 1588.

41 Robin Kayser and Mohamed Adhikari, 'Land and Liberty! The African People's Democratic Union of Southern Africa during the 1960s,' in SADET, *Road to Democracy*, pp. 319–39, 322–4; *State vs Alexander*, p. 1518; Scanlon, *Representation,* pp. 206–7.

42 SWAPO of Namibia, *To Be Born a Nation: The Liberation Struggle for Namibia*, Luanda: SWAPO of Namibia; London: Zed, 1981, p. 176.

43 Interview, Neville Alexander, Cape Town, 14 March 1988; interview, Kenneth Abrahams; Matsemela, interview, Alexander, A2.3, pp. 38–45; Matsemela, interview Fikile Bam, UCTCPM 104311, https://ibali.uct.ac.za/s/center-for-popular-memory/item/104311, accessed 2 September 2025; *State vs Alexander*, pp. 1661–62; Rassool, 'Individual,' pp. 465–8; Levinson, *Five Years*, pp. 149–53. 'Kenneth Abrahams,' in Leys and Brown, eds, *Histories* p. 144.

44 Matsemela, interviews, Ottilie Abrahams; interview, Ottilie Abrahams, Windhoek, February 1988; interview, Kenneth Abrahams; Yvette Abrahams, 'Tribute'; *State vs Alexander*, 1930–54.

45 Interview, Marsh; *State vs Alexander*, p. 1661.

Convent in Cradock and obtained her teaching certificate from Dower Memorial College in Uitenhage, joining the Teachers' League in 1956. In January 1960 she started teaching at Garden Village Methodist School in Maitland. After her brother's return, she accompanied him to lectures on international affairs, joining APDUSA around August–September. She joined an unofficial Lansdowne APDUSA group, which had several teachers and two students. Among them were Brian Landers, a student of University College of the Western Cape (UCWC), and Franz Lee, a clerk from an impoverished north-east Cape family. Fired and blacklisted, Lee enrolled at the distance-education University of South Africa. The Lansdowne group invited Neville Alexander and Kenneth Abrahams to lecture on Algeria, Cuba and South West Africa.[46]

Neville Alexander had already joined Wolhuter's study group.[47] In March 1962 Dorothy Alexander joined an Athlone caucus of discontented Apdusans, which included Elizabeth van der Heyden, September and Solomon. They invited Abrahams and Alexander to speak. As September put it, 'the [APDUSA] leadership ... had a bureaucratic hold over the organisation ... no progressive work could be done and the suspension of Drs. Alexander and Abrahams caused a rift in the organization ... many of the members were contemplating leaving.' The caucus met fortnightly to discuss revamping APDUSA.[48]

In April a new circle began meeting fortnightly at the Abrahams home. Initially, the group included Neville Alexander, Xenophon Pitt, a UCWC student and CPSU member from Queenstown, and Andreas Shipanga of SWAPO.[49] In May Kenneth Abrahams invited Solomon to join.[50] Bam, then boarding with the Abrahamses, began attending in June; since Archie Mafeje still supported Tabata, the two friends drifted apart.[51] SWAPO members migrant worker David Haufiku and, briefly, Peter Kaluma also joined in June. In mid-July Kenneth Abrahams invited van der Heyden after learning she had been reading independently about guerrilla struggles. The second woman in the group, she was 'eager for new ideas.' Bam suggested the group be called

46 *State vs Alexander*, pp. 1548–50; 'Franz J. T. Lee,' New York: Alexander Defense Committee, n.d., UCT BC1538 D6.

47 Allison Drew and Lungisile Ntsebeza, interview, Marcus Solomon, Rylands, Cape Town, 15 June 2018; interview, Fataar.

48 *State vs Alexander*, pp. 1562, 1519–20, 1663.

49 *Liberation*, 1, 1, February 1963, p. 5; *State vs Alexander*, p. 1663; Dennis Mercer, *Interviews in Depth – Namibia (SWAPO): Andreas Shipanga*, Richmond, BC: LSM, 1973, pp. 4, 6; *Namibian*, 21 February 2013, https://archive.is/20130221040735/http://www.namibian.com.na/news-articles/national/full-story/archive/2012/may/article/liberation-pioneer-dies, accessed 23 June 2020.

50 Drew and Ntsebeza, interview, Solomon, 15 June 2018.

51 Morrow, *Bams*, pp. 89–90; Nyoka, 'Mafeje,' p. 30.

Ingqungquthela yesizwe [unity of the nation]. But they decided on the Yu Chi Chan Club, after Mao Zedung's book; they nicknamed it YC3. Naming might be seen as important, but there is no indication they saw themselves as Maoist. Rather, they were intellectually eclectic, albeit broadly socialist. 'We felt armed struggle was inevitable and that we needed to be a part of it,' recalled van der Heyden.[52]

Strategies of armed struggle had been discussed in political circles since the 1961 sabotage attacks. The YCCC's approach was comparative. Mao's book concerned China's response to Japan's 1937 invasion: 'the guerrilla campaigns being waged in China today are a page in history that has no precedent,' he wrote. 'Their influence will be confined not solely to China ... but will be world-wide.' His book was 'the first systematic study of the subject,' according to its American translator Brigadier General Samuel B. Griffith in 1961.[53] In addition to Mao, they read Che Guevara's *Guerrilla Warfare*, Joan Gillespie's *Algeria: Rebellion and Revolution*, and Deneys Reitz's *Commando: A Boer Journal of the Boer War* about the 1899–1902 Afrikaner guerrilla war. Bam found Reitz's book to be especially important as a corrective to their thinking in that it reflected South African terrain and experience. The discussions must have been sophisticated, as well as accessible: the point was not to mechanically apply these cases to South Africa, Dorothy Alexander later explained, but to assess in what ways they might be applicable.[54]

They photostatted texts and published their own pamphlets, stimulating lively discussions with frequent disagreements. Each pamphlet was drafted by one person, with occasional input from others. Neville Alexander wrote *The Conquest of Power in South Africa*, and Kenneth Abrahams *Technical and Organisational Aspects of the Yu Chi Chan Club*, although Ottilie undoubtedly helped shape its ideas about South West Africa. Elizabeth van der Heyden drafted *Secret Communications*, lifted from the 1962 *Encyclopedia Britannica* section on 'codes and ciphers.'[55] The pamphlets' authorship was not directly

52 *State vs Alexander*, p. 1663; p. 1352, has *Indqindqthela yesizwe*; Ronald Dreyer, *Namibia & Southern Africa: Regional Dynamics of Decolonization, 1945–1990*, London: Routledge, 2016 [1994], p. 204, n.26; Randolph Vigne, *Liberals against Apartheid: A History of the Liberal Party of South Africa, 1953–68*, Basingstoke: Macmillan, 1997, p. 185.

53 Mao Tse-tung, *Mao Tse-tung on Guerrilla Warfare*, p. 3, and Griffith, 'Introduction,' p. 11.

54 *State vs Alexander*, pp. 1553, 1520–22, 1667, 1700; Matsemela, interview with Bam, UCTCPM, 104311.

55 Interview, van der Heyden; *State vs Alexander*, p. 1522; Matsemela, interview, Alexander, pp. 67–68; [YCCC-Neville Alexander], *Pamphlet no. II: The Conquest of Power in South Africa* [1962]; [YCCC-Kenneth Abrahams], *Pamphlet no. III: Technical and Organisational Aspects of the Yu Chi Chan Club* [1962]; [YCCC-Elizabeth van

gendered, but reflected that some members had the scholarly training to write long complex pieces and some did not. Nor was production gendered: Neville Alexander and Landers typed; Ottilie Abrahams cyclostyled; Solomon and Bam stapled.[56] Work in APDUSA continued: Neville Alexander and Solomon ran under-the-radar study groups; Elizabeth van der Heyden, Dorothy Alexander and September served on its finance committee; Van der Heyden and Pitt organized; September and Wolhuter convened meetings. They mimeographed documents at the van der Heyden home and in the Abrahams' garage, where they kept several typewriters, allowing production of the YCCC, NLF and SWAPO documents to be centralized.[57]

In November–December, Haufiku left for South West Africa, Bam to prepare for exams, and Pitt to teach in Queenstown. Those remaining disbanded the YCCC and decided to organize a network of cells called the National Liberation Front, after the Algerian FLN. They sought the widest possible basis for unity – prospective members had only to be anti-apartheid and interested in discussing guerrilla struggle. Its members had endured years of sectarian fighting within the Unity Movement, and they wanted no more arguments over the merits of either the Ten Point Programme or the Freedom Charter. Moreover, many of them were still in the Unity Movement or felt a sentimental attachment to it, and they did not want news of their activities to get back to Tabata. They didn't want to rock the boat, recalled Bam.[58] The decision to form the NLF was confirmed at an executive committee meeting on 16–18 January 1963. But setting off on their own had consequences, Alexander later conceded: 'We didn't have the maturity. We didn't have the resources. We didn't have the network.' Umkhonto, by contrast, had the support of the ANC and the SACP and, in turn, that of the Soviet Union.[59]

The National Liberation Front – structure and recruitment

The anonymous typescript 'When, Where, Why was the N.L.F. Formed?' describes the NLF's structure and aims. It was presumably a discussion document rather than a binding agreement adopted by the members. According to the document, the NLF aspired to link various anti-apartheid groups into a united front, 'organize in breadth not depth' and create a network of cells with ten regions, five zones, five areas, and one cell per area,

der Heyden, *Pamphlet no. IV: Secret Communications* [1962–63], all in UCTMA, A. H. Murray Papers [hereafter BC1253], A.1.1.

56 *State vs Alexander*, pp. 1411–12, 1744, 1755.

57 *State vs Alexander*, pp. 1519–20, 1701; interview, van der Heyden.

58 Matsemela, interview with Bam, UCTCPM, 104311.

59 Matsemela, interview, Alexander, A2.3, pp. 45, 81; At the trial Alexander denied the NLF was named after the FLN, *State vs Alexander*, pp. 1701–3, 1611.

i.e., *dorp* [small rural town or village], location or part of a town. Influenced by the FLN model, cells were to have a maximum of ten members – most were much smaller. Regional committees with two members from each cell would coordinate work by passing information to and from the cells.[60] Although some members had presumably been influenced by Trotsky's writing, their usage of 'united front' suggested an alliance based on shared interests in armed struggle rather than Trotsky's aim to promote working-class consciousness and common political action.

Significantly, the document stated: 'No sex discrimination … No age discrimination. No discrimination on grounds of political history.' Despite the stricture on age discrimination, the document suggested people between the ages of 20 and 35, as students were seen as 'usually too immature,' and older people, 'too fixed in way of thinking.' They sought people with political and organizational experience keen to form cells and study guerrilla struggle. New recruits were to be vetted by two individuals, but this was not always practised. The desired attributes were revolutionary ardour, honesty, integrity, intelligence, initiative and fearlessness; idealistically, each member was 'to devote 24 hours per day for revolution' and 'to work and play only when very necessary.' The document even questioned whether revolutionaries should have children, although the married Abrahamses already did.[61] Leslie van der Heyden married Ursula February, who taught at Grassy Park High alongside his sister Elizabeth and Wolhuter, while Elizabeth broke up with Bam.[62] In short, the NLF's young members were pursuing their romantic interests, but with very different conceptions of personal relationships. This suggests that 'When, Where, Why' was purely a draft for discussion.

Reflecting their concern with political education, they prioritized the production of literature. The NLF produced three issues of *Liberation* in February, April and May 1963. 'If any organization is to grow,' it exhorted, 'it must have a means of spreading its ideas amongst the people it wishes to interest.' After all, South and South West African political organizations had produced their own statements and newspapers. However, mentioning the recently banned *New Age*, and *The Torch* and *Soyan*, it felt that the liberation movement's literature was patchy, uneven and inadequate. The South and South West African movements 'are starved of recent, up to date literature,' and need a revolutionary publication. *Liberation* was to be an educational

60 BC1253, 'When, Where, Why was the N.L.F. Formed?' April 1962 [*sic*], p. 2; Marcus Solomon to author, 3 June 2020, thought that the document was collectively discussed; Scanlon, *Representation,* pp. 208–9.

61 *When, Where*, pp. 2–3, 9; Lissoni and Suriano, 'Married,' p. 138, for a similar view of revolutionary lives.

62 *State vs Alexander*, p. 380; interview, van der Heyden; Levinson, *Five Years*, pp. 9–13, 113–17.

and recruiting tool providing surveys of the various political organizations – Congress Alliance, SACP, Pan Africanist Congress (PAC), Poqo, SWAPO and Unity Movement and Anti-CAD.[63] The February issue highlighted the January conference recommendations concerning their literature and their paid organizer. They hoped to form cells in Wellington, Worcester, Port Elizabeth, Cradock and South West Africa and, within several months, in the Transkei, Natal and Johannesburg. Their paid organizer was trying to build cells in Kimberley and Barkly West, it reported.

Recruitment developed through personal networks, broadly following gender lines, with some exceptions. In van der Heyden's recollection they looked at CPSU and APDUSA members who would fit into the sort of organization they were envisioning. She recruited September, whom she thought was an adept organizer and administrator; September recalled learning that the NLF was a study group in January–February 1963 and joining in March because she 'was interested in learning.' Van der Heyden also recruited Dorothy Alexander and her own younger sister, Doris. A CPSU and APDUSA member, Doris had attended Athlone High and studied librarianship at UCT. In 1961 she became a library assistant at the Cape Provincial Library Services. Tired of APDUSA's 'continual bickering,' she joined the new group.[64]

Elizabeth van der Heyden met Dorothy Adams at an APDUSA meeting. Opinionated and outspoken from a young age, Adams had been born in 1928 and raised in the *verkrampte* [conservative] rural town of Wellington, some 43 miles north-west of Cape Town. Her great-grandfather, the West Indian photographer Francis McDonald Gow, had introduced the African-American-founded African Methodist Episcopal (AME) Church to South Africa. Her maternal grandfather was an AME minister, and her mother active in the church. The women in Dorothy's immediate family attended the AME church, and the men the Dutch Reformed Church, but Dorothy only attended church for special events. She studied at Athlone Teacher Training College in Paarl, nine miles south, teaching first in the tiny town of Wolseley, later returning to Wellington to teach at Pauw Gedenk Primary School, not far from her home on Kloof Street.[65]

Sorely disappointed by the reluctance of churches to challenge the 1950 Group Areas Act, which allowed the forced relocation of people according to the government's racial categories, Adams became active in the Teachers' League and APDUSA. In March 1963 the Wellington Apdusans invited Neville Alexander to lecture on Algeria. Adams set up an NLF cell with three stable and various floating members, and Alexander and Solomon visited occasionally

63 *Liberation*, February 1963, p. 15.

64 Interview, van der Heyden; *State vs Alexander*, pp. 1563–64, 1588, 1880–83.

65 Interview, Florence Adams, Woodstock, Cape Town, 22 May 2018; Clifford Williams, 'Dorothy Williams (née Adams) 1928–2011,' 2011.

to drop off literature.[66] Adams was motivated by a moral approach to politics and less self-consciously intellectual than van der Heyden. Nonetheless, she wanted to study and learn from other struggles: 'we decided on this organization that could look at … the successful revolutions: Cuba, Algeria, China.' But since anyone who spoke out could be banned, she explained, 'there would be no public meetings, it would have to be cells, and the cells would operate in their area and … have a representative in that area who [would] meet with other representatives.'[67]

Neville Alexander recruited his Livingstone colleagues Reginald Francke and Leslie van der Heyden, who already knew of the group from his sister Elizabeth. Leslie attended Athlone High, graduated from UCT with a BA in Native Law and Administration, and Constitutional History and Law, and obtained a teaching certificate. His brother-in-law, the activist Basil February, boarded with the van der Heydens; Basil and Solomon had been friends since boarding together at Zonnebloem Hostel.[68]

Alexander recruited Anti-CAD activist Gerald Giose, who taught with his mother Dimbiti Bisho Alexander at a Mowbray primary school; Giose's father, an AME minister and a communist, had ensured his children learned both the *Lord's Prayer* and the *Communist Manifesto*. Alexander went to Durban to discuss armed struggle with lawyer and Apdusan Kader Hassim, but his overtures were rejected. He approached Wolhuter, who was tired of endless conferences and meetings and thought guerrilla struggle was the only way forward. She was on the point of joining just before his arrest.[69]

Underground recruitment varied across the liberation movement but generally showed gendered patterns. For Umkhonto, Mandela prioritized male Second World War veterans who knew sabotage techniques, while the SACP prioritized ideological commitment, with veteran communists evaluating prospective

[66] Scanlon, *Representation,* 208; Kayser and Adhikari, 'Land,' pp. 324–5; *State vs Alexander*, p. 1714; interview, Fataar; 'Dorothy Adams,' *South African History Online*, https://www.sahistory.org.za/people/dorothy-adams, accessed 15 July 2020.

[67] Quoted in Scanlon, *Representation,* p. 209; discussion with Scanlon, Cape Town, May 2018.

[68] Drew and Ntsebeza, interview, Solomon.

[69] Vaughan Giose, *The Yu Chi Chan Club* [DVD], Cape Town: Rainbow Circle Films, n.d.; 'Gerald Giose, National Liberation Front/Yu Chi Chan Club – ANC/Umkhonto we Sizwe (Cape Town, 6 December 1995),' in Tor Sellström, ed., *Liberation in Southern Africa – Regional and Swedish Voices: Interviews from Angola, Mozambique, Namibia, South Africa, Zimbabwe, the Frontline and Sweden*, Uppsala: Nordiska Afrikainstitutet, 2002, https://www.diva-portal.org/smash/get/diva2:272726/FULLTEXT01.pdf, accessed 27 March 2023, pp. 122–7; Hassim to author, 27 July 2020; interview, Fataar.

recruits.[70] Jean Middleton and Sylvia Neame were recruited into the SACP. A young teacher and socialist, Middleton was in the ANC-aligned South African Congress of Democrats when Hilda Bernstein recruited her into a four-woman SACP cell. After training, including discussion of communist literature, Middleton moved to a mixed-sex cell. The cells were divided by tasks, ranging from slogan-painting to distribution of flyers to highly secretive document production. At the bottom of the SACP hierarchy were racially segregated area units and committees, reflecting residential apartheid. At the top were 'mixed race' district and central committees. Women were in the lower, racially based groups, excluded from the top tiers on the preposterous grounds that their presence would enable the police to charge people under the Immorality Act, which forbade sex between people of different racial groups. 'It's undeniable that the organization was dominated by men,' Middleton concluded.[71]

Neame had joined the Liberal Party while at Rhodes University, but switched to the Congress of Democrats when she moved to Cape Town. In August 1961 communist and trade unionist Reginald September invited her to join the SACP. She agreed, 'thrilled to bits and very proud to have been asked.' In January 1963 she moved to Johannesburg and joined a cell of young people in Hillbrow, before being drawn into the Rivonia network.[72]

By contrast, newly politicized UCT student Stephanie Kemp volunteered at the Defence & Aid Fund and was befriended by several older communist women – Ray Edwards, Dora Alexander and Sarah Carneson. They lent her Eddie Roux's *Time Longer than Rope*, and she began eating supper with the Carnesons. In 1962 Fred Carneson invited her to join the SACP. 'Becoming a Communist was easy,' she thought; 'Marxism-Leninism provided guidelines.' She joined a Party cell and read the few Marxist books she could find – many were censored. But there is no sense that the complexities of Marxism or of guerrilla struggle were discussed.[73]

That same year Kemp joined the National Committee for Liberation – without telling her SACP comrades. National Union of South African Students leader and Liberal Party member Adrian Leftwich invited her for coffee and asked if she would consider engaging in sabotage. Leftwich was 'a senior and I was some small fry student, so I was highly flattered,' she recalled. He insisted that she think about it, and she decided against it. But three weeks

70 Mandela, *Long Walk*, pp. 261–3; Joe Slovo, *Slovo: The Unfinished Autobiography*, Randburg: Ravan, 1995–1996, p. 153.

71 Jean Middleton, *Convictions: A Woman Political Prisoner Remembers*, Randburg: Ravan, 1998, pp. 12–29, quotes 22. Acker, 'Hierarchies,' p. 152, notes that claims that women have a sexually unsettling influence in organizations are common.

72 Sylvia Neame to author, 30 September 2020.

73 Stephanie Kemp, 'My Life: The Making of an Afrikaner Revolutionary in the South African Liberation Struggle,' *South African History Online*, 2018, pp. 61–4.

later Leftwich asked again. 'I just never could bring myself to say no,' she acknowledged. 'I wasn't sophisticated enough to really sort out what I was doing or who … for or anything like that.'[74] Men in the NCL recounted many political discussions, but these did not, evidently, include Kemp.[75]

National Liberation Front activities

Unlike those groups, the NLF's division of labour was not gendered, nor were its cells divided by task. Its members formed cells, read, held discussions and lectures, produced articles for *Liberation*, and fundraised. The first two cells were Athlone-Lansdowne and Cape Town central. The Athlone-Lansdowne group met weekly at the Alexander home, with Neville Alexander, Ottilie Abrahams, Solomon, Shipanga, and Kenneth Abrahams as chair. From February 1963 Shipanga attended sporadically as he was often in Ovamboland preparing for his return as a SWAPO field organizer. September, Dorothy Alexander and Doris van der Heyden began attending in March, later joined by teachers Leslie van der Heyden, Reginald Francke and Cyril Jacobs.[76] The group split; Elizabeth van der Heyden led the Athlone cell, and Neville Alexander the Lansdowne group.[77]

Solomon was by then teaching at Walmer Street Primary in Woodstock; once settled in Walmer Estate he brought his siblings from their orphanage to live with him. He formed a Cape Town central cell, which met weekly at his Walmer Estate home. The group initially included Elizabeth van der Heyden and Landers and, briefly, Philip April, as well as Apdusan Lionel Davis, who had recently completed his Cape Technical College junior certificate and was working as a storeman and clerk. Lionel's father's family came from Sierra Leone; his mother's was of slave, Khoisan and Dutch origins. His father died when he was four, and the impoverished family had lived in District Six, with its tightly packed semi-detached houses, 'dilapidated, but architecturally works of art,' recalled Richard Rive. District Six was lively, cosmopolitan, full of culture and generally tolerant but also, in Lionel's memory, marked by a colour hierarchy and its attendant name-calling. Lionel's family was itself split between lighter and darker skinned members, and Lionel was dark. By age thirteen, he was aware of the family division and as a result became very

74 Julie Frederikse, interview, Stephanie Kemp, London, 1986, South African History Archive, http://www.saha.org.za/nonracialism/transcript_of_interview_stephanie_kemp_htm, accessed 20 April 2019, pp. 6, 10–11; Kemp, *My Life*, pp. 63–4.

75 Baruch Hirson, *Revolutions in my Life*, Johannesburg: Wits University Press, 1995, p. 301; Daniels, *There & Back*, p. 105.

76 *State vs Alexander*, pp. 1706, 1757, 1632, 1638; Matsemela, interview, Alexander, p. 64.

77 *State vs Alexander*, pp. 1565, 1757.

anti-white. But he knew he needed to 'uplift himself,' so he went to night school.[78] Around March–April, Apdusan Yusuf Lucas and high school teacher Achmet Ajam joined the group, which began meeting at Ajam's house in Salt River. Kenneth Abrahams formed small groups in Maitland, led by Daniel Swabel and, in Elsies River, by Giose.

Learning was central to the NLF, and the cells were organized accordingly. Through their reading and discussions, cell members educated themselves and each other. As Lionel Davis recalled, they organized for APDUSA but received their political education in the NLF.[79] This was in marked contrast to Nelson Mandela's individualized, self-directed programme while he was launching Umkhonto. Of course, Mandela relied on suggestions from others and recommended some of his readings to other comrades. For example, in the 1950s, before Gaur Radebe became a Pan Africanist, he introduced Mandela to Marxist writings. Later Mandela asked Mac Maharaj to send him books from London. Mandela immersed himself in literature on guerrilla struggles, especially China's and Cuba's. He and his Umkhonto comrades discussed the Cuban case, but did not, apparently, organize study groups.[80]

The NLF cells were run in a participatory style, with standardized agendas covering four points – developments in the camp of the oppressed, developments in the camp of the *Herrenvolk* [master race], finances, and general.[81] The agenda and study topics were introduced by different people, broadening speaking opportunities. Women and men led discussions, lectured or gave short talks – helpful for those with limited public speaking experience. They studied the YCCC publications and comparative works on guerrilla warfare. Neville Alexander lectured on Mao Zedung; Ottilie Abrahams, who kept the group's library and lent September Mao's book, lectured on South West African politics; Elizabeth van der Heyden on secret communications and on APDUSA; Solomon on the PAC; and Landers on partisan warfare.[82]

78 Richard Rive, *Buckingham Palace, District Six*, Berlin: Cornelsen Verlag, 2006 [1986], p. 185; Drew and Ntsebeza, interview, Solomon; Davis, 'Telling My Story,' pp. 29–38; Tina Smith, 'Remembering District Six: The Restorative Art of Lionel Davis,' in Mario Pissarra, ed., *Awakenings: The Art of Lionel Davis*, Cape Town: Africa South Art Initiative, 2017, pp. 41–54, 41; Jane Harries interview Lionel Davis, UCT Centre for Popular Memory, 13 June 1997, PIN 11.05a and 11.05b.

79 Interview, Lionel Davis, Cape Town, 6 May 2019; *State vs Alexander*, pp. 1542, 1525–27.

80 Landau, *Spear*, pp. 111–23, esp. 115, 119, 121.

81 The NEUM used the Nazi term *herrenvolk* to describe white South Africans upholding white supremacy.

82 *State vs Alexander*, pp. 1565–66, 1620–21, 1683, 1709, 1887; Matsemela, interview with Bam, UCTCPM, 104311.

Doris van der Heyden made a presentation on the uprising in Paarl, a small town surrounded by vineyards and fruit farms, 36 miles north-west of Cape Town.[83] Poqo had been entrenched in Langa since 1961 and established in Paarl by mid-1962. By then Paarl's population included about 400 African families and 2,000 migrant workers, all unhappy with the town's resettlement schemes. The town had a tradition of organized protest with branches of the African Food and Canning Workers' Union, the ANC and PAC. On 22 November 1962 migrant workers from Mbekweni location marched on Paarl with axes, pangas [machetes] and homemade weapons to attack the police station and prison and to free prisoners. Forewarned, the authorities shot at the crowd, killing seven and wounding many others. Some of the marchers killed whites. The matter was often in the press; the government's Snyman Commission issued its interim report in March 1963, and a final report in June 1963.[84]

The NLF formed a regional committee to coordinate the cells; it held its first meeting in February. Initially Neville Alexander was to be the NLF's editor and represent the Athlone-Lansdowne group on the regional committee, along with Ottilie Abrahams. But he was drinking heavily – perhaps still stunned by the differences between West Germany and South Africa, or homesick for Europe, as Deirdre Levinson thought – and missed or came drunk to meetings. He was suspended, and Ottilie Abrahams became the editor and Athlone-Lansdowne delegate; every member was held accountable for their actions.[85]

As in the YCCC, women and men produced the literature. The articles were typed – Elizabeth van der Heyden recalls a group of them at the Alexander home, she dictating, while Neville Alexander typed – then duplicated through cyclostyling and later a Photostat machine. September, the 'post office,' received and distributed material. The articles were in English; Francke was planning to translate some literature into Afrikaans, which was widely spoken in the western and northern Cape and Namibia, but this never happened.[86]

Producing and distributing literature required money. To fundraise they sold literature and organized social events, such as rummage sales, concerts and *bobops* – dances at private homes where one paid to enter. Part of their motivation through these activities was to remain embedded in their local communities; they were popular, and the events were well attended. But their fund-raising – 38 Rands on one occasion – was paltry compared to the SACP,

83 *State vs Alexander*, pp. 1565–66, 1620–21, 1683, 1709, 1887.

84 Bianca Paigè van Laun, 'In the Shadows of the Archive: Investigating the Paarl march of November 22nd 1962,' University of the Western Cape, MA, 2012; Tom Lodge, 'The Paarl Insurrection' Paper presented to the Wits University African Studies Seminar, October 1979; Lodge, *Black Politics*, pp. 248–55.

85 *State vs Alexander*, p. 1705; interview, van der Heyden; Levinson, *Five Years*, p. 147; Morrow, *Bams*, p. 89.

86 Interview, van der Heyden; *State vs Alexander*, pp. 362–4, 499, 1411.

which received US$30,000 from the Soviets in 1960, US$50,000 in 1961 and, as sabotage increased, US$112,445 in 1962.[87] Lacking the support of a larger organization or international power, the NLF was indeed financially strapped.

Conclusion

The NLF was predominantly male, recalled van der Heyden, but 'it wasn't a matter of you are in that position because you are a male, you are a woman therefore you must be there … we were mostly men, but I think that was because of the mentality of the society at that time – women stayed home.'[88] Several factors explain why the NLF's practice did not follow the society's gender norms. First, the organization's lack of hierarchy and small cell size made participation easier for both women and men. Secondly, its stress on small group learning meant that while advanced education was an advantage in certain types of work, especially writing long documents, its lack was not a barrier to reading, speaking or writing shorter pieces. People were encouraged to speak, allowing women to collaborate equally within the cells. Thirdly, all the women had prior experience in student or political bodies. Lastly, most of them came from homes where they had been not only allowed but encouraged to voice opinions.

The NLF drew on the Unity Movement's tradition of study groups picked up in SOYA and other forums. But as young people freed from the Unity Movement's bureaucratic leadership, they reinterpreted its educational approach to suit the new underground political conditions. While the Unity Movement did not include political space for a women's group or discussions of gender, a tiny number of women intellectuals in Cape Town played public or behind-the-scenes political roles. However few, those visible women undoubtedly left an imprint on younger women intellectual-activists, not least in the belief that they could play active political roles.

Drawn together around the concern to study and consider new methods of struggle for national liberation, in its short lifespan neither the apartheid regime's misogyny nor the liberation movement's sexism were on the table for discussion. Nonetheless, while the NLF maintained the Unity Movement's idealized notion of revolutionary life premised on an abstract individual with traits associated with public, vocal male activists, it broke with the Unity Movement's gendered hierarchy. The NLF's non-hierarchical small group structure enabled women and men to participate as equal individuals, ensuring

87 *State vs Alexander*, pp. 1574–6, 348; Matsemela, interview with Bam, UCTCPM, 104311; Irina Filatova and Apollon Davidson, *The Hidden Thread: Russia and South Africa in the Soviet Era*, Roggebaai: Jonathan Ball, 2013, p. 341; Magubane et al., 'Turn to Armed Struggle,' p. 136.

88 Quoted in Scanlon, *Representation,* p. 208.

that its teaching and learning was egalitarian. However important that was, their activism had revolved mainly around student and teacher organizations, and in the underground conditions they had virtually no opportunity to broaden their experience beyond work with intellectuals. Their absorption with reading, writing and publishing eventually led to their capture and prosecution by giving the state tangible evidence of their thinking.

Chapter 3

The National Liberation Front and the South West Africa Question

For South African liberation activists, the Chinese, Cuban and Algerian revolutions demonstrated the real possibility of overthrowing repressive regimes. But the immediate catalysts for armed struggle were closer to home: the December 1959 Windhoek massacre and the March 1960 Sharpeville-Langa massacres. Those massacres set the scenes for the sabotage campaigns that began the next year in South Africa and provided the backdrop for the Yu Chi Chan Club (YCCC)'s and National Liberation Front (NLF)'s formation and concern with South West Africa. This chapter explores how South West African politics, carried to Cape Town by Namibian students and workers, was central to the formation of both groups. The NLF had two main aims: to build a united front of like-minded anti-apartheid groups and 'introduce the idea and techniques of armed insurrection into the national liberatory struggle.' The group hoped to have members in and to work with all organizations that supported those aims. Their publications indicated the importance of South West African events to their thinking and analysis – which the state could hardly miss, once discovered. South West Africa's anti-colonial struggle would give them an opportunity for the popular activism they needed if they were to grow. They had some influence in the Cape Town branch of the early South West Africa People's Organisation (SWAPO) which, they thought, offered 'ready soil' for their political approach based on Namibian agency, the need for a united front and the primacy of the internal guerrilla struggle.[1] However, their practical work in South West Africa was extremely brief due to arrest and exile.

As mentioned in Chapter 2, several YCCC and NLF members came from South West Africa, colonized in turn by the German Empire and the Union of South Africa. Windhoek's Old Location, where Ottilie Schimming grew up, was in the German Police Zone comprising the southern two-thirds of the territory and demarcated on maps by a red line.[2] Ottilie's father Otto

1 *Liberation*, February 1963, pp. 5–6.

2 Aisha Akoshile, 'An Age-Old Tug of War: Understanding the Intergenerational Conflicts of Southern African Nationalist Groups,' BA, History, Columbia, 2021, p.

Schimming was the son of a German soldier and Herero mother. The senior Otto Schimming divorced his Herero wife when South Africa voided marriages across the colour bar and sent her and her two sons to a reserve. But he later brought the boys back to attend school, and his multilingual son Otto studied at the Lovedale Mission in South Africa. On young Otto's return he settled in the Old Location and set up a school for Herero-speaking children, becoming Namibia's first black teacher. He had a dairy, so the family was comfortable compared to many of their neighbours, a status that Ottilie felt keenly. Her mother Charlotte was a Damara-speaker who fervently supported national liberation. At that time missionaries ran black education in South West Africa, and Ottilie attended mission school before continuing her studies in Cape Town.[3]

Andreas Shipanga, another YCCC and NLF member, was born in 1931 in Odangwa, south-east Ovamboland – north of the red line, where local affairs were run by chiefs and headmen in a system of indirect rule. One of six children, his parents were comfortable self-sufficient farmers. Shipanga's father had participated in a 1905 raid against the German seizure of land. His mother taught him to read in his mother tongue and encouraged formal education. He attended a Finnish mission school and taught himself to read English, subscribing to *Drum Magazine* and left-wing newspapers like *Advance*. Gradually politicized, Shipanga trained as a primary school teacher at Oniipa Teacher Training College, completing his studies in 1952. He began teaching at Iihongo but soon went abroad in protest against Bantu Education. In Bulawayo he began corresponding with the anti-colonial leader Andimba Toivo ya Toivo, whom he had met as a boy at Odangwa. He headed to Cape Town, where Toivo was based.[4] Of course, YCCC and NLF members had varied interests. Fikile Bam, for one, acknowledged that despite his friendships with Shipanga, Ottilie and Kenneth Abrahams and Ottilie's sister Nora Schimming, he did not follow Namibian politics, being more concerned with

15; Interview, Ottilie Abrahams, Windhoek, 28 February 1988, Basel Africa Library, TAA18_9_A, TAA18_9_B.

3 Interview, Ottilie Abrahams; 'Otto Schimming Dies,' *The Namibian*, 8 December 2005, https://www.namibian.com.na/11489/archive-read/Otto-Schimming-dies; Catherine Sasman, 'Otto Schimming: A self-made man,' *New Era*, 22 October 2012; 'Liberation pioneer dies,' *The Namibian*, 11 May 2012, https://archive.is/20130221040735/http://www.namibian.com.na/news-articles/national/full-story/archive/2012/may/article/liberation-pioneer-dies, accessed 22 June 2021; discussion with Kenneth Abrahams, Jr., Windhoek, 16 October 2022.

4 'Profile of Andreas Shipanga,' *Windhoek Advertiser*, 1 September 1978, p. 8, Andreas Shipanga Papers, National Archives of Namibia, NAN AACR LS 212; Andreas Shipanga with Sue Armstrong, *In Search of Freedom: The Andreas Shipanga Story as told to Sue Armstrong*, Gibraltar: Ashanti, 1989, pp. 1, 6, 18–20.

South Africa's Transkei and African townships.[5] Nonetheless, the group sought to study and understand South Africa's colonial relationship with its northern neighbour.

The development of Namibia's national liberation movement

A dry, sparsely populated land, much of it desert, the country now named Namibia was claimed as German South West Africa in 1884. The Germans were ruthless against the dispersed peoples protesting colonization. The multilingual strategist Jakob Marengo aimed to unite these groups in the 1904–1908 Nama-Herero guerrilla uprising, but the Germans crushed them with genocide, wiping out some 60 per cent of the population. Despite the uprising's tragic outcome, Neville Alexander described it as the 'crucible of Namibian nationality' in that for the first time the different peoples cooperated against their common German enemy.[6]

The Germans set up the Police Zone within which they settled and transformed the indigenous people into cheap labour.[7] Blacks in the Police Zone confronted racist laws daily and developed specific resistance strategies, using transnational tactics such as petitioning and letter-writing. According to Marion Wallace, the Germans did not occupy the north both because of the military strength of its Ovambo kingdoms and the need for labour. Whites were not allowed north of the red line; Africans could cross it only if contracted to work. So resistance in the north focused on labour.[8]

South Africa joined the First World War as part of the British Empire, its troops defeating the German forces in South West Africa in 1915. At the war's end, the Allied powers divided up Germany's former territories. Although South Africa hoped to incorporate South West Africa as a fifth province, in 1919 the Treaty of Versailles agreed that South Africa should administer South West Africa as a mandate in 'sacred trust.' This became law in December

5 August Matsemela, interview with Fikile Bam, UCT Centre for Popular Memory, item 104311, https://ibali.uct.ac.za/s/center-for-popular-memory/item/104311.

6 Neville Alexander, 'Jakob Marengo and Namibian History,' *Namibian Review Publications*, 1, June 1983, pp. 8–23, 17; Neville Alexander, 'The Namibian War of Anticolonial Resistance, 1904–1907,' *Namibian Review Publications*, 1, June 1983, pp. 49–70, esp. 54, where he argues that the centrality of land for the Herero, rather than wages or political rights, defined the uprising as anti-colonial; quote p. 64.

7 Richard Moorsom, 'Underdevelopment, Contract Labour and Worker Consciousness in Namibia, 1915–72,' *Journal of Southern African Studies*, 4, 1, October 1977, pp. 52–87, 55.

8 Hogan, 'Remov[e] Us,' pp. 39, 68, 381; Marion Wallace with John Kinahan, *A History of Namibia: From the beginning to 1990*, New York: Columbia, 2011, p. 199.

1920 when confirmed by the League of Nations.[9] After the transition from German to South African rule, South West Africa was raised continually at the League of Nations and later the United Nations (UN). So from early days, South West Africa's developing anti-colonial nationalism was buttressed by internationalism.[10]

For South West African blacks, the German defeat initially inspired hopes for positive change. The early 1920s saw the first efforts to transcend pre-colonial communal identities in the Police Zone, using new ideologies and structures and transnational networks developed over nearly 200 years by African-American seamen travelling from the United States and the Caribbean to Southern Africa. These networks bore fruit following the First World War in South West African branches of Marcus Garvey's Universal Negro Improvement Association and African Communities League (UNIA), and after the Second World War, in a branch of the African Methodist Episcopal (AME) Church.[11]

The coastal town of Lüderitz was especially important. In 1920 South African worker-activist James La Guma organized a Lüderitz branch of the Industrial and Commercial Workers Union, launched the year before in Cape Town. The UNIA's Cape Town activists set up branches in South West Africa, where West African and West Indian settlers also carried the UNIA message. The year 1922 saw the launch of the South West African National Congress modelled on, but independent of, the South African Native National Congress [from 1923 the ANC]. These initiatives soon collapsed. This phase of resistance ended when South Africa, backed by white settler opinion, crushed the 1923 Bondelswart uprising with machine guns and armed airplanes and the 1925 Rehoboth uprising with the threat of air attacks. Crucially, though, local people developed a consciousness of themselves and their own organizing efforts in contrast to South African-launched initiatives.[12]

9 Wallace with Kinahan, *History of Namibia*, pp. 217–18; Susan Pedersen, *The Guardians: The League of Nations and the Crisis of Empire*, Oxford: Oxford University Press, 2015, p. 113; Tor Sellström, *Sweden and National Liberation in Southern Africa*, vol. 1, Uppsala: Nordiska Afrikainstitutet, 1999, p. 256; Gerhard Tötemeyer, *South West Africa/Namibia: Facts, Attitudes, Assessment and Prospects*, Randburg: Fokus Suid, 1977, p. 17.

10 I am extending backwards in time from Robert H. Jackson and Carl G. Rosberg, 'Why Africa's Weak States Persis: The Empirical and Juridical and Statehood,' in Marc Williams, ed., *International Relations in the Twentieth Century: A Reader*, London: Macmillan, 1989, pp. 98–116.

11 Zedekia Ngavirue, 'Political Parties and Interest Groups in South West Africa: A study of a plural society,' DPhil, 1972, pp. 255–8; Hogan, 'Remov[e] Us,' pp. 133–73, 251–78, 381–4; Wallace with Kinahan, *History of Namibia*, p. 246.

12 Tony Emmett, 'Popular Resistance in Namibia, 1920–1925,' African Studies Seminar Paper 150, African Studies Institute, University of the Witwatersrand, June

After the Second World War, the UN's formation raised expectations that League of Nations mandates would become UN trust territories before their eventual independence.[13] The South African Army had recruited about 5,000 Namibian men during the war, the majority from Ovamboland. Indeed, many of them had joined the war expecting that their lot would improve afterwards. They were soon disillusioned. 'The soldiers returned with lots of literature and photographs – and, importantly, with politics. The seeds were sown,' recalled Shipanga.[14]

Refusing to consider South West African independence, South Africa imposed its own structures on the territory – apartheid structures from 1948. Apartheid imposed a climate of fear but also intensified the anti-colonial struggle. Namibians – especially chiefs in the Police Zone – petitioned the UN; as secretary to Herero Chief Hosea Kutako, Otto Schimming wrote the first such letter protesting South Africa's efforts to incorporate South West Africa.[15] Compared to the Police Zone, where Herero, Nama and Rehoboth leaders 'were speaking out against South African rule ... constantly petitioning the United Nations to expel South Africa,' thought Shipanga, 'Ovamboland was pathetic,' the people passive.[16]

The UN set up a Permanent Committee on South West Africa that ran from 1954 to 1961. In 1957 it formed a Good Offices Committee to negotiate with South Africa. The committee temporarily considered splitting the territory, giving the south, with the white-owned farms, to South Africa and allowing the north to be administered by South Africa as a UN trusteeship. But the Permanent Committee successfully argued that this conflicted with the UN mandate. Thereafter, South Africa strove to thwart the Permanent Committee.

African states in the UN placed white-minority regimes on the international agenda. In June 1960 Ethiopia and Liberia raised South West Africa at the International Court of Justice. Six years later the court decided that the two countries had no standing to bring the case. However, it ruled that the UN General Assembly should supervise South West Africa and receive reports from South Africa and petitions from Namibians. Supported by

---

1984, pp. 17–18, 27–28, 32–3; Vinson, 'Sea Kaffirs,' pp. 281–2; Pedersen, *Guardians*, pp. 114–28.

13 Post-Second World War Namibian history, esp. late 1950s and early 1960s, is still contested; see Wallace with Kinahan, *History of Namibia*, p. 243. Generally, I have followed Wallace for dates.

14 Shipanga with Armstrong, *In Search*, pp. 9–10; Wallace with Kinahan, *History of Namibia*, p. 241.

15 Chris Saunders, 'Some Roots of Anti-colonial Writing about Namibia,' *Journal of Namibia Studies*, 3, 2008, pp. 83–93, 87; Wallace with Kinahan, *History of Namibia*, p. 243; 'Otto Schimming Dies.'

16 Shipanga with Armstrong, *In Search*, pp. 18–19.

renowned anti-apartheid activist Reverend Michael Scott, Namibians increased their lobbying of the UN, which remained a key element in the territory's independence campaign.[17]

Two factors were crucial for the development of nationalist politics. One was the 'incipient Namibian intelligentsia' – students able to continue their education beyond mission school. South West Africa did not have a university, and the 1950s saw the first generation of black Namibians to attend post-primary school and university in South Africa, where in 1952 the short-lived South West Africa Student Body (SWASB) was launched, with Fanuel Jariretundu Kozonguizi as president and Ottilie Schimming among its founders. Its members were extremely impressed by the ANC's Defiance Campaign, hoping to apply its model to their own country. In 1955 SWASB became the South West Africa Progressive Association (SWAPA), which provided bursaries to study in South Africa and aspired to unite the territory's ethnic groups into a national movement.[18]

Many Namibian students in the western Cape joined the non-aligned Cape Peninsula Students Union (CPSU). The ubiquitous Ottilie Schimming joined the CPSU and Society of Young Africa (SOYA), attracted by their 'atmosphere of lively debate.'[19] Fellow Namibian Charles Kauraisa also joined the CPSU. Like Ottilie, Kauraisa had attended St Barnabas Anglican Mission School in Windhoek. He then went to the AME's Wilberforce Institute in Evaston, Transvaal and, finally, Lückhoff High School, which had opened in January 1935 as Stellenbosch's first secondary school for children classified Coloured and which also accepted Namibians. At Lückhoff, Kauraisa was profoundly influenced by his history teacher Ronnie Britten, who came from Paarl and had studied at the University of Cape Town (UCT). 'My political mentors were I. B. Tabata and Ronnie Britton [*sic*] of the Unity Movement,'

17 Wallace with Kinahan, *History of Namibia*, pp. 247, 261–2; J. H. P. Serfontein, *Namibia?* London: Rex Collings, 1976, pp. 15, 50; Tötemeyer, *South West Africa*, p. 19; Rodney Davenport and Christopher Saunders, *South Africa: A Modern History*, 5th ed., Basingstoke: Macmillan; New York: St Martin's, 2000, pp. 523–6; Jeremy Silvester, 'Forging the Fifth Province,' *Journal of Southern African Studies*, 41, 3, 2015, pp. 505–18.

18 Wallace with Kinahan, *History of Namibia*, p. 247; Ngavirue, 'Political Parties,' pp. 291–5, dates SWAPA's formation as 1958; *South West Africa*, 1, 1, 5 March 1960; Akoshile, 'Age-Old Tug of War,' p. 16; Thula Simpson, *History of South Africa: From 1902 to the Present*, Cape Town: Penguin Random House, 2021, p. 199. Kenneth Abrahams said SWASB was launched in Windhoek.

19 Interview, Kenneth Abrahams, Windhoek, February 1988, Basel Africa Library, TPA153_20_A; Matsemela, interviews, Ottilie Abrahams, UCTCPM, 104407, and Kenneth Abrahams, 104408 'Liberation pioneer dies.'

Figure 4: Ottilie Schimming, SWAPA Reception, International Hall, Windhoek, 3 July 1960. Source: *South West News*, 9 July 1960.

Kauraisa recollected. 'They were the people who exposed a number of us to the study of Marxism.'[20]

Politically engaged Namibian students may have faced more hurdles studying overseas than did their black South African counterparts. Neville Alexander had sailed for Europe in October 1958 without problems. Not so Hans Beukes from Rehoboth, South West Africa. The son of activist shoemaker Hermanus Beukes, Hans arrived at UCT in the late 1950s to study law, financed by a Rehoboth Community Chest loan. In 1959 he was awarded a three-year bursary from the Norwegian Students Union via the National Union of South African Students – Norway's attempt to counter the impact of university apartheid. Obtaining his South African passport, he was waiting to board a

[20] Tor Sellström, interview with Charles Kauraisa, Windhoek, 20 March 1995, https://nai.uu.se/library/resources/liberation-africa/interviews/charles-kauraisa.html, accessed 13 June 2021; interview, Charles Kauraisa, Windhoek, 20 October 2022.

Norwegian ship, when the police, concerned he would contact the UN when overseas, arrested him and seized his passport. Unsure if UCT would readmit him, Hans travelled clandestinely to Bechuanaland and overseas, arriving in Oslo on 11 September 1959 and leaving immediately for New York, where he addressed the UN General Assembly. But he paid a high price, unable to return home for decades.[21]

The other, perhaps more important, factor for Namibian nationalism was the organization of Ovambo contract workers in the north, where the underground resistance movement *Nghuwoyepongo* ['the call of an orphan who is rescued by God'] emerged in the early 1950s. The territory saw almost yearly strikes between 1946 and 1959, mostly on the mines. By the late 1950s Cape Town had some 230 Namibians, many having escaped from the hated contract labour system. Afrikaans-speaking, they passed themselves off as Coloured to avoid carrying passes as African men were compelled to, and they took Coloured names and married Coloured women. Some of them met socially at Timothy Nangolo's Barber Shop at 35 Somerset Road.[22]

They, too, were impressed by the Defiance Campaign and began making political contacts. The Food and Canning Workers Union's Frank Marquard had formed a Lüderitz branch in 1949, and the communist trade unionist Ray Alexander arrived in 1952; Namibians later met with her and her communist husband Jack Simons in Cape Town. But restrictions on the movement of Africans to the western Cape impeded the ANC's growth, so Liberal Party contacts were perhaps more significant.[23] Ottilie Schimming and Kenneth Abrahams attended discussions at Timothy's Barber Shop and brought

21 Hans Beukes, *Long Road to Liberation: An exiled Namibian Activist's Perspective*, CreateSpace Independent Publishing Platform, 2014, chaps. 2–3; Tore Linné Eriksen, 'The Origins of a Special Relationship: Norway and Southern Africa, 1960–1975,' in Tore Linné Eriksen, ed., *Norway and National Liberation in Southern Africa*, Uppsala: Nordiska Afrikainstitutet, 2000, pp. 9–87, 13–14, 23, 90; Werner Menges, 'UN petitioners retrace long road to freedom,' *The Namibian*, 24 September 2010, http://www.namibian.com.na/news/full-story/archive/2010/september/article/un-petitioners-retrace-long-road-to-freedom, accessed 19 July 2024.

22 Wallace with Kinahan, *History of Namibia*, pp. 246–7, 258–9; Shipanga with Armstrong, *In Search*, p. 35; Lauren Dobell, *Swapo's Struggle for Namibia, 1960–1991: War by Other Means*, Basel Namibia Studies Series, Basel: Basler Afrika Bibliographien, 1998, pp. 28–9; interview, Kenneth Abrahams.

23 Ngavirue, 'Political Parties,' p. 331; Wallace with Kinahan, *History of Namibia*, pp. 246–7; Ronald Dreyer, *Namibia and Southern Africa: Regional Dynamics of Decolonization*, 2nd ed., London and New York: Routledge, 2016, pp. 30–3. Ruth First, *South West Africa*, Harmondsworth: Penguin, 1963, pp. 196–7; Sifiso Mxolisi Ndlovu, 'African Leaders and the National Liberation Struggle in Namibia,' in SADET, *The Road to Democracy in South Africa*, vol. 5, part 2, UNISA Press, 2014, pp. 664–727, 668–9.

Namibian workers to Unity Movement meetings so they could develop their critical thinking skills.[24]

In 1957 Toivo and Solomon Mifima had launched the Ovamboland People's Congress (OPC), concerned, first and foremost, with the condition of Ovamboland contract workers; Ottilie Schimming was a founding member.[25] Toivo cut an impressive figure. Taught by Finnish and Anglican missionaries, during the Second World War he served as a corporal in South Africa's Native Military Corps, then worked as a teacher and on the mines before arriving in Cape Town to work on the railways. He became deputy chair of the Modern Youth Society, a cultural group with communist roots that was open to all youth.[26] Shipanga arrived in Cape Town that year, becoming known as Andries Cloete, joining the OPC and meeting communists and liberals. Kozonguizi, by then a UCT law student, lived with Toivo in Langa.[27]

The police often raided Timothy's Barber Shop. To protect itself from police crackdowns during the long-running Treason Trial, in 1958 the OPC became the Ovamboland People's Organisation (OPO), which organized in contract worker compounds on the mines and in towns. It included the north's underground resistance movement and rapidly become a mass organization with 'branch structure based solidly (though not exclusively) in the contract workers' compounds of the towns and mines.'[28] Crucially it was committed to independence. Its petitions to the UN led to Toivo's expulsion from South Africa, and Shipanga took over the Cape Town leadership. On 19 April 1959, with Toivo under house arrest in Ovamboland, Sam Nujoma launched the OPO in Windhoek's Old Location.[29]

24 'Kenneth Abrahams: A Doctor in the Struggle at Home and in Exile,' in Colin Leys and Susan Brown, *Histories of Namibia: Living through the Liberation Struggle – Life Histories*, London: Merlin: 2005, pp. 139–57, 139–41; photo of UCT's graduating medical class and discussion with Kenneth Abrahams, Jr.

25 Dobell, *Swapo's Struggle*, p. 28, n. 10 notes that sources vary on date of the OPC's founding; SWAPO of Namibia, *To Be Born a Nation: The Liberation Struggle for Namibia*, Luanda: SWAPO of Namibia, and London: Zed, 1981, p. 172.

26 Wallace with Kinahan, *History of Namibia*, pp. 246–7; First, *South West Africa*, pp. 198–9; Z. Pallo Jordan, 'Denis Goldberg and the Modern Youth Society,' https://www.sahistory.org.za/sites/default/files/2019-05/5_pallo_jordan_a5_rev.pdf; 'Andimba Herman Toivo Ya Toivo,' https://www.sahistory.org.za/people/andimba-herman-toivo-ya-toivo, both accessed 22 June 2021.

27 While Dobell, *Swapo's Struggle*, p. 28, n. 10, uses Toivo's claim of August 1957 for the OPC's founding, Shipanga with Armstrong, *In Search*, pp. 33–40, states the OPC was already formed when he arrived in Cape Town in April 1957; Simpson, *History of South Africa*, p. 199; 'Liberation Pioneer Dies.'

28 Moorsom, 'Underdevelopment,' p. 79; 'Kenneth Abrahams,' in Leys and Brown, eds, *Histories*, p. 143.

29 Ngavirue, 'Political Parties,' pp. 292–4, 302; Shipanga with Armstrong, *In Search*, p. 37; Wallace with Kinahan, *History of Namibia*, pp. 247–50; Roger Southall,

The December 1959 Windhoek Massacre and its reverberations

Since South Africa was imposing apartheid in both its own country and South West Africa, South Africans and Namibians were fighting a common enemy. By 1959, recalled Kenneth Abrahams, the situation in South West Africa

> was so bad they didn't even have signs up saying 'Blacks Not Permitted.' Blacks just knew that you couldn't go into a bank, couldn't go into a shop, couldn't go into a restaurant. I remember [Ottilie's] brother taking me to the railway station to see those contract workers. They were at the station with signs around their necks, you know, showing just a destination and numbers – people wearing sacking and just with their destination around their necks.[30]

Namibians launched their own defiance campaign. Protests intensified in opposition to forced removals and controls over beer, brewed by women. In August 1959 SWAPA and the Herero Chiefs Council formed a coalition with the OPO to establish the South West Africa National Union (SWANU), a federal body that held its first national convention in Windhoek on 27 September 1959. Kozonguizi was its president, Werner Mamugwe, a multilingual Oshiwambo speaker who subscribed to the left-wing *Spark*, its national organizer, and Nujoma a national executive committee member. In December SWANU organized a campaign against forced removals from the Old Location to *Katatura* ['we have no dwelling place'] which was much farther from Windhoek and ethnically divided into an Ovambo-*lokasie* [location], a Damara-*lokasie*, and so on. Women were at the forefront of forced removal protests. On 10 December 1959, police shot the protestors, killing thirteen and wounding more than fifty. Ottilie Schimming knew some of the dead and wounded; from then on, she recalled, women came to the fore in politics. Indeed, 10 December became known as the Day of the Namibian Women.[31]

Liberation Movements in Power: Party & state in Southern Africa, Woodbridge: James Currey; Pietermaritzburg: University of KwaZulu-Natal, 2013, pp. 40–1; Serfontein, *Namibia?* pp. 145–6; SWAPO, *To Be Born*, pp. 172–3; Dobell, *Swapo's Struggle*, p. 30; Dreyer, *Namibia and Southern Africa*, p. 29; Chris Saunders, 'SWAPO, Namibia's Liberation Struggle and the Organisation of African Unity's Liberation Committee,' *South African Historical Journal*, 70, 1, 2018, pp. 152–67, 155; Gwen Lister, *Comrade Editor: On Life, Journalism and the Birth of Namibia*, Tafelberg, 2021, p. 58. Sources vary as to location and dates of the OPC, OPO and SWAPO's formation. *Liberation*, 1, 1, February 1963, p. 14 dates the OPO's formation as August 1958, Cape Town.

30 'Kenneth Abrahams,' in Leys and Brown, eds, *Histories*, p. 142.

31 Interview with Harry Boesak, Windhoek, 16 October 2022; Interview with Ottilie Abrahams, Basel, TAA18_9_B; Martha Akawa, *The Gender Politics of the Namibian Liberation Struggle*, Basel: Basler Afrika Bibliographien, 2014, p. 31; Ngavirue, 'Political Parties,' pp. 296–7; Totemeyer, *South West Africa*, p. 83.

The shock was profound: the residents had assumed that since theirs was a mandated territory South Africa would not shoot them. They began moving to Katatura. Kauraisa had finished his studies and returned home a few days after the massacre, 'finding an upsurge of political militancy in the making.' He joined SWANU, but the massacre shattered its fragile coalition. At its second national convention that month it elected a moderate slate of leaders; the OPO's Nujoma felt that the Ovambos would be put off by the radical Hereros. To no avail. First the Herero Chief's Council, then the OPO pulled out, leaving the intellectuals on their own. Nujoma went into exile in February 1960.[32]

The massacre accelerated the spread of nationalist ideas, signalled by the launch of the trilingual English–Afrikaans–Otjiherero *South West News/ Suidwes Nuus* on 5 March 1960. An Old Location community newspaper with national and continental content, it billed itself as 'the only non-racial newspaper in the territory' ['*Mehindi o'Tjaitonga Indji aijerike ondjihina 'mbangu komihoko*']. Its multilingualism promoted nation-building: English was the main linking language of southern African politics, although hardly spoken in Namibia; Afrikaans the lingua franca of central Namibia; Otjiherero the mother tongue of the newspaper's founders and the Old Location elite. Namibia's first black social worker Zedekia Ngavirue had proposed such a newspaper the year before at a SWAPA function. Its volunteer staff were mainly Herero and SWANU office-holders. Work on the newspaper sped up after the Windhoek massacre: most of those associated with the newspaper had experienced it, and its first issue honoured the victims.[33]

South West News offered social and political coverage with photographs; its 9 July 1960 issue ran photos of sisters Ottilie and Nora Schimming at a SWAPA reception in Windhoek. It aimed 'to promote the social and educational well-being of all inhabitants of South West Africa, irrespective of race, colour or creed,' and especially, 'the majority of our people whose voices are silenced.' Initially unable to find a Windhoek printer who would produce a

32 Interview with Ottilie Abrahams, Basel, TAA18_9_B; Interview with Boesak; Sellström, interview with Kauraisa; Israel Goldblatt, *Building Bridges: Namibian Nationalists Clemens Kapuuo, Hosea Kutako, Brendan Simbwaye, Samuel Witbooi*, ed. by Dag Henrichsen and Naomi Jacobson, Basel: Basler Afrika Bibliographien, 2010, 1, https://doi.org/10.2307/j.ctvh9vw19, accessed 25 June 2021; Wallace with Kinahan, *History of Namibia*, pp. 249, 254; First, *South West Africa*, pp. 196–7; Serfontein, *Namibia?* pp. 142–5; Southall, *Liberation Movements*, p. 40; Lister, *Comrade Editor*, pp. 58, 65; Simpson, *History of South Africa*, pp. 199–200, dates Nujoma's exile as March 1960.

33 Dag Henrichsen, 'Historiography,' in *A Glance at Our Africa*, compiled by Dag Henrichsen and introduced by Zedekia Ngavirue, Basel: Basler Afrika Bibliographien, 1997, pp. 13–44, 17; Lauren Dobell, 'Review of Dag Henrichsen, *A Glance at Our Africa*,' *Journal of Southern African Studies*, 24, 4, December 1998, pp. 833–5.

black-run newspaper, its directors turned to Prometheus Printers and Publishers of East London, run by Unity Movement stalwart Enver Hassim. Prometheus printed the first two issues, but in the State of Emergency following the Sharpeville-Langa massacres its owners were detained, and production shifted to Windhoek. Emil Appolus, a founding member of the Cape Town OPC, was the first editor until he was forced into exile following the deportation of his activist South African wife, nurse Putuse Dwyili-Appolus; thereafter Appolus covered the unfolding Congo crisis.[34]

The newspaper was run on a shoestring, its editors suffering from state harassment and SWANU's discord. Not surprisingly, it soon folded, its ninth and final issue appearing on 3 September 1960.[35] Nonetheless, in exposing apartheid policies it made its mark. It ran an African writers series and promoted African unity: an interview with Chief Kutako, for example, proposed the unity of South West Africa and the British protectorate of Bechuanaland [now Botswana].[36] It covered Macmillan's 'Wind of Change' speech, and its trilingual column, 'A Glance at Our Africa,' provided readers with a table of independent African countries and those still struggling for freedom. Each issue was circulated and read by many people. Crucially, *South West News* enabled Namibians to compare their own evolving national struggle with others.

In June 1960 the OPO reconstituted itself as SWAPO to have a national profile. Although SWANU and SWAPO were both broadly social democratic, SWANU's leaders were intellectuals, often studying overseas. Striving to show their capacity for self-government, they stressed self-reliance and education and pursued international links, joining the All-Africa People's Conference, the Afro-Asian People's Solidarity Organisation and the Anti-Apartheid Movement. Without the chiefs it drifted to the left; around September 1960 its leader Kozonguizi attacked Western imperialism over Radio Peking. By contrast, SWAPO's leaders pragmatically saw the UN as pivotal in the quest for independence.[37]

Back in Cape Town, Shipanga, Ottilie Schimming, Kenneth Abrahams and Marcus Solomon, who had been recruited by his girlfriend, Ottilie's sister

34 Zedekia Ngavirue, 'Introduction,' in *A Glance at Our Africa*, pp. 7–12, 9–10; Henrichsen, 'Historiography,' pp. 14, 18; Marion Mboono Nghidinwa, *Women Journalists in Namibia's Liberation Struggle, 1985–1990*, Basel: Basler Afrika Bibliographien, pp. 25–6; Akawa, *Gender Politics*, p. 48; 'Putuse Dwyili-Appolus, the Benevolent Meekulu of the Struggle (1930–1986),' https://neweralive.na/posts/putuse-dwyili-appolus-benevolent-meekulu-struggle-1930-1986, accessed 14 August 2021.

35 Henrichsen, 'Historiography,' p. 22.

36 *South West News*, 5 March 1960, 1, 1.

37 Ngavirue, 'Political Parties,' pp. 300–4, 335–8; 407–11; First, *South West Africa*, p. 201; Sellström, *Sweden and National Liberation*, pp. 263–5; Serfontein, *Namibia?* pp. 148–9; Dobell, *Swapo's Struggle*, pp. 32–3.

Charlotte, worked with SWAPO. Alexander joined them after his return from Germany. They criticized SWAPO's external leadership, which, 'now completely out of touch with the general membership, still has faith in U.N.O. as a liberatory force.' But, interestingly, they preferred SWAPO to the more intellectual SWANU, presumably because SWAPO had a migrant labour base, and they had close contact with migrant workers in Cape Town. 'S.W.A.P.O. has grown from a small group of people in Cape Town to a wide organization with branches throughout S.W.A., S. Africa and Bechuanalan,' wrote the NLF's monthly organ *Liberation*. Headquartered in Windhoek, SWAPO's strongest branches were in Walvis Bay, Oranjemund, Lüderitz, Tsumeb and Ovamboland, but the Cape Town branch was the most influential, it reported. It had twenty-two branches with about 90,000 members.[38]

Shipanga was in Cape Town during the Windhoek massacre, but he witnessed the march from Langa Township to Cape Town following the Sharpeville-Langa massacres. For him the Windhoek massacre showed, first, that labour needed to align with the national movement; secondly, that Namibians could not rely primarily on the UN, which did little but denounce the killings; finally, that passive resistance was limited: 'we could not push our people into the muzzles of machine guns; we had to confront guns with guns.'[39]

Pressure for armed struggle mounted after the massacres. South Africa's liberation movement launched sabotage actions in late 1961. External SWAPO leaders pushed armed struggle, which SWAPO endorsed in 1961–62, although it was not launched for several years. When the YCCC was formed in 1962, its members shared SWAPO's support for armed struggle. By contrast, SWANU did not think armed struggle was needed then, particularly one launched from outside the country.[40] Yet when communist journalist Ruth First toured Windhoek in 1962 in preparation for her book *South West Africa*, she found the distinctions between SWANU and SWAPO reflected personality and nuance rather than policy. The SACP initially preferred SWANU, whose acting chairman Mamugwe showed First around during her visit; she reportedly asked him to set up a Namibian branch of the SACP. SWANU leaders criticized SWAPO's reliance on petitions to the UN. As Mamugwe told First, external support should supplement actions inside the territory.

38 *Liberation*, 1, 1, February 1963, p. 14; Ngavirue, 'Political Parties,' p. 303; interview with Boesak.

39 Shipanga with Armstrong, *In Search*, pp. 38, 41–2, 50.

40 'One of two remaining Maoist Swanu China trained cadres laid to rest,' *Windhoek Observer*, 24 January 2022, https://www.observer24.com.na/one-of-two-remaining-maoist-swanu-china-trained-cadres-laid-to-rest, accessed 24 October 2022; SWAPO, *To be Born*, p. 176; Serfontein, *Namibia?* pp. 148–9; Shaun Whittaker, 'Namibian Moments in the Life of a Socialist Educator,' *Education as Change*, 17, 2, 2013, pp. 261–73.

Otherwise, 'United Nations promises cool the courage and spirit of the people, and they do not realize that *they* must do something themselves to attain their freedom.' First found that 'S.W.A.N.U.'s plan proceeds from a country-wide South West African popular consultation on forms of government; S.W.A.P.O. from U.N.-organized elections.' Nonetheless, she thought, they had more to unite than to divide them.[41]

South African liberation movements and the South West Africa question

According to Kenneth Abrahams, by the very early 1960s two schools of thought on South West Africa had emerged within South Africa's liberation movement. One saw the territory as South Africa's fifth province, its liberation dependent on South Africa's. The other supported an independent Namibia. Over time, as SWAPO developed, that second approach became dominant.[42] Perhaps some did initially see South West Africa as a fifth province; evidence is scanty. But this did not include the SACP, which endorsed Lenin's call for the right of national self-determination and in 1962 insisted that a future democratic South Africa should 'proclaim and scrupulously observe the right of self-determination and independence of South West Africa, Basutoland, Bechuanaland and Swaziland.'[43]

Nonetheless, Abrahams contends, the ANC hoped to form an Ovamboland branch, a bid rejected by Toivo.[44] Instead, pushed by Ghana's Kwame Nkrumah, the ANC organized the South Africa United Front (SAUF), launched in Addis Ababa in June 1960 to promote the liberation movement overseas. It included the ANC, Pan Africanist Congress (PAC), South African Indian Congress, SWANU and, from January 1961, SWAPO; like the SACP, the ANC supported SWANU until it aligned with China.[45] In September 1960, SAUF cautiously proposed that the UN take control of South West Africa 'as a first step towards

41 Interview, Boesak, who was Werner Mamugwe's son; First, *South West Africa*, p. 22, quotes pp. 204, 206, emphasis in original; Wallace with Kinahan, *History of Namibia*, p. 259; Saunders, 'Some Roots,' pp. 8–9, n.30; First was evidently pressured by SWAPO to revise the book but to her credit refused.

42 Interview, Kenneth Abrahams.

43 South African Communist Party, *The Road to South African Freedom: Programme of the South African Communist Party*, London: Inkululeko Publications, 1962, p. 34; Allison Drew, *Discordant Comrades: Identities and Loyalties on the South African Left*, Aldershot: Ashgate, 2000, p. 129; SADET, *Road to Democracy*, vol. 1, pp. 90, 428–30; Dreyer, *Namibia and Southern Africa*, pp. 32–3; Southall, *Liberation Movements*, p. 41; *South West News*, 5, 9 July 1960.

44 Interview, Kenneth Abrahams; Tötemeyer, *South West Africa*, p. 62; I have not found confirming evidence for Abrahams' claim.

45 Sellström, *Sweden and National Liberation*, pp. 262–3.

the granting of the complete independence of the territory.' Unfortunately, SWANU-SWAPO tensions limited its work on South West Africa. Its dissolution in February–March 1962 was attributed to ANC-PAC rivalry, especially after the PAC's rapid growth following the Sharpeville-Langa massacres.[46] Nonetheless, its brief existence signalled that some liberation movement leaders supported a united front.[47]

In contrast to SAUF, the factionalized Unity Movement saw the UN as pro-imperialist and SWAPO's reliance on the UN as collaborationist. Ottilie and Kenneth Abrahams were adamant that Tabata did not see the need for an independent Namibian organization, insisting that he wanted them to form an APDUSA branch in Namibia and develop APDUSA, rather than SWAPO. 'Tabata was very clear … This came as a shock to us,' recalled Kenneth Abrahams. 'That even those in the leadership of the black … national movement in South Africa regarded Namibia as a fifth province.' Cape Town SWAPO members were adamant that Namibians must decide whether they wanted their own liberation struggle and whether to choose independence or to federate with a post-apartheid South Africa.[48] Although Tabata might have built on the presence of young Namibians in the Unity Movement and their connection to SWAPO, he evidently chose not to.

The Unity Movement's position on South West Africa had certainly evolved since 1946 when its central executive committee had resolved:

> In view of the [government's] proposals to incorporate S. West Africa as a fifth province of the Union, the Non-European Unity Movement wishes to declare its emphatic opposition … on the grounds that it will be detrimental to the people in the Protectorates and to the Non-Europeans in the Union.[49]

By the Unity Movement's ninth national conference in January 1962, neither Jane Gool's address 'The International Situation' nor Tabata's 'The National Situation' mentioned South West Africa. Tabata evidently held a classical

46 Arianna Lissoni, 'The South African Liberation Movements in Exile, c.1945–1970,' PhD, SOAS, University of London, 2008, pp. 93–8, 101–2, 112–16, 123–4; Landau, *Spear*, pp. 64–7.

47 Similarly, Jean-Michel Mabeko-Tali, 'Dreaming Together, Fighting for Freedom Together: African Progressive Nationalism and the Ideology of Unity in Portugal's African Colonies in the 1950s and 1960s,' *Journal of Southern African Studies*, 46, 5, 2020, pp. 829–44, points to aspirations for unity in Lusophone African colonies during this period.

48 Interviews, Ottilie Abrahams; interview, Kenneth Abrahams; I have not found confirming evidence for this claim.

49 Non-European Unity Movement, *Proceedings of 5th Unity Conference*, 20–21 December, 1946, City Hall, Kimberley, p. 5.

Marxist view that during a revolution the army would go over to the people. He was scathing about '"bomb throwing" or "terror" ... They think this is also a method of work, a way to liberation. So they are going to throw bombs here and bombs there.'[50] Just a few days before, at SOYA's annual conference, Kenneth Abrahams and Neville Alexander had been suspended over SWAPO and armed struggle.[51]

In April 1962 Tabata addressed APDUSA's first national congress. APDUSA aimed to fight 'for the liquidation of the national oppression of the oppressed people in Southern Africa' and the 'acquisition by the whole nation of those democratic rights enjoyed at present by ... the white people,' he stated. Heretofore, Unity Movement leaders had referred to the South African nation. Tabata did not explain the shift to Southern Africa, rather stressing the African in APDUSA's 'aptly chosen' name: the organization represented all those 'who accept this country as their home and ... regard themselves as Africans.' However, he did discuss Southern Africa from the perspective of the South African economy, arguing: 'If all the neighbouring States decide to broaden their boycott of South African goods ... to include the stoppage of their labour supplies ... it is not difficult to imagine the reeling blow that would be dealt to South Africa.'[52]

The Eastern Cape Unity Movement activist Livingstone Mqotsi critiqued the state's plan for self-governing Bantustans. The regime's plan for the Transkei, he argued, was 'a blueprint for the regimentation and control of the minds and bodies of all the Non-Whites in South Africa and in South-West

50 I. B. Tabata, 'The National Situation,' January 1962, Speech to the Non-European Unity Movement Conference, p. 7; Jane Gool, 'The International Situation in 1961: An analysis presented at the Ninth National conference of the Non-European Unity Movement,' Edendale, Pitermaritzburg, 3–5 January 1962; Allison Drew, ed., *South Africa's Radical Tradition: A Documentary History, vol. 2, 1943–1964*, Cape Town, Buchu, Mayibuye and UCT, 1997, pp. 30–1.

51 'Kenneth Abrahams,' in Leys and Brown, eds, *Histories*, p. 144; interview, Alexander, 14 March 1988. The suspensions were for one year but became de facto permanent as this was the final SOYA conference. I have been unable to obtain minutes of the SOYA or NEUM conferences that year. Alie Fataar, *The Disintegration of the U.M.S.A. Abroad*, July 1974, p. 2, https://disa.ukzn.ac.za/rep19740700026044000. Abrahams and Alexander were not the first youthful critics to be suspended or expelled; see *The Soyan* [February 1959], pp. 9, 15. However, Bobby Wilcox, 3 November 2014 to author, disputes that they were suspended over SWAPO, claiming instead they were suspended for organizing in APDUSA circles and thus confusing its members.

52 NEUM, *Ninth National Conference*, Edendale, Maritzburg, 3–5 January 1962; I. B. Tabata, 'Presidential Address,' APDUSA, Cape Town, April 1962, pp. 1, 12. Robin Kaysar and Mohamed Adhikari, 'Land and Liberty!,' p. 324, suggest that Tabata, influenced by Trotsky's permanent revolution thesis, thought a revolution in South Africa would spread because of regional integration.

Africa.' He expanded: 'there will be self-government for Griquas, Muslims, Basutoes [*sic*], Bechauanas, Zulus, Hereros, Ovambos, and so on … We in APDUSA believe that the whole of Southern Africa belongs to the nation of Southern Africa.' Yet APDUSA's leaders did not conceptualize this southern African nation or, apparently, discuss the matter with SWANU or SWAPO.[53]

Ottilie Abrahams had valued the Unity Movement's 'constructive criticism,' but when it suspended Alexander and her husband, she said, they 'came to a parting of the ways.' In her words, 'we were not going to get our freedom without some sort of armed struggle … we felt that this was the only way out … it was something we grew into.'[54] The Abrahamses published the cyclostyled *South-West Commentator*, launched in November 1961 by the S. W. Discussion Group – in fact, Cape Town SWAPO – whose contact was a Mr Roberts [i.e. Kenneth Abrahams] at a post office box in Cape Town's Rondebosch suburb. Although mainly English language, readers wrote letters in various South West African languages. SWAPO member Paul Helmut arranged for the issues to be smuggled by boat into South West Africa. The police tried in vain to make local Namibian labourers disclose who was behind the *Commentator*.[55]

Unlike the *South West News*, the *Commentator* was strictly political. Despite the Abrahamses' break with the Unity Movement, the *Commentator* showed its political and linguistic influence. It was scathing about the UN. In 1962 the South African government finally allowed a UN mission to visit the territory, but this lost credibility when it issued a joint statement with the apartheid government. The *Commentator* berated the UN as 'a weapon in the hands of [the] Imperialists,' rejected 'a system of UN trusteeship' and demanded 'Independence now.'[56] It also criticized 'quisling chiefs' – quisling being a key Unity Movement term.[57] Although chiefs had played a crucial role in the territory's early anti-colonial struggles, some northern chiefs were rejected

53 L. Mqotsi, 'Bantustans, Colouredstans & Indianstans,' Speech delivered at the African People's Democratic Union of South [*sic*] Africa Conference [1962], pp. 3–4, https://disa.ukzn.ac.za/spe19620400026044000, accessed 3 September 2025; Southall, *Liberation Movements*, p. 114.

54 Matsemela, interviews, Ottilie Abrahams, Kenneth Abrahams; Yvette Abrahams, 'Tribute to "Mother of Education",' *The Namibian*, 4 July 2018, https://www.namibian.com.na/179164/archive-read/Tribute-to-Mother-of-Education, accessed 3 August 2020; *State vs Alexander*, pp. 1930–54.

55 Interview, Ottilie Abrahams; 'Kenneth Abrahams,' in Leys and Brown, *Histories*, p. 143; *South-West Commentator* was published until at least May 1962.

56 Wallace with Kinahan, *History of Namibia*, 261; *South-West Commentator*, 16 May 1962, pp. 1–2.

57 Drew, ed., *Radical Tradition*, vol. 2, pp. 24, 155, n. 6; see also I. B. Tabata, *The Boycott as a Weapon of Struggle* [June 1952], pp. 5–6, https://www.sahistory.org.za/sites/default/files/The%20Boycott.pdf, accessed 16 August 2021.

by local people because they policed the contract labour system. Moreover, under the Odendaal Plan, South Africa was extending its Bantustan system into South West Africa. The *Commentator* opposed attempts to partition the territory and enhance chiefly power, castigating the announcement of a planned Bantustan in the north along the lines proposed for the Transkei. It cited a 'C.T. SWAPO official, originally from Ovamboland,' who argued that the government's development proposals would be merely 'a showpiece to exhibit to foreign visitors.' The people want a democratic government and franchise, 'not various Bantu Authorities and the dying system of chieftainship. We support them in all their efforts to ensure that the proposed Northern Bantustan will be a dismal failure!' The Odendaal Plan was nonetheless implemented.[58]

Yet in contrast to the Unity Movement, the *Commentator* supported armed struggle. The Algerian Front de Libération Nationale (FLN) and the French government had just agreed to a cease fire on 18 March 1962 – the Evian Accords. The *Commentator*'s 28 March editorial 'Salute the F.L.N.' underlined: 'We learn … that freedom and independence have to be wrenched from the Imperialist powers, at a very heavy cost indeed … There are far too many in our country who still believe that the Government will grant us freedom if only we ask long enough and loudly enough; or if we offer to cooperate and be "nice" to the white-man.' But peace did not mean freedom, it added, as the Evian Accords gave too much power to French imperialism. However, the Algerian war showed the need for an organization of all the oppressed with a programme 'to raise as a banner so that all may follow.' Neither the *South-West Commentator* nor the YCCC or NLF understood the FLN's conception of unity, which was not based on a pluralist assembly of groups, but rather on the dissolution of all other groups and the adherence of their members directly into the FLN.[59]

The Abrahamses, whose first child, Kenneth, Jr, was born in January 1962, held a fortnightly study group at their home – the YCCC. As Shipanga recalled: 'A group of us from several different political parties formed the *Yu Chi Chen* [*sic*] Club. There were a few of us from South West Africa, but because it was dangerous we did not want to associate SWAPO with the name. I was the only member of the SWAPO leadership to belong to *Yu Chi Chen* [*sic*].' He stressed the importance of education for guerrilla struggle: 'This was only a study circle, but … it was forming cadre who were to become the instructors and leaders of our guerrillas.'[60] Keen to gain exposure to a wide variety

58 *South-West Commentator*, 28 February 1962, pp. 3–4; Wallace with Kinahan, *History of Namibia*, pp. 259–65.

59 *South-West Commentator*, 28 February 1962, pp. 1, 3–4; 28 March 1962, pp. 1, 5–7; Drew, *No Longer in France*, pp. 184–209.

60 Shipanga with Armstrong, *In Search*, pp. 50–1; Dennis Mercer, *Interviews in Depth – Namibia (SWAPO): Andreas Shipanga*, Richmond, BC: LSM, 1973, p. 6;

of approaches, Shipanga, Haufiku and Kaluma – the Swapos, as SWAPO members were informally called – were also Liberal Party members. These Namibians opened the group to the Namibian struggle.[61]

Along with Shipanga, the Abrahamses also organized SWAPO study groups. In Ottilie's words, 'we tried to introduce an analytical element into SWAPO.' At the time, she explained, SWAPO membership 'was more a loyalty to liberation.' People would not analyse speeches or pose questions. So, they wanted to teach SWAPO members how to 'look critically at issues' and to familiarize them with voting procedures.[62] They produced *SWAPO (Cape Town Branch)*, which succeeded the *Commentator*. After the documents were produced, often in the Abrahamses's garage, they were shipped clandestinely to Walvis Bay and into South West Africa.[63]

SWAPO (Cape Town Branch) pushed armed struggle. It mentioned the Afro-Asian Bloc pressure, the increasing disillusionment with the UN, the recognition that trusteeship was not necessary and the 'growing demand for independence NOW!' It bemoaned SWAPO's internal divisions, its leadership's contradictory statements and the lack of contact between the branches and national executives inside and outside the territory.[64] The Cape Town branch called for immediate independence, full democracy and an increased living standard through armed struggle, pressure on the UN and unity: 'We must establish a firm basis on which to collaborate with SWANU; and this must be seen as a prelude to a firm organic union of our organisations.'[65] It also proposed that the South and South West African liberation movements unite:

> No attempts have been made in the past to bring about a firm, organic unity of the struggle in South Africa and South West Africa … The only concrete attempt at unity was via the SA United Front and even then [t]his had absolutely no effect on the position at home.

Finally, it insisted, the external SWAPO must be under the control of SWAPO inside the country, and funds must go to the internal struggle.[66]

Namibian, 21 February 2013, https://archive.is/20130221040735/http://www.namibian.com.na/news-articles/national/full-story/archive/2012/may/article/liberation-pioneer-dies, accessed 23 June 2020.

61 Dreyer, *Namibia & Southern Africa*, p. 204, n.26; Randolph Vigne, *Liberals against Apartheid: A History of the Liberal Party of South Africa, 1953–68*, Basingstoke: Macmillan, 1997, p. 185; Shipanga with Armstrong, *In Search*, p. 39; *State vs Alexander*, p. 1663; *South-West Commentator*, 16 May 1962.

62 Interview with Ottilie Abrahams, TAA18_9_B.

63 *State vs Alexander*, pp. 1519–20, 1701.

64 *SWAPO Cape Town Branch*, n.d. [c. 1962–63] pp. 1, 3.

65 *SWAPO Cape Town Branch*, p. 10.

66 *SWAPO Cape Town Branch*, pp. 5–8, 10.

The Yu Chi Chan Club and the South West Africa question

South West Africa's colonial status certainly shaped the YCCC's thinking on guerrilla struggle. Alexander's pamphlet, *The Conquest of Power in South Africa*, provided a theoretical rationale for guerrilla warfare in South and South West Africa. Both had a history of guerrilla struggles – the Afrikaners against the British in the South African War, the Nama-Herero against the Germans and later the Mpondoland and Ovamboland struggles. Difficult reading, *Conquest* shows the influence of Mao and Guevara. The need for guerrilla warfare was shaped by South Africa's racially divided society, Alexander began. Class struggle had been 'blurred by the historical accident of race' and the ruling class use of 'colour groupings.' This was 'the colour-caste, capitalist system.' Since the white working class had been bought off, 'the most revolutionary sections of South African society are to be found among those ... called the Non-Whites. The most exploited classes ... are at the same time racially or nationally oppressed.'[67]

Guerrilla warfare was 'a weapon that a nation inferior in arms and military equipment may employ against a more powerful aggressor nation,' Alexander continued, quoting Mao's *Yu Chi Chan*. Unlike Europe, where the army could go over to the popular classes, the white South African army would never support the black masses, he maintained. Algeria, Cuba and to an extent Angola showed 'that guerrilla bands of vanishing magnitude were turned into regular armies in the course of the struggle through desertions, political propaganda and state repression of the civilian population.'[68]

Unusually, Alexander stressed the parallel between South Africa's colonial relationship with South West Africa and France's colonial relationship with Algeria: South Africa saw South West Africa as a fifth province, just as France claimed Algeria as a French Department. South West Africa was South Africa's Achilles heel. Although he hoped that the two struggles could be conducted as one and that each could reinforce the other, this was unlikely. More likely, he thought, guerrilla war could 'bring about some kind of "Algerian" Independence.' Although not satisfactory in the long run, 'from the point of view of providing a strong liberated area ... it will be an invaluable gain for the struggle as a whole.'[69] Ovamboland was 'one of the most natural guerrilla areas in Southern Africa.' The Ovambos, well-armed and aimed at independence, had a popular political movement, whose programme needed 'some tightening up.' Ovamboland and Mpondoland, with their quasi-guerrilla traditions, and the

67 [YCCC-Neville Alexander], *Pamphlet no. II: The Conquest of Power in South Africa* [1962], p. 1. This is an early articulation of Alexander's ideas about colour-caste and racial capitalism.

68 YCCC-Alexander, *Conquest*, p. 3.

69 YCCC-Alexander, *Conquest*, p. 7.

Transkei, with its mountainous areas, coastline and proximity to Basutoland, would be primary fields of operations.[70]

Paramilitary cells that studied military tactics and strategy could become 'the nuclues [*sic*] of a guerrilla unit.' The rural masses would provide the base of the guerrilla army for some time, meaning that education was crucial. 'The fight against rural illiteracy starts during the revolution, not afterwards. The raising of the cultural level, apart from bringing our ideas to the masses on a higher level will also instil discipline into the soldiers and into the masses.' Guerrilla teachers would 'be among the most powerful agents of the political, social and cultural revolution.' In cities, guerrillas would work in political and trade union organizations. Crucially, he stressed, 'no guerrilla unit should ever forget its fundamental political character … To forget this would mean to fall back into primitive militarism.'[71] Their immediate task was to form cells in all strategically important areas and synchronize their own guerrilla units with those of other organizations, Alexander concluded, ever mindful of his Unity Movement lessons: 'Guerrilla warfare in South Africa, is the continuation of the policy of Non-Collaboration in a specific form towards the achievement of … democratic aims.'[72]

Kenneth Abrahams' pamphlet, *Technical and Organisational Aspects of the Yu Chi Chan Club*, stressed education, but particularly propaganda and persuasion. 'Our primary task is to do ALL that is necessary to prepare for, plan and carry through the military phase of the Revolution in South Africa,' the pamphlet began boldly. Their group envisioned ten regions in which to form cells – 'always for our purposes including South West Africa.' Each region would have at least one professional revolutionary working in a political organization 'to set members of this organization on the revolutionary road, make them aware of the necessity for an armed insurrection.' Although the typical guerrilla would 'be an ardent agrarian revolutionary fighting for land,' during the next year they would not fight but would instead train leaders who would recruit their own people: 'most guerrilla activity does not involve fighting! Much time is spent spreading political propaganda, winning support for the Revolution and weakening the influence of the enemy. A guerrilla … is creating a new society.'[73] Indeed, the idea of guerrilla teachers would

70 Interview with Alexander, c. April 1988, Basel Africa Library, PA 153, TPA153_8_A; YCCC-Alexander, *Conquest*, pp. 6–7; Allison Drew, 'Visions of liberation: The Algerian War of Independence and its South African reverberations,' *Review of African Political Economy*, 2015, 42, 143, March 2015, pp. 22–43, 36.

71 YCCC-Alexander, *Conquest*, pp. 5–6.

72 YCCC-Alexander, *Conquest*, pp. 4–5; see also Neville Alexander, 'Aspects of Non-collaboration in the Western Cape 1943–1963,' *Social Dynamics*, 12, 1, 1986, pp. 1–14.

73 [YCCC-Kenneth Abrahams], *Pamphlet no. III: Technical and Organisational Aspects of the Yu Chi Chan Club* [1962], pp. 1–2.

have been especially attractive to the group, given their Unity Movement background and stress on education. Guerrilla teachers would have been a means of bridging the intellectual-activist divide that had impeded the Unity Movement's development.

Returning to South West Africa

After the YCCC disbanded, the NLF was launched as a network aiming to extend beyond the western Cape. As Alexander recalled:

> the basic idea was to … create political infrastructure to indentify [*sic*] individuals who could be recruited into military organisations eventually. And that way to prepare the ground for the launching of guerrilla warfare in 3 or 4 years … We always thought in terms of preparations over a period of 3 or 4 years.[74]

Shipanga and Ottilie Abrahams felt strongly that SWAPO had to be built inside their country, not just outside. SWAPO activists had been campaigning in Ovamboland since 1961, and Shipanga was called back to organize. Returning in early 1963 with a copy of Mao's *Yu Chi Chan*, he met with SWAPO leaders in Windhoek and discussed the December 1959 massacre. In his words:

> I did not want to tell my colleagues about *Yu Chi Chen* [*sic*] directly, but only to test the ground. I said: 'What do you think? Can we still call our people out to protest peacefully?'
>
> A woman replied:
>
> 'No. We cannot call people out when they have nothing to defend themselves with … Let us have guns. If you men are not up to it, we women will wage war while you look after the children.'[75]

Liberation reported that their member [Shipanga] arrived in South West Africa on 28 February and attended a two-day regional congress in Ovamboland, presenting NLF views while not identifying the organization. He explained that he and his comrades opposed the UN because imperialist and colonialist ventures in South West Africa such as the Tsumeb Corporation and Consolidated Diamond Mines would 'control UNO and divide – even

74 Matsemela, interview with Alexander, A.2.4, p. 88; Drew, 'Gendered Approach,' p. 195.

75 Shipanga with Armstrong, *In Search*, p. 51; cf. Mercer, *Interviews in Depth – Namibia (SWAPO): Andreas Shipanga*, p. 21. Wallace with Kinahan, *History of Namibia*, p. 260.

partition the country. This would result in a bloodbath – as in the Congo.'[76] Studying Mao's book, Shipanga met with Toivo and others, often in private homes, to convince people that Namibia, like other African countries, should get its freedom.[77]

Liberation's discourse, like the *Commentator*'s, still showed Unity Movement influence, whether in castigating popular protests or the leaders of other organizations. Its 'Brief Survey of the Revolutionary Movement in S.W.A.' characterized the Windhoek massacre in typical Unity Movement terms as 'an unsophisticated Herrenvolk response to the people's naïve adventuring.' The Namibian leadership arising from the 1959 struggles had thrown itself behind the UN, *Liberation* maintained, and organizations inside the territory were left 'wandering around in circles ... the lack of purposive activity ... inversely proportional to the rising militant mood of the people.' SWAPO had a large Ovambo membership, yet its influence among Coloured and Rehoboth people was 'virtually nil.' Although its leadership was 'making an effort,' it remained in 'suspended animation.' SWANU's leadership, by contrast, represented only 'scattered groups of dissatisfied Herero people' and 'exist[ed] from one depressing discussion to the next.'[78]

Namibians still hoped the UN would help them gain independence if they documented South Africa's atrocities, claimed *Liberation*. There was some thought of armed struggle, but this was 'more of a hangover from the wars of conquest than a modern solution to the problem of liberation. However, the impact of revolutions in Cuba, Algeria and Angola, plus the turbulence in SA (Transkei, Poqo), is making itself felt.'[79] The article recommended greater emphasis on political education rather than military work for 'the next year at least.' That would entail using existing platforms and producing underground literature. Then, hopefully, NLF guerrillas could infiltrate other organizations to fight pro-UN and pro-imperialist tendencies, again stressing political education: 'To recruit guerrillas who are still politically raw would be in opposition to our policy of training leaders.' Notwithstanding the NLF's talk of a united front, it added that the absence of other anti-apartheid military groups in the territory meant that if those groups eventually tried to recruit South West African guerrillas, it would be able 'to stifle any such activity.'[80]

In May 1963 the Abrahamses left for South West Africa, their second child, Yvette, having been born that January. Neville Alexander became *Liberation*'s

[76] 'Short Report on Activity in S.W. Africa (Ovamboland),' *Liberation*, 1, 3, May 1963, p. 3.

[77] Shipanga with Armstrong, *In Search*, pp. 53, 55.

[78] *Liberation*, April 1963, pp. 7–9.

[79] *Liberation*, April 1963, pp. 8–9; Matsemela, interview with Alexander, A2.4, pp. 89–90.

[80] *Liberation*, April 1963, pp. 7–9, and 1, 3, May 1963, p. 3.

editor. The Abrahamses moved to Rehoboth in central Namibia, some fifty-six miles south of Windhoek. Rehoboth had had limited self-rule since 1870, including the right to bear arms and grant citizenship. Ottilie's father had acquired a farm there and through this, citizenship. In turn, Ottilie became a citizen and through her, so did her husband Kenneth, the only doctor for some 30,000 people. Once settled, they began recruiting for SWAPO, hoping to build its support there. However, the South African police contended that Kenneth was in the territory illegally, although the Rehobothers had granted him citizenship. A lengthy court case ensued.[81]

On 20 July the police attempted to arrest Kenneth. But hundreds of Rehobothers arrived with guns and gathered in front of the Abrahams home, refusing to allow the police to remove their only doctor. Ottilie created a diversion by driving off in their red Volkswagen, and Kenneth fled through their back door, where the local priest was waiting in his *bakkie* [pick-up truck]. Kenneth climbed in, soon joined by his neighbour, 'Old Man' Hermanus Beukes, father of student Hans. The priest drove off, and at every residence Beukes called out: 'The day of the revolution has broken!' Other men jumped on board. They camped in the hills for several days. The authorities backed down and allowed Kenneth Abrahams to return. Finally, reported the *Cape Times* of 2 August, the Deputy Minister for South West Africa Affairs allowed him to remain in Rehoboth if he worked solely as a medical practitioner.[82]

Conclusion

Once back in South West Africa, Shipanga and the Abrahamses organized for SWAPO. However, that work was very soon cut off by their arrests and exile. As a result, the NLF had no direct impact in the territory. Yet it is interesting because it offered an intermediate position between SWANU's call for self-reliance and work inside the territory and SWAPO's subsequent externally based guerrillas. The NLF aspired to help Namibians become conscious of their own agency rather than relying solely on the UN. Against the backdrop of sabotage attacks unfolding in South Africa, its members introduced ideas about democracy, united fronts and guerrilla struggle to Cape Town SWAPO members. Its relationship with Cape Town SWAPO was presumably due to the relative fluidity of the new Namibian liberation organizations compared to the rigidity and rivalry of the older South African organizations. By 1962

81 First, *South West Africa*, pp. 41–5; 'Kenneth Abrahams,' in Leys and Brown, *Histories*, pp. 145–8; Matsemela, interview, Alexander, A2.4, p. 88; *State vs Alexander*, pp. 379, 1753–54, 1763, 1884.

82 *Cape Times*, 20 July, 2 August 1963; 'Kenneth Abrahams,' in Leys and Brown, *Histories*, pp. 145–8; Abrahams states he went to Namibia in January 1963, and Shipanga, earlier. Those may have been preliminary visits.

SWAPO had decided to pursue political and military efforts 'concurrently' rather than rush into armed struggle – eventually launched on 26 August 1966, the month after the International Court of Justice rejected Ethiopia and Liberia's case.[83] But SWAPO's approach to armed struggle was not the NLF's vision of a guerrilla war that relied on guerrilla teachers. Nor were the NLF's hopes for a united front realized.

Notwithstanding SWAPO's strength among migrant workers, its eventual dominance of South West Africa's liberation movement was ensured by international developments. The first development was the Cold War and the early 1960s Sino-Soviet rivalry. Despite the SACP's initial preference for SWANU, as the Sino-Soviet rift deepened, the Afro-Asian People's Solidarity Organisation split. The Chinese camp claimed SWANU, and in turn the Soviets claimed SWAPO, swiftly followed by the SACP. Western powers, too, preferred SWAPO's pragmatism. SWANU became ever more isolated.[84]

The second development concerned the Organisation of African Unity (OAU), launched in Addis Ababa in May 1963. Initially the OAU recognized both SWANU and SWAPO as liberation organizations. In October 1963 SWANU and SWAPO's internal executives formed the South West African National Liberation Front in Windhoek. However, not unlike the South Africa United Front's dissolution, it collapsed after SWAPO's external leaders, notably Nujoma, rejected it. That same year the OAU formed the Liberation Committee, headquartered in Dar es Salaam, to promote the end of white minority rule on the continent. The Liberation Committee stipulated that its recognition was premised on support for armed struggle and asked SWANU and SWAPO for their plans. SWAPO's plan indicated that it had been training soldiers since 1962. SWANU replied that it was not prepared for military activity and did not wish to conduct armed struggle from exile, although a few members underwent military training – four trained in China in 1964, for example. Rather, it wished to organize people inside the country.[85] In late 1964 the Liberation Committee derecognized SWANU, deemed SWAPO to be the territory's sole legitimate and authentic liberation movement and allocated funds solely to SWAPO.[86] This curtailed any possibility of a Namibian

83 Dreyer, *Namibia and Southern Africa*, p. 37; Saunders, 'SWAPO,' p. 157; Wallace with Kinahan, *History of Namibia*, p. 268.

84 Dobell, *Swapo's Struggle*, p. 34.

85 First, *South West Africa*, p. 204.

86 Saunders, 'SWAPO', pp. 155–6; Simpson, *History of South Africa*, p. 200, states the OAU stopped funding SWANU on 2 August 1965 but did not derecognize it. According to Jeremy Friedman, *Ripe for Revolution: Building Socialism in the Third World*, Harvard University Press: Harvard University Press, 2021, p. 174, the Liberation Committee recommended that Holdon Roberto's *Govêrno revolucionário de Angola no exílio* be recognized and aid given exclusively to his *Frente Nacional de Libertação de Angola*.

united front and split SWANU's intellectuals off from organized labour and political pragmatists. That year the Abrahamses were expelled from SWAPO for promoting a SWANU-SWAPO united front.[87]

Ironically, the very internationalism that had initially promoted Namibia's anti-colonial struggle impeded its national struggle. Squeezed between the South African state's brutality and SWAPO's external power politics, the YCCC and NLF's ideas about guerrilla struggle and united fronts were fleeting. Nonetheless, their written words on South West Africa's anti-colonial struggle remained. For the apartheid regime these would be further evidence of their thought crime.

[87] Tor Sellström, interview with Ottilie Abrahams, Windhoek, 16 March 1995, https://nai.uu.se/library/resources/liberation-africa/interviews/ottilie-abrahams.html, accessed 25 June 2021, also in Tor Sellström, ed., *Liberation in Southern Africa: Regional and Swedish Voices*, Uppsala: Nordiska Afrikainstitutet, 2nd ed., 2002, pp. 59–62; Sellström, *Sweden and National Liberation*, pp. 264, n.1, 272, n.1; Ngavirue, 'Political Parties,' pp. 277, 304, 339; Saunders, 'SWAPO,' pp. 154–6, 166; interview with Kauraisa.

Chapter 4

Things Fall Apart

A tiny new group lacking a larger, parent organization could hardly hope to get a foothold in early 1960s South Africa or South West Africa when the police state was ever more powerful. After all, the Unity Movement, with an institutional culture dominated by a few strong personalities, had rejected the young people who formed the Yu Chi Chan Club (YCCC) and National Liberation Front (NLF). Yet, in Fikile Bam's recollection, most NLF members were still imbued with the Unity Movement's philosophy and commitment to non-collaboration. As activists they sought to extend its approach with new ideas and methods. Guerrilla struggle was an unconventional form of war, and they believed it could be adapted to 1960s South Africa.[1] They looked especially to Algeria, whose history of mass expropriation, migrant labour and a rigidly divided working class showed striking parallels with their own country. However, settler societies such as Algeria and South Africa lacked the classical Marxist proletarian vanguard: workers of European descent could not lead national liberation struggles, and the indigenous majorities were still predominantly rural and often aspired to be self-sustaining peasants. Still, China, Vietnam, Cuba and Algeria conjured visions of urban and rural guerrillas who could substitute for an urban proletarian vanguard. Notwithstanding scholarly debates over whether the liberation movement's turn to violence was a strategic or tactical mistake, anti-apartheid activists had examples of successful armed struggles before their eyes.[2]

South African communists likewise studied these experiences. Reflecting the country's divided left, two visions of armed struggle developed. Rooted in the pragmatic Congress Alliance tradition, Umkhonto we Sizwe launched sabotage attacks before developing a strategy for guerrilla war. Sabotage, although inspiring, did not involve the masses. Instead, it led to an emphasis on military training over political education and, crucially, intensified state repression. As a result, by late 1962 many activists saw it as counterproductive. By contrast, despite the NLF's bold written rhetoric, its members generally

1 Matsemela, interview with Bam, UCTCPM, 104311.

2 Thula Simpson's, 'Mandela's Army: Urban revolt in South Africa, 1960–1964,' *Journal of Southern African Studies*, 45, 6, 2019, pp. 1093–10, 1094–5 provides an effective summary of these debates.

believed that an immediate armed struggle was premature. So they tried to build an underground network and educate members about guerrilla strategy, stressing the need for guerrilla teachers who linked political education and activism. This chapter discusses their efforts.

Perceptions and misperceptions

The NLF's monthly organ *Liberation* styled itself as an 'illegal newspaper,' but its hand-drawn cover brashly announced it as the NLF organ for ten cents. It was dense, with single-spaced typed pages numbering in the teens and unattributed articles reflecting the knowledge and interests of each author. The first issue reported on the 16–18 January executive committee meeting, describing the NLF as a paramilitary organization with military and political aims. 'We accept into our organization all those who are trustworthy and convinced opponents of the Herrenvolk Government and accept the policy of armed insurrection,' it stated baldly, hoping to build a united front with other similar anti-apartheid groups.[3] Although the NLF's name echoed the Algerian Front de Libération Nationale (FLN), it did not evidently theorize united fronts nor understand that the FLN was based on a unitary rather than pluralist conception of unity and so did not accept other organizations. Rather, individuals left their organizations, which were expected to disband, and joined the FLN directly. By contrast both the Congress and Unity movements had pluralist traditions of unity based on alliances of organizations.[4]

Building a united front necessitated an understanding of other anti-apartheid groups. Although the NLF recognized that members of those groups might have differing and evolving viewpoints, its analyses did not always reflect this. The South African left had a history of sectarian division, broadly reflecting the articulation of communism and Trotskyism with national liberation politics. Two decades earlier, Peter Abrahams had lamented that although activists Johnny Gomas and Goolam Gool were both 'sincere and honest in their strivings for non-European emancipation ... each was all that was untrustworthy to the other. Labels had conquered the men.' Socialists, like other political activists, fit information into pre-existing theories and frameworks, which in turn influence what they deem significant. This is apparent in the NLF's writings. Nonetheless, the NLF's aspiration to transcend the left's longstanding sectarianism was important, even if not realized.[5]

3 *Liberation*, February 1963, p. 5.

4 Drew, *No Longer in France*, pp. 184–5, 188–9, 269.

5 Peter Abrahams, *Tell Freedom: Memories of Africa*, London: Faber & Faber, 1954, p. 276; Robert Jervis, 'Hypotheses on Misperception,' *World Politics*, 20, 3, April 1968, pp. 454–79 and Robert Jervis, *Perception and Misperception in International*

Since YCCC documents had already discussed guerrilla struggle, *Liberation* began with a series of articles on other anti-apartheid organizations. Its survey started with the Communist Party. Before its 1950 banning, the Communist Party of South Africa (CPSA) had prioritized working class and trade union struggles, the article began, but its successor, the South African Communist Party (SACP), pushed 'class alliance and organizational merging even though … the building up of independent organizations in the rural and urban proletariat was possible.' That approach inspired 'enormous popularity for Congress and the C.P. at the expense of the worker's [*sic*] struggle.' The Treason Trial of Congress Alliance leaders had further increased the SACP's visibility, although it had shocked some of its older members 'into inertia.'

This assessment is problematic. The seeming 'inertia' perceived by the NLF may well have reflected concern that the state was shrinking public political space, making open opposition far riskier than heretofore. The Congress movement had been concerned about secrecy throughout the 1950s. In 1953 Nelson Mandela proposed his M-Plan for the ANC's expansion through an underground cell structure. Although implementation faltered, there was some success around Durban and in the Eastern Cape, where communist Govan Mbeki organized study groups. Mandela continued the work in 1961–62, after the post-Sharpeville clampdown, but his comrades often resisted his efforts. The tiny underground SACP, for its part, did indeed promote class alliances over working-class independence – after all, organized black labour was a small proportion of the population. But it scrupulously avoided a public profile, leading to internal disagreements, and when it launched the *African Communist* in October 1959, it was without attribution. Only in July 1960 did it finally issue a flyer in its name and in September claim responsibility for the *African Communist*. By the early 1960s repression had forced many 1950s Congress activists, including communists, to flee the country.[6]

The sabotage attacks launched by the SACP and Umkhonto were 'not inspired by organisations of the masses,' *Liberation* continued, but rather aimed 'to bring the masses on collision with the state.' They aimed to provoke a UN intervention – the July 1960 intervention of UN peacekeeping forces

Politics, Princeton, NJ: Princeton University Press, 1976, new edition, 2017 concern international relations, but the main idea is applicable to socialist politics.

6 *Liberation*, February 1963, p. 8; Drew, 'Visions,' p. 24; Thomas Karis and Gail Gerhart, 'The Congress Movement,' in Thomas Karis and Gail Gerhart, eds, *From Protest to Challenge*, vol. 3, Stanford: Hoover Institution, 1977, pp. 3–98, 35–40; Lodge, *Black Politics*, pp. 75–6, 231; Lodge, *Red Road*, pp. 315, 331; Paul S. Landau, 'The M-Plan: Mandela's Struggle to Reorient the African National Congress,' *Journal of Southern African Studies*, 45, 6, 2019, pp. 1073–91, 1073–8, 1090.

in newly independent Congo was very much in NLF minds.[7] But was the SACP seeking such a collision? It had formally accepted the use of violence at its December 1960 conference, although with little discussion, and began preparations on a need-to-know basis; after all, ANC-aligned organizations were under pressure from the armed actions of other groups, notably the National Committee for Liberation and Poqo. In November 1961 the SACP secretary-general Moses Kotane told Soviet officials in Moscow that the Party had agreed to limited violence. It would begin training cadres in the use of explosives, but there was no suggestion of 'full-scale guerrilla war.' Although Kotane thought violence unavoidable, over the next few years he was still critical of its use. Despite this caution, the Party had agreed to establish Umkhonto, which the next month set off explosions around the country.[8]

In contrast to the NLF's interest in united fronts, Umkhonto had no interest in aligning with other armed struggle groups: 'It was not connected in any way with a so-called Committee for National Liberation [*sic*] whose existence has been announced in the press,' stated its manifesto. Umkhonto leaders had considered sabotage, guerrilla warfare, terrorism and revolution. They thought terrorism would undermine their attempts to build public sympathy, while the disappointing turnout for the 31 May 1961 stay-at-home – organized by the ANC's Mandela and opposed by Poqo – suggested to them that the masses were not ready for a revolutionary uprising. So they decided on a rolling sabotage campaign as the least harmful to human life. Recent research suggests that Umkhonto initially used violence to inspire and promote non-violent protests, such as stay-at-home strikes and boycotts.[9]

However, Umkhonto faced internal pressure to shift to guerrilla struggle. On 20 July 1962 Mandela returned home after a trip across Africa to raise support for the armed struggle. In late March he and his comrade Robert Resha had visited the FLN's army camps in Morocco. The mood was jubilant: the Evian Accords were signed on 18 March, and a ceasefire declared the next day. Mandela was extremely impressed by their ideas about guerrilla war. Reporting back to his comrades at Rivonia, he stressed the need for unity, political education, and coordination of rural and urban struggles. Although some comrades felt that sabotage still offered possibilities and that guerrilla

7 *Liberation*, February 1963, p. 8; Republic of the Congo, ONUC Background, https://peacekeeping.un.org/sites/default/files/past/onucB.htm, accessed 28 May 2025.

8 Drew, 'Visions,' p. 25; Lodge, *Red Road*, pp. 320–2.

9 'Manifesto of Umkhonto we Sizwe issued on December 16, 1961,' in Brian Bunting, ed., *South African Communists Speak: Documents from the History of the South African Communist Party 1915–1980*, London: Inkululeko, 1981, pp. 274–6; Simon Stevens, 'Violence, Political Strategy and the Turn to Guerrilla Warfare by the Congress Movement in South Africa,' *Journal of Southern African Studies*, 47, 6, 2021, pp. 1011–28, 1017–18; Drew, 'Visions,' pp. 26–7.

struggle was premature, given the lengthy period needed for guerrilla training, they agreed to proceed. Mbeki had been writing a book about the eastern Cape Mpondo uprising against Bantu Authorities, which had begun in the 1950s, peaked in 1960 and finally been suppressed in 1961. He thought that 'sabotage activities were not proving very successful as from '61 through the end of '62.' So, he proposed to his comrades in Johannesburg, 'let's get on to the next phase, which is the armed struggle itself.' Mandela was arrested soon after, on 5 August.[10]

It is not known whether NLF members had read the SACP's programme, *The Road to South African Freedom*, adopted at its sixth congress in October 1962. The programme elaborated the 'colonialism of a special type' thesis that national democracy was a precondition for socialism and called for continued alliance with the ANC. Since the government was using more violence, it argued, 'the people could no longer rely on traditional non-violent methods of struggle and protest, but would have to find new answers if their cause was to be victorious.' Over the long term, the people 'must find mass methods of struggle, both violent and non-violent, into which the whole democratic movement and all its supporters can be drawn.'[11]

The SACP stressed the parallels between South Africa and Algeria, where 'the racial situation is closest to our own' and the working class had 'strong unions and its own political party.' Moreover, it was in Algeria that South African communists found most sympathy for their non-racial policy, which was criticized in other parts of the continent. The party's short-lived publication *Assagai* [Spear] referred to the Algerian experience, stressing the need to combine urban and rural work. Although the *Johannesburg Star* claimed that underground politics had moved from the cities to the countryside, *Assagai* noted in March 1963 that urban sabotage attacks were occurring alongside rural guerrilla activities. Interlinking urban and rural struggles would rally the people: 'sabotage in the towns destroys the property of the rulers, disturbs their communications and forces them to employ large numbers of men in trying to track down the attcakers [*sic*]. Like-wise guerilla activities in the country harasses [*sic*] their army and breaks [*sic*] down the machinery of administration

10 Drew, 'Visions,' pp. 29, 33–4; Nelson Mandela Notebook, Nelson Mandela Centre of Memory, Johannesburg, pp. 54–7; Landau, 'M-Plan,' pp. 1090–1; Magubane et al., 'Turn to Armed Struggle,' pp. 138, 60; Govan Mbeki, *South Africa: The Peasants' Revolt*, Harmondsworth: Penguin, 1964; Drew, 'Mbeki's *The Peasants; Revolt*,' p. 68.

11 Drew, 'Visions,' p. 34; Lodge, *Red Road*, pp. 315, 326; SACP, 'A Landmark in South Africa's History: The Sixth National Conference of the South African Communist Party,' International Bulletin, no. 4, December 1962, in Allison Drew, ed., *South Africa's Radical Tradition: A Documentary History, vol. 2, 1943–1964*, Cape Town: Buchu, Mayibuye and UCT, 1997, pp. 358–64; Howard Barrell, *MK: The ANC's Armed Struggle. London: Penguin*, 1990, p. 11.

... This two-pronged strategy formed the basis of the successful Algerian Revolution.'[12] So despite *Liberation*'s speculations, the SACP's position showed much thought and a desire to coordinate different methods of struggle.

Members of the NLF knew of the SACP's ongoing debates about armed struggle, and they interpreted them through the prism of Soviet policy. There were 'unofficial groups with a guerrilla warfare orientation,' *Liberation* acknowledged, but they were 'apparently frowned upon by the executive.' The SACP was following the Soviet peaceful coexistence strategy, it stressed, and notwithstanding the Freedom Charter's calls for nationalization, the NLF believed its demands were 'bourgeois democratic.' The SACP had superseded the ANC, *Liberation* claimed, which aside from occasional speeches by Chief Luthuli, 'has virtually been burned out of existence as a force in the politics of the country.'[13]

Liberation's April issue discussed Umkhonto, whose leadership, it noted, came from the SACP – a view upheld by later scholarship.[14] Umkhonto leaders in the western Cape were reportedly more concerned with developing political cadre than was the case in Johannesburg, where the leadership stressed military training. Perhaps the NLF was aware of this. Still, it thought that Umkhonto aimed to be 'a pressure group with effective striking power and ... a large underground army.' It had begun military and practical training internally and abroad and had developed a course for which students were screened and had to pass a fitness exam.[15] This presumably referred to the December 1962 training camp run by Denis Goldberg and Looksmart Ngudle near Mamre, about thirty miles north of Cape Town. Many attendees were from Nyanga Township, but some, including Basil February's friend James April, were in the South African Coloured People's Congress. The training included calisthenics, judo, squad drill and lectures on first aid, the field telephone, the duplicator for disseminating news, the petrol engine for repairing transport, security, and weapons and explosives training. The communist lawyer Albie Sachs lectured on political economy; Elias Motsoaledi, Wolfie Kodesh, and Second World War veterans Jack Hodgson, Harold Strachan and Ben Turok were involved. At night they discussed news and listened to recordings of freedom fighters

[12] SACP, 'Landmark,' p. 361; 'The Peasants' Struggle,' *Assegai* [*sic*], 2 March 1963, in Drew, ed., *South Africa's Radical Tradition*, vol. 2, pp. 369–72, 371–2; Drew, 'Visions,' p. 34.

[13] *Liberation*, February 1963, pp. 8–9.

[14] Lodge, *Red Road*, p. 324; *cf.* Landau, 'M-Plan,' p. 1090.

[15] *Liberation*, April 1963, pp. 5–6, thought it was a three-month course; 'James April,' in SADET, ed., *The Road to Democracy: South Africans Telling their Stories*, vol. 1, Houghton: Mutloatse Arts Heritage Trust; Hollywood, CA: Tsehai, January 2008, pp. 47–59, 54, says it was a ten-day course interrupted after several days. Drew, 'Visions,' p. 38.

from around the world. However, the police discovered the camp soon after it began and interrogated a participant who had been recruited at a Coloured People's Congress meeting in mid-1962.[16]

Despite their common interest in the Algerian struggle, the NLF found 'no evidence' that Umkhonto interpreted guerrilla warfare as it did. Umkhonto worked with two main principles, *Liberation* stated: first, 'to publicise its existence and to give it prestige in the eyes of the oppressed'; secondly, to pressure the state for concessions. 'They are most likely planning for foreign UN intervention' and would presumably support a liberal capitalist regime against workers and peasants, 'unlike the NLF, which is fighting for a socialist democracy.' Nonetheless, NLF sources felt that some SACP and Umkhonto members might be receptive to its propaganda.[17] While the ANC's Lobatse conference on 27–28 October 1962 had affirmed sabotage as its main form of struggle, a few months later Umkhonto announced: 'we see this [sabotage] activity as only the beginning of a movement which will grow in size and scope.'[18]

Basil February must have been a key source. He knew the NLF well. He and Marcus Solomon had been friends since school, when they both boarded at Zonnebloem Hostel. February had matriculated at Trafalgar High in 1960 with five distinctions and was in Trafalgar High teacher Hassan Bavasah's Marxist study group. February applied to study law at UCT, but the Deputy Minister of Education, Arts and Science refused his application, so he registered for medicine instead. By then boarding with the van der Heydens, he became Leslie's brother-in-law following his sister Ursula's marriage. Fed up with the Unity Movement's abstentionist politics, February joined the Coloured People's Congress in 1963. February and Neville Alexander argued vehemently about politics; on at least one occasion when they were in a car together, their discussion became so heated that February insisted on getting out. Ursula Wolhuter described a similar encounter between February and Alie Fataar, with February demanding that Fataar stop the car.[19]

[16] *Cape Times*, 1 November, 18 December 1963; Lodge, *Red Road*, pp. 324–5; Joffe, *State vs. Mandela*, pp. 111–18; Janet Smith and Beauregard Tromp, *Hani: A Life Too Short*, Johannesburg and Cape Town: Jonathan Ball, 2009, pp. 43–4. Looksmart Ngudle went underground but was arrested in August 1963 and died in prison the next month.

[17] *Liberation*, April 1963, pp. 5–6.

[18] Simpson, 'Mandela's Army,' p. 1104; Stevens, 'Violence,' pp. 1020–3.

[19] *State vs Alexander*, p. 1020; Interview, van der Heyden; Drew and Ntsebeza, interview, Solomon; interview, Fataar; discussion with Norman Bromberger, Stellenbosch, June 2018; Nicole van Driel, 'The Journey to Wankie: A biography of James April,' BA Hons, University of the Western Cape, 1990, p. 23. Teacher Hassan Bavasah was noted for his insights into Marxism.

Around this time Umkhonto was discussing Operation Mayibuye [Let Africa Return], a plan to facilitate the transition from sabotage to guerrilla struggle. Drafted between late March and early July 1963 by Mbeki and Joe Slovo, it reflected their understanding of the Algerian and Cuban revolutions, as well as the Mpondo uprising. The two communists had complementary views: Mbeki emphasized the rural population's peasant aspirations. Slovo believed most rural dwellers were peasant-workers, but he acknowledged land hunger and felt it necessary to appeal to rural people based on their aspirations.[20]

Criticized by key SACP leaders as overly ambitious given the balance of forces at the time, Operation Mayibuye was evidently never adopted by either the SACP or Umkhonto.[21] However, it shows how some of their leaders were thinking. The plan began with a reference to Potlako Leballo's 24 March 1963 announcement of a nationwide Pan Africanist Congress (PAC) insurrection; not to be outdone, in April the ANC endorsed sabotage as the first stage of armed struggle. Although the state smashed the PAC, Operation Mayibuye conceded that Leballo's announcement had struck an emotional chord and that the people showed the preconditions for a 'revolutionary situation': disillusionment with legal methods, belief that change needed force and readiness to follow a lead. It called for guerrillas to spark the uprising and arm the people. With international support – including military intervention in South West Africa – the liberation movement could establish an external political authority on friendly soil. Foreign-trained guerrillas could then infiltrate the country to 'attack … pre-selected targets with a view to taking the enemy by surprise, creating the maximum impact on the populace, creating as much chaos and confusion for the enemy as possible.' Rural areas would be the initial focus of guerrilla activities, but would be complemented by urban sabotage. The regime's isolation might 'result in such massive assistance … that the state structure will collapse far sooner than we can at the moment envisage.' Clearly, the SACP and indeed all the other early 1960s underground groups underestimated state capacity.[22]

20 Z. Sanders [Zena Susser], 'Aspects of the Rural Problem in South Africa,' lecture delivered to the Johannesburg Discussion Club on 1 December 1952, *Viewpoints and Perspectives*, 1, 1, 21 February 1953, in Drew, ed., *South Africa's Radical Tradition*, vol. 2, pp. 316–21, 321; Clingman, *Bram Fischer*, p. 313.

21 Drew, 'Visions,' p. 34; Stevens, 'Violence,' pp. 1023–5; Lodge, *Red Road*, p. 329; cf. Joe Slovo, *Slovo: The Unfinished Autobiography*, Randburg: Ravan; London: Hodder & Stoughton, 1995, p. 146.

22 'Operation Mayibuye,' Document found by the police at Rivonia, 11 July 1963, in Thomas Karis and Gail Gerhart, eds, *From Protest to Challenge*, vol. 3, 1977, pp. 760–68, 762–5; Barrell *MK*, pp. 13–17; Mandela, *Long Walk*, pp. 336, 343–4; Slovo, *Slovo*, p. 146; Allison Drew, 'Govan Mbeki's *The Peasants' Revolt*: A Critical Examination,' in Thembela Kepe and Lungisile Ntsebeza, eds, *Rural Resistance in*

Both Operation Mayibuye and Alexander's *Conquest of Power in South Africa* stressed the predominantly rural nature of guerrilla struggle, but nonetheless there were notable differences. For the NLF, guerrilla struggle encompassed political education, while Operation Mayibuye saw it as a 'spark,' prioritizing military action over political education. Moreover, while the NLF stressed Namibian agency and potential for guerrilla warfare, Operation Mayibuye's stress on UN military intervention in South West Africa might imply Namibian passivity.[23] Although not official policy, Operation Mayibuye was evidently influential and pushed Umkhonto further in a militaristic direction. Simon Stevens suggests that it 'formalized the lack of interest in organizing mass non-violent action that had characterised the practice of the high command since MK's formation.'[24] Despite Umkhonto's increasingly militaristic approach and the NLF's stress on political education, these differences should not have precluded discussions between the organizations, assuming political will.

Liberation also covered the PAC and Poqo. Apart from Basil February, NLF members had scant contact with the Congress Alliance. But they knew PAC and Poqo members through their earlier Society of Young Africa (SOYA) work in Langa and Nyanga, where both Neville Alexander and Fikile Bam had organized. The PAC lacked a clear policy and was rent by tensions about either a quick insurrection or a long guerrilla struggle, *Liberation* maintained. There were differences over UN intervention and divisions between the regions, national committee and overseas representatives. Racialism was 'very much to the fore,' notwithstanding the enrolment of Coloureds and Indians and the 'ideological twists and turns by the P.A.C. intellectuals.'[25]

Poqo, by contrast, was a terrorist organization that nonetheless had an emotional impact on the liberation movement, *Liberation* continued. Poqos – as its members were known – used homemade weapons to kill chiefs and headmen and force people to join. But forced recruitment was 'very unhealthy.' Those compelled to join Poqo would never fully understand its aims and policy, and it could not count on their loyalty, as shown by the many members who gave evidence against it in trials around the country. 'The first requirement of any revolutionary and guerrilla is that he be sure of the necessity of the armed insurrection, and his joining the organisation must be voluntary,' it stressed.[26] Moreover, Leballo's announcement of a national uprising was irresponsible. If such intended plans could not be carried out,

---

South Africa: The Mpondo Revolts after 50 years, Leiden: Brill; Cape Town: UCT Press, 2012, pp. 67–89, 84–5.

23 Drew, 'Visions,' p. 37; Lodge, *Red Road*, p. 328.

24 Stevens, 'Violence,' p. 1025.

25 *Liberation*, February 1963, pp. 10–11.

26 *Liberation*, April 1963, p. 12.

local groups might 'take matters into their own hands.' Armed insurrection 'is an art which must go hand in hand with political policy and strategy,' it emphasized. Each cell must understand its function within the organization, but the enemy should never be told. Since the November 1962 Paarl uprising, 'there is close to chaos in Poqo,' not least due to indiscipline and police success in infiltrating and bribing members: 'The local riots, terrorism and killing of whites are but a waste of valuable energy in that they are not directed against the very pillars of the fascist state – the police force, defence force, navy and air force,' it cautioned. 'If we are ever to gain freedom, these pillars will have to be fought and smashed.'[27] The people are ready for the NLF, it wrote with the arrogance of youth, 'the best organization to take over from the PAC/Poqo and to succeed where the latter had failed.'[28]

But how accurate were *Liberation*'s claims about Poqo and how could the NLF have taken over from PAC and Poqo without roots in their migrant labour communities and fluency in their language, isiXhosa? As noted in Chapter 2, NLF members had already discussed the Paarl uprising. At the time, aside from newspaper articles, the South African Institute of Race Relations (SAIRR) and the Snyman Commission provided the main written sources. The Snyman Commission noted Paarl's municipal corruption but argued that rural people resorted to terrorism due to the burdens of modernization. The SAIRR report, however, contended that the cruel migrant labour system and living conditions led people to join Poqo voluntarily. Tom Lodge maintains that the Snyman Commission ignored the SAIRR's conclusion, instead finding that people were coerced into joining. State witnesses also stressed coercion. Bianca Paigè van Laun points to Poqo's heterogeneity, which may explain its members' diverse motivations in supporting Poqo. In stressing Poqo's use of coercion, the NLF presumably relied heavily on the Snyman Commission report. The belief that a tiny, largely Coloured and English- and Afrikaans-speaking group could lead Poqo reflects both arrogance and extraordinary naivety.[29]

Of the Unity Movement affiliates, *Liberation* disparaged the Anti-CAD's methods as unchanged since its 1943 formation and the AAC's affiliates as virtually indistinguishable. SOYA and APDUSA's student wing were the most important due to their intellectual training. But the Unity Movement leadership remained obstinate and beset by internal squabbles, so no work was being done.[30] A piece on the Unity Movement's 'New Line' argued that the NLF's propaganda among Apdusans was succeeding. In September 1962 Jane Gool had complained to Tabata that Alexander and his supporters aimed to 'wreck'

27 *Liberation*, April 1963, pp. 12–13, 9.

28 *Liberation*, May 1963, p. 5.

29 Lodge, 'Paarl Insurrection,' pp. 3, 8, 11–12, 15; van Laun, 'In the Shadows,' pp. 65–68, 146–51.

30 *Liberation*, February 1963, pp. 12–14.

APDUSA.[31] Late that year Tabata secretly left the country to seek external support. The Algerian government promised to help train Unity Movement soldiers. As a result, in January 1963 – a year after the Abrahams and Alexander suspensions – an extended executive meeting accepted 'armed insurrection as the only method of struggle against the Herrenvolk State' and stipulated that APDUSA would organize a people's army.[32] But APDUSA's new members were soon disillusioned by the leadership's failure to announce a plan of action. Speculating that the new policy was simply a gesture to prolong the Unity Movement's life, the article concluded that the NLF should recruit from outside APDUSA. Still, almost all NLF recruits came from the Unity Movement, and although its original members were 'under a cloud,' they had 'succeeded in drawing many members from the NEUM [Non-European Unity Movement] into the cells,' noting that 'we now have the majority in the local NEUM.'[33]

Liberation published several articles on the political situation in South West Africa and, not surprisingly, was most enthusiastic about the South West Africa People's Organisation (SWAPO), which had seen very rapid growth, with the Cape Town branch 'the most influential.' As a new organization, it was less bureaucratized than the Congress Alliance or Unity Movement, although its leadership was 'completely divorced from the membership,' but the NLF still found it receptive to its ideas.[34] *Liberation* also covered other themes. An article entitled 'The "law-less" and the law' boldly declared: 'we have dedicated ourselves to the task of destroying the state machinery by armed insurrection … we have divested ourselves of any protection under the law.' Noting the seventeenth-century English expression 'the law is an ass,' the article proceeded to outline some of the country's remaining rights.[35] The next issue appeared after the Ninety Day Act became law on 2 May 1963. It published an English translation of French philosopher Jean-Paul Sartre's introduction to Algerian communist Henri Alleg's book, *La Question*, in which Alleg recounted his experience of torture by French paratroopers during Algeria's liberation war. While not agreeing with all Alleg's political views, it stated, 'we believe that the feelings of those who have suffered for liberty are by and large the same.' This was followed by an article entitled 'Torture in South Africa,' especially its de facto legalization under the Ninety Day Act. Although torture had 'long been known to have been used on prisoners' – the article provided several graphic examples – it had to be done away from the courts and the public eye. Now, however, individuals 'can be detained

31 Rassool, 'Individual,' pp. 468–9; Levinson, *Five Years*, p. 149.

32 Kayser and Adhikari, 'Land,' pp. 324–5; *Liberation*, February 1963, p. 13.

33 *Liberation*, February 1963, pp. 6, 10.

34 *Liberation*, February 1963, pp. 5, 14; *Liberation*, April, May 1963.

35 *Liberation*, April 1963, p. 11.

for ninety day periods for questioning, without ever appearing in court. This will, in fact, mean indefinite periods of torture.' The piece argued, perhaps naively, that a state uses torture 'when it is with its back to the wall, when it is struggling for its very existence.'[36] The apartheid regime undoubtedly felt threatened by the sabotage attacks around the country, but it was definitely not struggling for its existence.

Building a network

Organizing the NLF in the Cape went relatively smoothly, especially in the Cape Peninsula, where most of its members lived and which they knew well. By April–May 1963 the NLF had tiny groups or cells in Athlone, Bellville South, Cape Town Central, Elsie's River, Lansdowne, Maitland, Queenstown, Wellington and possibly Kimberley. As one example, the Bellville South Cape Peninsula Students Union (CPSU) branch, whose members were also in APDUSA, had been politicized by the CPSU's Frank van der Horst, a frequent speaker. The branch became an NLF cell with library science student Frank Musson, from Kimberley, August Matsemela, Ambrose George and Desmond Moodley, all from Port Elizabeth. They were joined by Gerald Giose and Gordon Hendricks from the Elsie's River branch. Giose had recruited Hendricks; they were both active in the Elsies River Parent-Teachers' Association, which was fighting the transfer of Coloured children's education to the Coloured Affairs Department. The group met at Musson's lodging in Bellville South and discussed local issues with the goal of revolution. Musson became the Bellville South and Elsie's River representative on the regional committee.[37]

For the north-west Cape, the NLF employed a paid organizer, Don Davis. Born in 1920, Davis was older than the other members and had grown up in the diamond mining centre of Kimberley, attending St Francis Xavier's Mission School and Perseverance Training School. But he dropped out in 1937 after his father's death and became an apprenticed plumber. In 1940 he joined the Cape Corps, which attracted Coloured and Indian men in Kimberley, and served in the Second World War Africa campaigns until his 1944 discharge. After studying at the Transvaal Bible Institute, he began preaching interdenominationally in Pentecostal churches, also working as a truck driver and lab assistant. He met Kenneth Abrahams in August 1962 through their mutual friend Giose, and like Giose and Hendricks, was in the Parent-Teachers' Association.

Don Davis' evangelical work took him often to the rural and semi-rural areas of the north-west Cape and along the west coast. In Kimberley, forced

36 *Liberation*, May 1963, pp. 7, 12.

37 Interview, Frank Musson, Cape Town, 10 August 2022; Marcus Solomon to author, 10 July 2024.

removals had preceded the launch of apartheid and the Group Areas Act. Its diverse multicultural Malay Camp, which dated from the 1870s, was razed in the 1940s – so harshly that even mosques, temples and churches were removed. Most of the inhabitants were relocated to Florianville Township, called Floors because it was built on the original mine floor area. Davis' aunt and niece lived in Floors, and his brother lived north-west of Kimberley in the alluvial diamond mining site of Gong-Gong, named after the sound of rocks clanging in the Vaal River.[38]

Davis was a 'very unorthodox and eccentric sort of preacher,' remembered Neville Alexander, and the NLF thought he would be able to identify people amenable to their ideas – figuring out 'who was who and what was what in the countryside.' Armed with the YCCC and NLF's mimeographed literature, Davis set out to make contacts in the north-west.[39] But he lacked experience, and on 5 May the interim national executive decided to forego paid organizers. Agreeing that organizers living in the area would be more effective, they planned to set up a school for volunteers using NLF officials and at least one representative from each cell. They did not know that Davis would inadvertently recruit a police informer.[40]

The NLF had friendly relations with Cape Town's Fourth Internationalists, especially Kenneth Jordaan and Enver Marney. 'They have assisted us in some practical ways, but we have not yet ascertained in how far it is possible to work with them on a political level,' noted *Liberation*.[41] For communication between Cape Town and Johannesburg, the NLF relied on Edmond Trosée. Born in Leiden, Netherlands in December 1930, Trosée and his family had immigrated to South Africa soon after the Second World War, and he spoke English with a strong Dutch accent. Trosée attended Grey College in Bloemfontein, then enrolled at the University of the Witwatersrand (Wits) in 1949 and 1950. He dropped out and moved to Cape Town, staying with his mother and niece in Hopeville Mansions. Profoundly affected by the treatment of European Jews during the war, Trosée contacted South African leftists, especially the Fourth Internationalists, but other groups as well. A white person with freedom of movement, Trosée worked with Neville Alexander, as well as Marcus Solomon, who met him on the Cape Town Parade to

38 Allen, Vida and Tanja Kruger, *Malay Camp: A Forgotten Suburb*, Departments of Sport, Arts & Culture and Tourism, Environment & Conservation, Kimberley: McGregor Museum, 2006, esp. pp. 12–14, 54–6, 64; *State vs Alexander*, pp. 1499–1500, 1510.

39 Matsemela, interview, Alexander, A.2.3, pp. 62–63; Matsemela, interview with Bam.

40 *Liberation*, May 1963, p. 13.

41 *Liberation*, February 1963, p. 5.

exchange information and teased him that his name sounded like Trotsky.[42] In Johannesburg, Baruch Hirson remembered that shortly after the Sharpeville-Langa massacres Trosée criticized him and his comrades for not issuing statements supporting Kgosana's march to Cape Town and the ensuing strike.[43]

People assumed that Trosée's skin colour would protect him from police suspicion, but that was not so. He had evidently been working as an actuary for a large firm, but the Special Branch began following him, and he lost his job. 'A more security conscious person we could not imagine,' recalled Roseinnes Phahle:

> He would arrange with me where to meet him – usually on the grounds of Wits, a multi-racial campus where a meeting between blacks and whites did not raise suspicions. But on seeing us at a distance walking towards him, he would start walking ahead of us in the opposite direction. He would turn this corner and that corner, always looking behind and around him, until he found a point he thought was safe for meeting and talking.[44]

The NLF also had comrades in West Germany. Franz Lee had received a bursary or scholarship to study at the University of Tübingen and left for West Germany in October 1962, where he joined socialist students in the SDS (Socialist German Students' Union). By then Irmgard Bolle was in the SDS Office for International Affairs with responsibility for Africa. Bolle and Lee set up the NLF's tiny German cell, which sent literature to Cape Town. There was also a plan for NLF representatives to tour Europe and Africa.[45]

To expand underground, especially outside the western Cape, the NLF needed to approach people without raising suspicion and make preliminary assessments of their political views – expanding semi-political space above ground. They formed the Rover Soccer and Excelsior Table Tennis Clubs to fundraise and, drawing on their experience on the CPSU's bursary fund and APDUSA's finance committee, in April 1963 they set up the South African

42 Discussions with Eefka Trosée Young, Lorette Trosée Espi, Cape Town, August 2022.

43 Matsemela, interview, Alexander, A.2.4, p. 80; Hirson, *Revolutions*, pp. 279, 301; Roseinnes Phahle, 'Reminiscences of the Arrest of Fikile Bam & Marcus Solomon in 1963,' August 2019, *South African History Online*, https://www.sahistory.org.za/archive/reminiscences-arrest-fikile-bam-marcus-solomon-1963-roseinnes-phahle-august-2019, accessed 15 November 2022.

44 Phahle, 'Reminiscences.'

45 Matsemela, interview with Alexander, A.2.3, pp. 62–3; A.2.4, pp. 77–8; Klimke, *Other Alliance*, pp. 31, 255, n. 77; Svenja Kunze, Hamburger Institut für Sozialforschung, to author, 3 February 2020; Hergen Junge to author, 6 May 2024; *Liberation*, February 1963, p. 7.

Students Bursary & Loan Fund (SASBLF) to cover travel costs for overseas study. Solomon drafted the bursary fund's constitution, which was modified and approved at the first meeting. The fund was established with 'a view to raising the low standard of living among the majority of the population,' the constitution stated. 'While it shall not be run on a sectional/racial basis it shall … assist such students as would not otherwise be able to finance their studies … The administrators … shall remain loyal to the non-partisan traditions of true educational enlightenment.'[46] Reginald Francke was the chair, Landers, the treasurer, and September, the secretary, who circulated funding appeals, organized events, collected monies, paid the expenses, checked the post office box, and signed the paperwork. Alexander was arranging bursaries for South Africans to study at West German universities, and the fund was to pay for their airfare.[47] While their bursary fund provided a means to meet people and assess their political views, it was very much a legal educational organization.

In addition to South West Africa, the NLF felt that rural Transkei would be an important base. Bam was the NLF's link to the region. He made two trips to the Transkei and after his exams spent two months in Tsolo, Umtata, Matatiele and other villages interviewing civil servants, administrators, journalists, businessmen, protest leaders and headmen. He was writing a prize essay for UCT that assessed urban and rural African politics in Langa and Nyanga in Cape Town, Alexandra in Johannesburg and the Transkei. 'I had an hypothesis on what was happening in the Transkei,' Bam explained, 'and what I was really doing was to test out and confirm some of my own opinions.' But he was also keeping his eyes open on behalf of the NLF. In December he travelled to Durban with attorney Andrew Lukele and then on to Polela, where his mother was staying, some forty miles from Pietermaritzburg. Group Area operations were ongoing. Further north in Natal, in late February 1963, about 2,000 Africans were evicted from their homes in Besterspruit Township, Vryheid, where they had freehold rights, and moved to two tent camps, one of which was 28 miles from Vryheid, where they worked. Journalists were not allowed on site, so they flew above with cameras showing row after row of tents on barren, shadeless ground, 'reminiscent of concentration camps set up during the South African (Boer) War,' wrote the *Johannesburg Star*.[48]

46 *State vs Alexander*, pp. 1577–9, 1556; Interview, Marcus Solomon, Kenilworth, Cape Town, 21 June 2018. These clubs, societies and bursary funds were not uncommon; Richard Rive, *Emergency*, Cape Town and Johannesburg: David Philip, 1988 [1964], p. 26, mentions two in a discussion of left-wing organizations.

47 Interview, Solomon, 21 June 2018; *State vs Alexander*, pp. 1580–1, 1766; Alexander evidently received confirmation from Tübingen for the funding of thirty bursaries at West German universities on 11 July 1963.

48 *State vs Alexander*, pp. 1468–70, 1491–95; 'South Africa: Air view of tent towns for Africans evicted from township,' https://www.britishpathe.com/asset/247668, 28 February 1963, accessed 13 September 2024.

Bam returned to Cape Town in early March 1963 in time for classes. That same month Kenneth Abrahams asked him to give a lecture on the Transkei for interested individuals in Cape Town. But due to the doctor's work they arrived too late, so the talk was postponed. However, an article in *Liberation*'s April issue found little evidence of underground military groups in the Transkei. Neither Poqo nor Umkhonto had established a 'solid "network".' The press had exaggerated the PAC's presence while there seemed to be no knowledge of Umkhonto outside Alice, home of Fort Hare College, in the Ciskei. Through Bam, the NLF evidently had a few contacts in the Transkei. But, the article argued, because it was to be their 'primary field of operation … the work done thus far must be regarded as grossly inadequate.' The severe repression and lack of development meant the region would be dependent on urban cells until a wide and effective network could be established, *Liberation* concluded.[49]

On 18 June, Bam convened a meeting at Bosch Villa in Bishop Lavis Township. Organizing in Langa and Nyanga, he formed his own study group of young people from the CPSU, Congress Youth League, ANC, and PAC. In keeping with the NLF's united front aspirations, he invited members of his study group and of the NLF to the meeting, which was attended mainly by students and teachers planning to travel during the school break.[50] The meeting agreed that people would visit their political contacts, assess the local situations and set up cells where relevant. Four of Bam's students were travelling, and he asked them to find out about the politics in the areas where they were going. Elizabeth van der Heyden, the only woman present, was to go to South West Africa; she had a sister in Swakopmund, where Shipanga resided, and a school friend in Rehoboth, where the Abrahams family had settled. Landers was to go to Upington; Solomon to George, Cradock and Graaff-Reneit; Alexander to Kimberley and Johannesburg; and Bam to Johannesburg via Natal. They were to introduce their bursary fund to new acquaintances and advise their contacts to appoint local people to its committee. To people who seemed interested in politics, they would discuss the NLF, explain its aims and meetings, and ensure the supply of literature, upon payment. Once back from their travels, according to Bam, they planned to hold a conference in Cape Town to assess the state of their network; this would presumably be a preliminary step towards their hoped-for tour of Europe and Africa, which never materialized.[51]

Around 26 June, Kenneth Jordaan drove Alexander, Francke, van der Heyden, and Solomon to Wellington to supply Dorothy Adams with literature. From Wellington they drove north-west to De Aar in the sheep-farming semi-desert Karoo – literally thirsty land. It was a long drive, some 446 miles. De

49 *State vs Alexander*, pp. 1337–42, 1468–70, 1491–5; *Liberation*, April 1963, pp. 6–7.

50 *State vs Alexander*, pp. 1342–5, 1417–25.

51 *State vs Alexander*, pp. 365–8, 1344–8, 1532; Matsemela, interview with Bam.

Aar was an important rail junction, and they dropped Solomon and van der Heyden at the railway station. Solomon left for the Midlands, and van der Heyden for South West Africa, where she met the Abrahamses but learned that Shipanga was travelling.[52]

Leaving De Aar, Jordaan, Alexander and Francke continued north some 220 miles to Gong-Gong, where Don Davis' brother lived, then thirty miles south to Kimberley, where Francke remained. The next day Jordaan and Alexander drove north-west 290 miles to Johannesburg with their remaining documents.[53] They liked to laugh, but they also must have had intense discussions. Jordaan was not an NLF member – he did not think guerrilla struggle was relevant to relatively proletarianized and urbanized South Africa, and he and Alexander often debated this. Indeed, in 1951 Jordaan had written 'of the forces which are driving more and more Africans irresistibly forward into the capitalist economy as proletarians. The great task of the liberatory movement is to facilitate this development' – by making Africans full and equal citizens. Just five years before that article, on 12 August 1946, the great African mineworkers strike had erupted on the Witwatersrand. It was the biggest strike of black mineworkers since that of February 1920. Jordaan believed in the power of organized labour. But Alexander remained mesmerized by the Cuban and Algerian experiences, seeing rural proletarians and semi-proletarians – but not peasants – as the main base of South Africa's future guerrilla struggle.[54]

Reaching Johannesburg, they stayed in Alexandra Township with Martin and Deborah Mabiletsa. When Bam arrived, he went to his family in Soweto. Alexander and Bam 'had contacts in Johannesburg,' recalled Phahle, who lived next door to the Mabiletsas. 'For the five days they were in Johannesburg, they spent each day and each evening pursuing their contacts and holding meetings with them.'[55] They met Phahle's friend Arthur Magerman, who was close to Dan Mokonyane and, like him and the Mabiletsas, had been in the Movement for a Democracy of Content. Martin Mabiletsa took them to the home of one Douglas Smith, where they met with some National Union of South African Students (NUSAS) delegates. In June 1961, CPSU and the Durban Students Union had rejected an invitation to the July Congress of NUSAS, which they called 'liberal' and 'paternalistic.' But the government

52 *State vs Alexander*, pp. 1746–7; interview with van der Heyden; Allison Drew, 'Marcus Solomon,' May 2019, *South African History Online*, https://www.sahistory.org.za/people/marcus-solomon.

53 *State vs Alexander*, pp. 369–72, 1502, 1747, 1750.

54 K. A. Jordaan, 'A Critique of Mr. W. P. van Schoor's "The Origin and Development of Segregation in South Africa,"' *Discussion*, 1, 3, June 1951, in Drew, ed., *South Africa's Radical Tradition*, vol. 2, pp. 249–62, 261; Drew, *Discordant Comrades*, pp. 49, 256; interview, Alexander, c. April 1988, Basel Africa Library, TPA153_8_A.

55 *State vs Alexander*, pp. 1750–51; Phahle, 'Reminiscences.'

clampdown was radicalizing NUSAS; Minister of Justice and Police John Vorster called it a 'cancer' to 'be cut out.' This radicalization was presumably not lost on Alexander. After these meetings they returned to Cape Town leaving their documents with Phahle.[56]

The arrests begin

The NLF's efforts to build a network quickly collapsed. On Monday 8 July 1963 Don Davis was detained at Vredendal in the Oliphants River Valley, some 188 miles north of Cape Town. It was the first NLF arrest. Undercover Police Constable Jacobus Kotzee accompanied him to his residence to obtain some political pamphlets. Forty minutes after Kotzee left, police surrounded the house and picked up Davis. The next day Lieutenant S. I. Sauerman and his team came up from Cape Town. Davis had been preaching at Vredendal and Doornbaai [now Doringbaai], a small coastal fishing village 36 miles away. The police drove him to Doornbaai and searched his residence. They seized several letters, one stating that 'the family' was pleased to get his letter. They also found two diaries, one mentioning a 'bedding boy' taking 'fresh fish' from Cape Town to Johannesburg by train. Sauerman told Davis that he would not be charged if he gave evidence. Davis evidently replied: 'if it was a choice between giving evidence and being shot I would choose the bullet.' They took him to Cape Town, where he was charged with belonging to an illegal organization. That charge was later dropped, and on 17 July he was put in ninety-day detention.[57]

When news of the arrest reached Cape Town, Gerald Giose told Neville Alexander the police thought Don Davis was in the Communist Party.[58] When they met on Friday the 12th, were they discussing the arrest, and had they heard yet about the raid at Lilliesleaf Farm in Rivonia, Johannesburg just the day before? They did not seem worried. When Lieutenant Sauerman and his team arrived at the Alexander home at 8 Swiss Road, Lansdowne in the Cape Flats, Neville Alexander answered the door. At the Lieutenant's order Alexander took him to the living room where Leslie van der Heyden, Francke

56 *State vs Alexander*, p. 1751; *An Open Reply to NUSAS' Invitation to the Cape Peninsula Students Union and Durban Students Union*, 29 June 1961, author's possession; NUSAS, *57 Years of NUSAS – Have we learned our lessons?* 1981, pp. 2–3, https://disa.ukzn.ac.za/sites/default/files/pdf_files/cnf19811100.026.022.000.pdf, accessed 18 August 2024. Alexander, interview of 14 March 1988 with author, cited in Drew, 'Visions,' p. 37, suggests 30 cells in various locations. This was no doubt an exaggeration.

57 *State vs Alexander*, pp. 1513–14.

58 *State vs Alexander*, pp. 1514, 2012; Matsemela, interview with Alexander, A2.3, p. 60; A2.4, cassette 5, side 2, pp. 13–14, 22.

and Giose were seated around a table. On the table were half a bottle of brandy, a bottle of wine and a book titled *The Red Army of China*, according to a press report. They had been drinking; the mood – up to that point – had been 'buoyant.' In fact, the police had just raided Dulcie September's home. They found nothing: she routinely dispatched her documents immediately and had cleverly slipped her few remaining papers under her robe. As soon as they left, she called Neville and warned him that 'Sabena' was coming – their code for the police – but Alexander and Francke laughed it off. September then sent her sister to Ursula Wolhuter's house asking her to warn Alexander. Wolhuter and Alie Fataar drove to Alexander's home, but again he laughed it off.[59]

Sauerman asked Alexander about the large number of books, pamphlets and documents on and in the sideboard. 'I don't know,' he replied. 'I am an avid scholar and get a lot of publications which I read. That is all I have to say about the publications,' Alexander responded to Sauerman's continued questions. Asked about yet another document, he stated: 'I do not know where I have seen it before … I don't know what the hell is in my possession. I am a doctor of philosophy and people send me a lot of stuff … I don't know the damn thing … I wouldn't know what the hell it is.' The police took the visitors home and Alexander to jail, seizing his books and documents – the start of a cloudy, rainy winter weekend.[60]

That Sunday Francke, September, Dorothy Alexander and Doris van der Heyden met at Leslie van der Heyden's place. They discussed the question of giving evidence in court and decided to see Advocates Dullah Omar and Ben Kies, both in the Unity Movement; Kies, Omar's former teacher, had trained as a lawyer after being expelled from teaching. Francke said it would be unwise to make further statements to the police: 'No one knows how he is going to react … in certain fixed circumstances.' He himself was later detained but released.[61] Solomon had not yet returned to Cape Town. After meeting people in Graaff-Reinet, Queenstown and East London, he circled back to visit his uncle in Pacaltsdorp, a Coloured township on the outskirts of George in the western Cape. It was there that he saw the headlines about the arrest of a prominent Cape Town academic and realized it concerned Alexander. But he had left political literature in Cape Town, so he returned to collect it and then took the train to Johannesburg.[62]

59 Interview with Fataar who thought Kenneth Jordaan was with Alexander; *World Outlook*, 2, 1, 3 January 1964, pp. 2–11.

60 *Cape Argus*, 8 November 1963; Matsemela, interview Alexander, A2.4, cassette 5, side 2, pp. 14–15, 17; Alexander thought they traced him and September through Don Davis.

61 *State vs Alexander*, pp. 423–4.

62 Drew, 'Marcus Solomon.'

The press went crazy. Cold War hysteria and white supremacy were mutually reinforcing. Black resistance was stereotyped as communist, whether Soviet or Chinese; fighting black resistance was equated with fighting communism. As the government distributed pamphlets warning Africans that the ANC was controlled by Soviet 'Reds,' the *Cape Argus* railed about a 'Chinese Poqo': 'Peking-oriented Yui Chiu [*sic*] Chan … the latest underground terrorist organization to be in South Africa.' The *Sunday Express* warned of '"Red China" Men in South Africa.' The *Star* proclaimed a 'New Terrorist Group Uncovered in Time – trained in Peking.' The *World*'s headline read simply: 'Trained in China.'[63]

On Thursday Elizabeth van der Heyden was called to her principal's office at Grassy Park High, where Major R. A. Coetzee and Warrant Officer Botha were waiting. When the principal asked van der Heyden if she wished to accompany the police, Coetzee replied: 'She has no choice.' They took her to Caledon Square Police Station, where her brother Leslie van der Heyden and Brian Landers were held. Leslie was released on 27 July but detained a second time on 10 September, both times under the Ninety-Day Act.[64] Gordon Hendricks had been asked to report from his job at Maister Publicity to Caledon Square at precisely three o'clock on 19 August. He did so and was promptly detained and held in solitary for fifty days, until 8 October.[65]

A spiral of arrests followed: activists, intellectuals, and those just plain unlucky, some detained and released, others detained and charged. In the aftermath of the Rivonia raid and other arrests, hundreds of Africans, some as young as 17 or 18 years, were detained without charge. ANC trade unionist Elijah Loza, who had been tasked with implementing the M-Plan in the western Cape, was rearrested for a second, then a third spell of ninety-day detention. Bam's friend Archie Mafeje had been carrying out Masters fieldwork in the Transkei while also conducting research for American political scientist Gwendolyn Carter. Mafeje was arrested on 16 August in Cape Town for having attended illegal meetings in Bizana and Flagstaff and was denied bail on the 24th. Coincidentally, his professor and co-author Monica Wilson was then testifying on African customs at a Poqo trial, and extracts from their book *Langa* were read in evidence. On 25 August, Mafeje was taken by train to stand trial in Flagstaff. He pled guilty to having held an illegal meeting at Sigcau High School the year before, in July 1962 – the school principal had not given permission for the meeting.[66]

63 *Sunday Express*, 14 July 1963; *Cape Argus*, 15 July 1963; *Star*, 15 July 1963; *World*, 15 July 1963.

64 *Cape Times*, 5 December 1963; *State vs Alexander*, pp. 658–62, 1021.

65 *State vs Alexander*, p. 1831.

66 *Cape Times*, 21, 24, 26 August, 23 September 1963; Landau, 'M-Plan,' p. 1077; Bongani Nyoka, 'Archie Mafeje: An intellectual biography,' DLitt et Phil, University

Bam, for his part, had fled Cape Town for Johannesburg, staying underground in Soweto. Later, thinking it was safe, he returned to Cape Town. On 6 August, just back at his lodgings at 70 Sheldon Road, coffee cup in hand, he spied the police out front and jumped through the back window – forgetting jacket and pass book – and hopped the train to Johannesburg. He headed for Soweto, living clandestinely, seeking a way out of the country. He contacted Phahle and began meeting Phahle and Magerman in Johannesburg for lunch every Friday. Trosée kept Phahle informed of Cape Town developments.

Phahle learned that another Cape Town comrade would be arriving at Park Station. This turned out to be Solomon, who contacted Bam, and through him, Phahle. He too was seeking to flee the country. Solomon stayed in Riverlea, a new Coloured township near mining dumps – where no one wanted to live – some six miles south-west of downtown Johannesburg. His host was a Public Utility Transport Corporation bus driver whose route took him between Soweto and central Johannesburg. Phahle, in the meantime, had moved from Alexandra to Phefeni, Soweto, where he rented a room from Martha Matlhaku, an activist in the ANC and Federation of South African Women, banned for her work with the Garment Workers' Union. Phahle asked for her help arranging an escape route for Bam and Solomon. She and her exiled husband were from Zeerust, bordering Bechuanaland. Her relatives had helped ANC members arriving by train to cross the border. But Bam was worried about taking the train.[67] Matlhaku's willingness to help irrespective of political affiliation was noteworthy. While the SACP's reliance on a non-communist MK organizer [Joe Modise] to organize cross-border escapes might have indicated its diminished networks, as historian Tom Lodge argued, it also suggested a lack of sectarianism, a moment of political fluidity that allowed anti-apartheid activists to help each other irrespective of their political affiliation.[68]

To test the route's safety Phahle's friend and comrade mathematician Ismail Mohamed went by train to Zeerust, crossed the border with his passport and returned. This information was relayed to Bam, who nonetheless insisted on going by car to Zeerust. Through social worker Ann-Marie Louw, who knew both Bam and Winnie Mandela, it was arranged that Winnie would arrange transport. However, Winnie told Bam that she wanted evidence of their political engagement – namely the YCCC and NLF documents. Bam approached Phahle, but he refused to give up the documents; he had been forewarned by Cape Town comrades that the documents were being used as

of South Africa, 2017, pp. 50–1.

67 Phahle, 'Reminiscences'; Gisèle Wulfsohn, 'Malibongwe: Let us Praise the Women,' https://www.apartheidmuseum.org/uploads/files/Malibongwe_-Let-us-praise-the-women.pdf, accessed 10 December 2024.

68 Drew, 'Visions,' pp. 22–3, 39; Lodge, *Red Road*, p. 333.

proof of involvement. After all, the NLF arrests were widely covered in the press, and Winnie knew Bam's family and had no need of evidence.[69]

On 30 August Bam went to Solomon's safe house in Riverlea and told him they were being driven up north. Winnie Mandela was outside in her black and silver Fiat, her friend Brian Somana at the wheel, her two daughters in back. They were stopped soon after on the Main Reef Road, and Bam and Solomon arrested, taken to Marshall Square Police Station in Johannesburg, then transferred to Caledon Square in Cape Town. Somana, it turned out, was a police informer. Had Phahle given up the documents, they would have been used as evidence against him. News of Winnie's involvement in the arrests travelled swiftly across Soweto, infuriating many ANC Women's League members.[70]

The police continued their efforts in Johannesburg. On 2 September Phahle left his home and saw Deborah Mabiletsa through her kitchen window. She held her hands up together as if in cuffs to signal that the police were inside. Phahle spotted a car with a Cape Town registration on the license plate. 'It was the Cape Town police,' he realized, 'no doubt the special branch interrogating Martin inside his home.' He proceeded on his way and escaped interrogation.[71]

Back in Cape Town Lionel Davis was arrested at his home in early September. He was held in solitary and interrogated at Caledon Square. On 3 October he was charged and sent to Roeland Street Prison.[72] Neville's sister Dorothy Alexander was arrested at September's home by Major Coetzee and Sergeant van Wyk on 4 September. She was taken to Caledon Square and held in solitary. She had already been interrogated there twice before, and she was again interrogated on 10–11 September. Denied her medicine, she suffered severe headaches and sleeplessness. She finally made a statement, expecting to be released so she could resume her meds. Instead, she was charged on 8 October.[73] September was charged the same day, having been arrested the day before. Doris van der Heyden was detained that same month. As the police escalated their activities, other authorities were planning to remove more and more Africans from the western Cape.[74]

At some point the Cape Town police detained Kenneth Jordaan, who told them he did not agree with guerrilla warfare. This substantiated their belief that the NLF was planning armed action. Jordaan was released and subpoenaed

69 Phahle, 'Reminiscences.'

70 Phahle, 'Reminiscences.'

71 Phahle, 'Reminiscences.'

72 Tina Smith, 'Remembering District Six: The Restorative Art of Lionel Davis,' in Mario Pissarra, ed., *Awakenings: The Art of Lionel Davis*, Cape Town: Africa South Art Initiative, UCT, 2017, pp. 41–54, 41; *State vs Alexander*, pp. 919, 1544–8.

73 *State vs Alexander*, pp. 1557–9; *Torch*, 11 September 1963.

74 *State vs Alexander*, pp. 1513–14, 1547, 1557, 1580, 1584–6, 1880; *Cape Argus*, 14 September 1963.

to be a state witness. In the meantime, on 4 August, February and his friends Neville Andrews and April had been charged with painting 'Free Detainees' and 'Resist for your Liberty' on walls and roads in Wynberg and Claremont. They appeared before the Wynberg magistrate. In his defence, February claimed 'considerable emotional strain' due to arrest of his landlady's daughter and son – his brother-in-law – and 'the disruption and distress that had been caused to their families.' The magistrate found them guilty of 'malicious damage to property.' They were given bail, but April spent several months in prison for attending the Mamre training camp. Once free, February, April, Jordaan and a man called 'Army' fled Cape Town with the help of Abbas Gadief. In Johannesburg they were assisted by Suliman Babla Salooje and Molvi Ismail Ahmed Cachalia of the Transvaal Indian Congress. They moved around for a few days then took a bus to Zeerust and crossed the border into Bechuanaland.[75]

With the Cape Town arrests underway, the police refocused on Rehoboth. They had already tried to arrest Kenneth Abrahams for being illegally in South West Africa, but he was able to stay while the case was appealed. Shortly before the court decision, the police arrived and surrounded the community but were compelled to back down. Fearing another attempted arrest, Kenneth Abrahams left clandestinely for Windhoek, where he was joined by Shipanga, Hermanus Beukes and Paul Smit, all SWAPO organizers planning to flee. They drove to the Aminuis Reserve, crossed the Kalahari Desert on foot and finally reached Ghanzi in Bechuanaland. The District Commissioner agreed to arrange transport to Francistown.[76]

A week later, they set off in the mail truck. Once out of town, the truck stopped in front of a *bakkie* blocking the road. The four men were forced into a lorry at gunpoint and driven back to South West Africa. Bail was denied on the grounds they would flee. Shipanga, Beukes and Smit appeared before Chief Magistrate J. N. Marais in Gobabis, charged with leaving and re-entering the territory without the required documents. Abrahams was charged under the Suppression of Communism Act and flown to Cape Town, where he was put in the Woodstock Police Station and held in solitary for three weeks. Ben Kies represented Abrahams in court, where Mr Justice Diemont stated that the kidnapping was a *habeas corpus* matter and had to be dealt with before

75 *Cape Argus*, 28 September, 26 October 1963; 'James April,' p. 55; van Driel, 'Journey to Wankie,' pp. 25–7. Phahle, 'Reminiscences,' thought they stayed in Kliptown, Soweto, but April mentions several other townships.

76 'Kenneth Abrahams,' in Leys and Brown, eds, *Histories*, pp. 146–8; *Cape Times*, 2 August 1963; Shipanga with Armstrong, *In Search*, pp. 55–67; Jack Halpern, *South Africa's Hostages: Basutoland, Bechanualand and Swaziland*, Harmondsworth: Penguin, 1965, pp. 37–49; Saunders, 'SWAPO,' p. 154; Beukes, *Long Road*, chap 7.

the sabotage charges, which were still under investigation. The anticipated NLF trial was postponed.[77]

This was not the first time the apartheid regime had kidnapped South African activists from a British protectorate. The ANC activist and Mpondo leader Anderson Ganyile had been kidnapped from Basutoland two years earlier. After legal action, the South African government apologized and returned him.[78] According to journalist Jack Halpern, the Ganyile case set three precedents: the right of anti-apartheid activists to seek asylum in British High Commission Territories; Britain's willingness to provide asylum; and the powerlessness of South African police authorities once asylum was granted. 'Another Ganyile?' asked the *Rand Daily Mail* about Abrahams.[79]

The apartheid regime was concerned about activists fleeing South Africa into Bechuanaland where they could go into exile and be sent for training overseas: communists Joe Slovo and Jack and Rica Hodgson had fled there, where the Hodgsons were organizing escapes. Abrahams' kidnapping was an affront to the British government, which would provide asylum to 'genuine political refugees,' reported the *Cape Times* on 28 August, 'as long as they refrain from political activity.' The protectorates were not to be used as pipelines allowing activists to flee and receive guerrilla training. The British authorities evidently decided that Abrahams and the three Namibians were genuine refugees. Abrahams was flown back to Gobabis and, together with the three Namibians, returned to Bechuanaland.[80]

In the meantime, Ottilie Abrahams fled to Francistown, staying at a house run by the South West African Refugees' Organization. Always the activist, she contacted South West African National Union's Fanuel Kozonguizi, practising law in London, and asked him to raise the kidnapping with British Parliamentarians.[81] On 31 August British Pathé News showed the couple's reunion: Ottilie, bespectacled like her husband, hair in curlers covered by a kerchief, was pouring hot drinks for her husband and two other men outside a one-storey whitewashed house in Gabarone. Soon thereafter the

77 'Kenneth Abrahams,' in Leys and Brown, eds, *Histories*, pp. 148–50; Shipanga with Armstrong, *In Search*, pp. 59–61; Beukes, *Long Road*, chap 7.

78 Halpern, *South Africa's Hostages*, pp. 3–18, 39, 46

79 Halpern, *South Africa's Hostages*, pp. 18, 46; Shipanga with Armstrong, *In Search*, pp. 64–5; 'Basutoland: Ganyile interviewed after release from South African Gaoll [*sic*] (1962),' https://www.britishpathe.com/asset/245374/, accessed 12 September 2024.

80 *Cape Times*, 27, 28 August 1963; Lodge, *Red Road*, p. 330; South African Refugees in Bechuanaland, https://www.britishpathe.com/asset/117967/, accessed 12 September 2024.

81 'Kenneth Abrahams,' in Leys and Brown, eds, *Histories*, p. 150; *Cape Times*, 5, 19, 21 August 1963.

Abrahamses and Shipanga went to Dar es Salaam, where most southern African liberation movements had bases.[82]

Conclusion

As colonialism was ending across much of Africa, apartheid was growing stronger, and anti-apartheid groups were collapsing under the pressure. The tiny NLF lacked any tangible connection to a popular movement with the brief exception of SWAPO and so was far more isolated than either Poqo, connected to the PAC, or Umkhonto, linked to the ANC and SACP – notwithstanding the state's repression of those groups. Yet despite its isolation, the NLF aspired to build a network of activists supporting guerrilla struggle and a united front with like-minded groups. Hypothetically, groups with similar aims should have been able to join forces. But alongside the NLF's scepticism of the SACP, the SACP itself had a thick culture shaped by its long-term relationship with the Soviet Union.[83] That culture penetrated Umkhonto through its communist leadership and financial reliance on the Soviets, precluding alliances with other socialist groups. While NLF activists initially found it easier to work in the newly formed SWAPO, those who went to South West Africa were forced into exile, and SWAPO became mired in its own internal power struggles and Cold War politics. The fate of the ephemeral South West African National Liberation Front illustrated that united fronts were not viable when national organizations were concerned with their own power.

Perhaps the reasons for the NLF's capture are to be found within the group. Former NLF member August Matsemela asked Fikile Bam what mistakes he thought the group had made that led to their arrests. Bam replied, first, that most were from middle-class backgrounds and lacked experience dealing with the police. Secondly, they were young and lacked the street smarts of the older ANC members. Moreover, they had not sufficiently prepared themselves psychologically for arrest. Finally, he concluded, they had not followed their own security rules, and trusted people too quickly – this became apparent at

82 *Cape Times*, 28 August 1963; 'Kenneth Abrahams,' in Leys and Brown, eds, *Histories*, p. 150; Johann Alexander Müller, *'The Inevitable Pipeline into Exile': Botswana's Role in the Namibian Liberation Struggle*, Basel: Basler Afrika Bibliographien, 2012, pp. 83–4; https://www.britishpathe.com/asset/242804/ and https://www.britishpathe.com/asset/117967/ <accessed 31 December 2023>.

83 For example, 'Strive for World Communist Unity,' statement by the Central Committee of the South African Communist Party, *The African Communist*, January–March 1964, in Brian Bunting, ed., *South African Communists Speak*, London: Inkululeko, 1981, pp. 335–41, 339.

their trial. Dulcie September was more succinct: 'All the rules we made, they [the members] ignored every one of them.'[84]

Yet those internal factors were not sufficient to explain why the state was able to shovel up all the underground groups. South Africa had evolved rapidly into a police state; people who needed money willingly spied for the police. Although the state was far stronger than any of these groups, they all underestimated its power and resolve and overestimated their own capabilities. Mandela's ultimately unsuccessful efforts to implement his M-Plan showed how difficult it was to shift from public to underground activity. No individual could prepare him or herself for long-term solitary confinement; no organization could quickly replace layers of imprisoned leaders. Joe Slovo contended that the SACP's influence was greatest between 1960 and 1963, when the ANC was banned and before the Rivonia trial and exile. After exile, he maintained, the ANC's external mission had virtually complete control of Umkhonto.[85] Ultimately, the SACP survived through Soviet support, while the NLF lacked similar support.

'As a result of the arrests, the NLF, which was barely a year in existence, practically ceased to exist,' Roseinnes Phahle remarked. 'In Johannesburg, it was nipped in the bud even before it could claim an existence.'[86] Yet this did not make this minute band of intellectuals any less of a threat in the eyes of the state as it prepared for trial. Their publications posed crucial questions about South Africa's racial capitalist system, its colonial relationship with South West Africa and the suitability of guerrilla struggle. Even thinking about those questions was a challenge to a minority regime whose power rested in part on social acquiescence.

84 Matsemela, interview with Bam; interview with Van der Heyden.
85 Slovo, *Slovo*, p. 145; Lodge, *Red Road*, pp. 21, 341.
86 Phahle, 'Reminiscences.'

Chapter 5

The Trial

On 27 September 1963 several detectives and a policeman steered 26-year-old Neville Alexander into the Cape Town Magistrate's Court. Wearing a dark brown jacket and fawn trousers, he carried a small suitcase and a paper-wrapped parcel, ready and hoping to go home. Arms crossed protectively against his chest, rocking gently back and forth in stress and trauma, he faced Judge H. J. Powell. His parents were there, watching, hoping.

Representing Alexander, Advocate M. J. Richman of Ress, Richman & Company, argued for bail. Alexander had been in solitary for seventy-six days. Unaware that his comrades had been arrested, he spent thirty-five days in a nine-by-five-foot cell at Caledon Square Police Station being intensively interrogated. Then he spent another forty-one days in Maitland Police Station. Despite the sabotage charge, Alexander had only distributed pamphlets, Richman pointed out. He would accept stringent conditions and refrain from seeing his associates, he promised. His parents depended on his salary, and time at home would enable him 'to readjust mentally for his trial.' Moreover, he added, several other Livingstone High teachers had been detained, and the students would suffer from the continued absence of their teachers. But state advocate D. B. Brunette worried that Alexander would abscond. The police were continuing their wide-ranging investigations, and there was no need for concern about Alexander's mental well-being. Bail was denied.[1]

The state and its laws

Following the Sharpeville-Langa massacres, the state brutally clamped down on civil society and political protest. Opponents to white supremacy were cast as criminals and condemned to prison in criminal trials relying on hastily passed statutes. Two cases illustrate the rapidly changing laws and increasingly severe punishments. The first is the Pan Africanist Congress (PAC)'s Robert Sobukwe and twenty-two others, charged after the Sharpeville and Langa massacres with both pass law violations and incitement to violate pass laws. Like the 1952–53 Defiance Campaign, when the arrested volunteers had usually served two to

1 'Brilliant city man accused of sabotage,' *Cape Times*, 28 September 1963; *State vs Alexander*, p. 1767.

three months, the PAC had hoped that filling up the prisons would cause the pass law system to collapse. However, the charge of incitement was much more serious than the relatively minor charge of contravening pass laws: the maximum penalties were respectively five years and one month. The activists refused to plead to white laws that oppressed blacks, and – reflecting their slogan, 'no bail, no defence, no fine' – they did not appoint a lawyer. From the dock Sobukwe explained their political position, stating: 'We believe in one race only – the human race to which we all belong … our organisation aims at the overthrow of white domination, and the establishment of a non-racial democracy.' On 4 May 1960 the judge found most of them guilty. Sobukwe was sentenced to three years, eighteen others to up to two years and four were acquitted. But Potlako Leballo's announcement of a PAC uprising came shortly before Sobukwe's release. The police cracked down on the PAC and Poqo, which was smashed by March 1963. The government passed an amendment to the Suppression of Communism Act that allowed the state to extend an individual's imprisonment indefinitely in the hypothetical possibility that he would violate the act should he be released – applied only to Sobukwe, the amendment became known as the 'Sobukwe clause.' The state skipped the court process outright.[2]

The second case, the *State against Nelson Mandela and Nine Others* – the Rivonia Trial – opened in Pretoria soon after Alexander's court appearance; the year before, on 7 November 1962, Mandela had been sentenced to five years for incitement and illegally leaving the country. The UN Security Council appealed in vain on 7 August 1963 that 'all persons imprisoned, interned or subjected to other restrictions for having opposed the policy of *apartheid*' be released. The UN was then scrupulous about giving attention to the many political trials, most of which have been forgotten in the historiographical focus on Rivonia. On 11 October 1963 its General Assembly called on South Africa to abandon the Rivonia Trial and release all political prisoners.[3]

Unlike the earlier Treason Trial, the ten Rivonia accused were charged not with treason but with conspiracy and sabotage (221 acts, reduced to 193) aimed at catalysing violent revolution. In contrast to the Sobukwe trial, the Rivonia

2 Le Roux and Davis, *Lawfare*, p. 66; Tembeka Ngcukaitobi, 'Legality of Evil: Robert Sobukwe and the Apartheid Legal Order,' *Mail & Guardian*, 4 March 2023, https://mg.co.za/opinion/2023-03-04-legality-of-evil-robert-sobukwe-and-the-apartheid-legal-order, accessed 26 March 2025; Benjamin Pogrund, *How Can Man Die Better... Sobukwe and Apartheid*, London: Peter Halban, 1990, pp. 148–54, 159, 180–5; Johnson, *Dreaming*, pp. 147–8.

3 United Nations, *Fascist Terror in South Africa: Report of the United Nations Special Committee on Apartheid*, March 23, 1964, pp. 62–97, 62–63, https://www.sahistory.org.za/sites/default/files/archive-files4/Acn1764.0001.9976.000.017.Apr1964.8.pdf, accessed 28 April 2023; Simpson, 'Mandela's Army,' p. 1103.

accused had a distinguished legal team – by now, the use of statute law and the harsher penalties imposed by the state made legal defence imperative. The lead Rivonia defence counsel, communist Bram Fischer, applied for a postponement to consider the charges and get them quashed – a tactic successfully used in the Treason Trial. Even during the early 1960s, write le Roux and Davis, 'the state was obligated to let the accused know in clear terms what case they were required to meet in court.'[4] Their case was remanded until 29 October. But no sooner did the judge quash the charges than the police rearrested the group while they were still in court – an open contest between the judiciary and the police. The new charges were also unclear, but the defence failed to get them quashed. Mandela pleaded not guilty – the government should be in the dock, he stated. But the accused could hardly deny the many sabotage acts carried out by Umkhonto we Sizwe, and they used the trial to explain rather than deny responsibility for their actions. The defence, for its part, hoped to avoid the death penalty.[5]

The National Liberation Front (NLF) trial was concerned neither with incitement nor acts of sabotage, but rather with thinking and political education – the state aimed to criminalize political thought. This can be seen as a continuation and indeed a culmination of the laws promoting inferior education and censorship. These three trials illustrate the apartheid state's attacks on three different methods of struggle: incitement, sabotage and thinking.

The dramatis personae

Before the NLF trial began, legal representation was a problem. The Unity Movement would not help even though most of the accused were members. So Arthur Magerman and Roseinnes Phahle approached the International Defence and Aid Fund (IDAF) in Johannesburg. 'We were told that it could not come to their assistance if they were not members of the ANC,' Phahle recalled. The IDAF told them that legal fees for a trial would run to R50,000 (approximately R6 million or 300,000€ in 2025), but they could only raise R300. Phahle approached human rights lawyer David Soggot, a former Unity Movement/Progressive Forum member. He immediately agreed to represent the NLF *pro bono* with reimbursement for air fare. But then they learned from Fikile Bam's friend Ann-Marie Louw that the Special Branch knew of their efforts and that Alexander's West German supporters had agreed to cover the

4 Le Roux and Davis, *Lawfare*, pp. 72, 89; Swart, 'Road to Freedom,' p. 165.

5 *Cape Times*, 27 November 1963; Le Roux and Davis, *Lawfare*, pp. 76–7, 79–80; Broun, *Saving Nelson Mandela*, pp. 44, 117–18; Joel Joffe, *The State vs. Nelson Mandela: The Trial that Changed South Africa*, Oxford: Oneworld, 2007.

legal fees and were forming an Alexander Defence Fund. The German press carried reports of the arrests and forthcoming trial.[6]

The trial opened in the Supreme Court of South Africa (Appellate Division) on Keerom Street, Cape Town on 4 November. Advocate Gerald Gordon, QC, led the defence team.[7] Born in January 1909, Gordon was a first-generation South African raised in a family with a strong Jewish culture. His father came from the scholarly town of Salant, Lithuania, in the Russian Empire, his mother, from Wales and a long line of Welsh and English Jews. The couple met in Wales and later settled in a working-class area of Kimberley, where his father ran a small liquor business, and his mother was a homemaker and artist. At the Kimberley Boys' High School, Gordon won the London College of Preceptors' prize for best in the British Empire in Latin and Greek, the Kimberley Dux medal, and the De Beers and Diamond Scholarships, but he did not receive a Rhodes Scholarship – perhaps due to antisemitism, he felt. Despite his success he seems to have felt a bit of an outsider.

At the University of Cape Town (UCT) Gordon read classics in his first year, winning the top place in Latin and sharing the Governor-General's prize for the best BA student. Then he switched to law, winning medals, distinctions and first place in his final BA year. In 1930 he received the LLB and was admitted to the Bar. He soon published a massively influential tome on insurance law. Motivated by the desire to fight Nazism and antisemitism, during the Second World War he served in North Africa, rising rapidly through the ranks to captain, and on his way home he visited Palestine. Becoming a King's Counsel in 1949, he was also politically engaged: vice-chair of the War Veterans' Torch Commando, founding member of the Liberal Party and, after the Liberals' 1958 electoral defeat, joining the new Progressive Party. He had drifted from his parents' staunch religious upbringing: his wife, literary critic

6 Roseinnes Phahle, 'Reminiscences of the Arrest of Fikile Bam & Marcus Solomon in 1963,' August 2019; *Cape Times*, 1 November 1963; 'Memories of David Soggot, "the frugal hedonist",' *Mail & Guardian*, 4 June 2010, https://mg.co.za/article/2010-06-04-memories-of-david-soggot-the-frugal-hedonist/, accessed 10 February 2025. On German news reports see, for example, *Dienstag*, 6 August 1963 and *Schwäbisches Tagblatt*, 31 October 1963. My thanks to Dr Susanne Rieß-Stumm, Universitätsarchiv Tübingen and Prof. em. Dr. Bernd Jürgen Warneken, Eberhard Karls Universität Tübingen, for sending me the file on *Proteste um Dr. Alexander* concerning German solidarity efforts.

7 *State versus Neville Alexander and Ten Others* (Supreme Court of South Africa, Appellate Division); *Sunday Times*, 27 October 1963; Alexander Defense Committee, *Injustice in South Africa: The case of Dr. Neville Alexander*, New York, c. 1965, Berta Green Langston Papers, Holt Labor Library Digital Collection, HLL_BGL_01_01_015.pdf, Cal State University Dominguez Hills Archives and Special Collections; Interview, Judge Robin Marais, Cape Town, 21 September 2022; Interview, Lionel Davis, Cape Town, 6 May 2019.

Nancy Baines, was Anglican. By the time Gordon took the NLF case, he had won several important civil rights cases, including Rex vs Abdurahman (1950), which concerned the Train Apartheid Resistance Campaign. He had published several other legal books and two extremely successful novels. His meticulously organized law office, whose staff ranged from African messengers and tea servers up to white advocates, mirrored apartheid's social hierarchy; indeed, African employees were sometimes given English names to use at work, instead of their own. His home office in Clifton had a clear view of Robben Island; he used to stare at the island and think of its prisoners while completing his third novel, *Four People*, an account of two couples, one white, one black, set during the 1960 Langa Massacre.[8]

Gordon was assisted at trial by Robin Marais and Herschel Strauss, all instructed by Ress, Richman & Company. Coincidentally, Marais had taught Bam public and international law at UCT, and Bam had taught Marais isiXhosa. The three advocates represented eight of the accused, excluding Solomon, Hendricks and Doris van der Heyden, who were represented by Marais and Strauss. The accused had left ample evidence of their thinking in their writings, so their advocates were not optimistic.[9]

Andrew Beyers, QC, Judge President of the Cape Provincial Division of the Supreme Court, allocated the NLF trial to Justice Hermanus Arnoldus van Heerden, just appointed full-time judge in February 1963 – a hard-working junior judge.[10] Born in April 1920, the son of an attorney, van Heerden grew up in Bredasdorp a small town near Hermanus. After matriculating in 1936, he worked as a bank clerk in Somerset West and studied for a BCom through the University of South Africa. He then went to UCT for his LLB, playing rugby for UCT and western province, and graduating around 1947. He became Queen's Counsel a decade later. Despite being Afrikaner, he was not a member of the notorious Afrikaner secret society, the *Broederbond*, or of any other

8 Ellison Kahn, 'Honour for Gerald Gordon QC,' *South African Law Journal* 113, no. 3, August 1996, pp. 520–5; 'In Memoriam Gerald Gordon QC,' *South African Law Journal* 116, 1, 1999, pp. 141–47; Eve Horwitz, interview with Gerald Gordon, April 1985, UCT Kaplan Centre for Jewish Studies, mss_bc949_ct_tr_gordon_g, pp. 1–6, 28, 35, 60; 28, 60; Robertson, *Liberalism*, pp. 54 n. 3, 56 n. 3, 162, 184–203; Chris Chivers, 'Nancy Gordon,' *Daily Maverick*, 20 November 2023, https://www.dailymaverick.co.za/article/2023-11-20-nancy-gordon-a-literary-life-filled-with-love-laughter-and-the-light-of-still-point, accessed 6 October 2024; Justice Dumisa Ntsebeza, 'They Called Me Dennis – A Journey from Messenger to Justice,' Address given to the Notre Dame Law School, 30 January 2023, https://www.youtube.com/watch?v=iAEbh50CPjg, accessed 22 January 2025.

9 Interview, Marais.

10 Interview, Murray van Heerden, Cape Town, 10 August 2022; Gerald Friedman and Jeremy Gauntlett, *Bar, Bench & Bullshifters: Cape Tales, 1950–1990*, Cape Town: Siber Ink, 2013, pp. 35, 60; *Cape Times*, 6 November 1963.

Afrikaner group: his wife was English-speaking, and they spoke English at home. At the trial van Heerden was assisted by two assessors, Mr E. A. Wollaston and Mr J. J. Groenewald, whom the defence felt were very extreme. In theory assessors dealt with questions of fact, not law; in practice the line was often blurry.[11] Deputy Attorney General Mr J. E. Nöthling and Advocate Mr D. B. Brunette represented the state.

The charges

'Big Cape Trial on Monday,' read the *Post* in capital letters on Sunday 3 November: 'Charges of plotting violent revolution.' The apartheid regime was deadly serious. Just two days before, Lennox Madikane, Vevile Felix Jaxa and Mxolosi Damane had been hanged in Pretoria Central for their role in the Paarl uprising – the country's first hangings for sabotage.[12]

That Monday morning librarian Frank Musson of the Bellville South NLF cell was en route to the Groote Schoor Library in a mainly Coloured area. Apartheid's tentacles were squeezing the life out of civil society organs: the South African Library Association had just voted to implement separate libraries for the four supposed racial groups.[13] Walking past the court building, Musson spotted Mrs Dimbiti Alexander, Neville's mother, and stopped to talk. Just then he spied Detective-Sergeant J. P. 'Spyker' van Wyk pointing at him. Spyker – literally nail – was well known among western Cape prisoners as a torturer. Indeed, recalled Albie Sachs, Spyker's 'name invariably cropped up when there was mention of violence.'[14] Van Wyk knew Musson had denied knowing the Alexanders. Musson had been working at the Cape Town Municipal Library when the police rolled up, took him to the Caledon Square Police Station and interrogated him about Alexander and the NLF. Musson said he didn't know them. The police asked why people in the NLF were saying they knew him. He replied they were probably trying to find someone else to blame for their problems. He was released. Now van Wyk approached and questioned Musson, who said he had become interested in the trial after his detention and so had stopped to speak to Mrs Alexander.[15]

11 Interview, Marais; van Zyl Smit and Isakow, 'Assessors and Criminal Justice.'

12 *Cape Times*, 1 November 1963.

13 *Nature*, 199, 24 August 1963, pp. 746–7; *Cape Times*, 6, 10 September, 8 October 1963.

14 Albie Sachs, *Stephanie on Trial*, London: Harvill, 1968, pp. 15–16, 34. According to the TRC Final Report, p. 402, para 58, https://sabctrc.saha.org.za/reports/volume3/chapter5/subsection8.htm, accessed 3 November 2023, 'Spyker van Wyk [was] the individual most consistently associated with torture in the Western Cape over a thirty year period.'

15 Interview, Frank Musson, August 2022; *Post*, 3 November 1963.

The defendants were charged with contravening section 21 (1) of the 1962 General Law Amendment Act no. 76 – the Sabotage Act – and thus with conspiring to commit certain wrongful and wilful acts. Between 1 April 1962 and 12 July 1963, they were alleged to have conspired at meetings in the Wynberg, Cape Town and Bellville districts, so that they would have endangered public safety, law and order and property and overthrown the government by violent revolution and in the process kill and steal. Moreover, Don Davis, accused number 2, had distributed the group's literature between 1 December 1962 and 9 July 1963 at Gong-Gong, Barkly West, Vredendal and Kimberley. Finally, each of the accused had identified themselves with aims of the Yu Chi Chan Club (YCCC) and NLF. There were also three alternative charges. First, under the same section of the Sabotage Act they were charged with inciting, instigating, commanding, advising or encouraging others to commit certain wrongful and wilful acts. Secondly and thirdly, they were charged under sections 2a and 2b of the Suppression of Communism Act with furthering the aims of communism.[16]

The courtroom was packed – white and black observers separated, whites on the main level, friends and families of the accused in the public gallery upstairs. On 24 July, a Livingstone High faculty committee had asked Minister of Justice B. J. Vorster to free their detained teachers – Neville Alexander, Reginald Francke and Leslie van der Heyden – on the grounds that the students' education was suffering. The students had organized a stay-away, placing placards in the school courtyard, but decided against a protest march to Cape Town; the police had warned that organizers could be charged with incitement. Now, some forty students entered the courtroom – all in school blazers, the girls wearing dresses and boater hats, the boys, trousers, shirts and ties. They were ordered out because of their age. Their principal, the unpopular Mr Balie – a Coloured Affairs Department appointee who caned students and spoke with a strong Afrikaans accent – was told to compile a list of those students who had tried to attend.[17]

The trial was adjourned to Tuesday, 5 November. Similar to the moves of the Rivonia defence, Gordon applied to quash two of the three charges and to allow separate trials for each of the accused. He contended that the main charge of sabotage was vague, embarrassing and prejudicial to the accused. On the first alternative charge he contended that the State had failed to provide information critical to the defence and had wronged the accused in

[16] *State vs Alexander*, pp. 14a-14j, 819, 1966–67.

[17] *Cape Times*, 25 July, 5 November 1963; *Torch*, 13 November 1963; Simon Banda, 'My Senior Certificate Years (Standards 8, 9 and 10) of the Early Sixties,' n.d., courtesy Simon Banda; Shadley Fataar to author, 5 April 2024; Wieder, *Teacher and Comrade*, pp. 90–1.

Figure 5: High school students on the steps of Cape Town's Supreme Court at the start of the NLF trial. Source: *Cape Argus*, 4 November 1963.

the indictment. Further, alternative charges two and three were based on a wrongful misjoinder of cases.[18]

But three days later Justice van Heerden rejected Gordon's application to quash. If the State did not know certain things, it could hardly tell the accused, van Heerden contended. It was not obliged to inform the accused of every detail of its case, but only to allege in general terms. Indeed, he claimed, 'in doing what they were alleged to have done,' the accused 'became associated

[18] *Cape Argus*, 5, 8 November 1963; *Cape Times*, 9 December 1963; *Torch* 13 November 1963.

in an unlawful purpose.' Nor did he see that the accused were prejudiced by their cases being joined.[19]

The prosecution

Unlike the Rivonia accused, who were charged with plotting and engaging in completed acts of violence, the NLF members had never engaged in armed actions.[20] So the state was only dealing with hypothetical armed actions that might occur in the future. Hoping to avoid prison, much like the Rivonia trialists, the accused pled not guilty and explained their political engagement. The state's case depended on demonstrating a conspiracy to engage in a future armed struggle. It sought to show the group's commitment to armed struggle through its literature, and its use of conspiracy through meetings, discussions, and efforts to expand. Its concern with secrecy and code names further signalled this conspiracy, the prosecution contended, as did the formation of the South African Students Bursary & Loan Fund (SASBLF), allegedly a cover organization to finance the NLF's political ambitions.

The trial was conducted in English, which all the accused spoke, although some witnesses, especially the police, spoke Afrikaans; Advocate Gordon understood but evidently did not speak Afrikaans well, so having other advocates who could was helpful.[21] Deputy Attorney General Nöthling and Advocate Brunette began reading aloud over fifty documents that Lieutenant Sauerman had taken from Neville Alexander's home. It is not known whether the published works were legally available or had been banned; Alexander did not think they were banned, as the police had apparently not been aware of them until then.[22] Although the accused insisted they were concerned with both the study of guerrilla warfare and the formation of united fronts, the

19 *Cape Argus*, 8 November 1963.

20 Broun, *Saving Nelson Mandela*, p. 53.

21 *Sunday Times*, 27 October 1963; Interview, Marais.

22 Matsemela, interview with Alexander, A2.3, pp. 56–7. According to Christopher Merrett, email to author 23 June 2021, 'There was a list of banned books called *Jacobsen's Index* but unfortunately for the historian it was cumulative and (sort of) alphabetical. Every week we would receive a replacement set of pages and throw away old ones. That means it was not possible to achieve a snapshot of any particular period. So the old and very dusty volume still in the local university library is not of much help. It simply reflects what was still banned at the date of the final issue around 1990. The only definitive record of books banned under the Customs Act of 1955 and from 1963 under successive Publications Acts (there is no such record of titles banned under security legislation) is the *Government Gazette*. Friday by Friday it listed books banned and occasionally unbanned.' I have not been able to consult the *Government Gazette* from the late 1950s–early 1960s.

reading material contained virtually nothing on the latter. The literary focus on armed struggle to the neglect of united fronts strengthened the state's case and weakened that of the defence. Nöthling and Brunette started with Mao Tse Tung's *Strategic Problems of the Anti-Japanese Guerrilla War* and continued with Lenin's *The Paris Commune*. The courtroom atmosphere was initially electric, but as they droned on, by Friday afternoon the large crowd that had turned out on Monday dwindled to some twenty-three. The next week they carried on with Mao's *Yu Chi Chan* and copies of *Liberation*, finally concluding with Guevara's *Guerrilla Struggle*. The *Cape Times* noted *Liberation*'s account that two South African army officers and one police officer had been sent to Algeria in 1959 to study French torture methods.[23] The state also introduced a two-page report on the NLF's literature written by Professor Andrew Howson Murray, head of UCT's Philosophy Department and considered an expert on communism.[24]

Next, the state called its witnesses: police and informers, YCCC/NLF members testifying in exchange for immunity, and various individuals who confirmed details of alleged NLF activities, such as room bookings for fund-raising dances. Three men testified that Don Davis had given them books on guerrilla warfare. Then Police Constable Jacobus Kotzee and police informer Cecil Dempster claimed the group was preparing a Coloured uprising against whites to take place in January 1964 – an echo of Leballo's call for an African uprising.[25] They were apparently the only ones to make this absurd claim, the NLF being non-racial and concerned with longer-term guerrilla struggle. During his testimony Constable Kotzee referred to notes he had made from his earlier discussion with Don Davis. The defence requested the notes, but the judge refused to compel the police to produce them.[26]

Unable to find sufficient work as a mason, Kimberley resident Dempster had been a police informant since 1958. On 18 February 1963 he approached a Detective Warrant Officer Botha with a copy of Mao's book. Botha instructed Constable Kotzee to join the organization. On 12 April Kotzee followed Don Davis and Dempster from Kimberley to Cape Town, where Kotzee obtained political documents and gave them to Botha, who later saw Bam waiting for Dempster in Kimberley. Dempster first denied but later admitted to being in Cape Town, claiming that the police had instructed him to keep his Cape Town

23 *Cape Times*, 5, 6, 9, 11, 12, 13, 14 November 1963; *Liberation*, 1, 3, 1963; United Nations, *Fascist Terror in South Africa*, p. 75; Marcus Solomon to author, 1 May 2019.

24 A frequent state's witness, Murray did not appear at the NLF trial. A. H. Murray Papers, UCTMA BC1253, Alexander case; Teresa Barnes, 'The Curious Case of Prof. A. H. Murray in South African Political Trials, 1956–76,' Paper presented to the 'Rivonia Trial 50 Years On' conference, University of Pretoria, 18–20 June 2013, pp. 3–8.

25 *Cape Times*, 16 November 1963.

26 *State vs Alexander*, pp. 309–10; Heads of Argument for Appellants, para 16–17.

trip secret. When he picked out Marcus Solomon in the courtroom, Solomon said, '*Ja, vark*' ['Yes, pig']. Then, Dempster alleged, an accused man said: 'You are a Boere spy … Your life is in your hands.' The judge reprimanded Dempster for lying but deemed the remarks of the accused to be witness intimidation and adjourned to allow defence counsel to confer with their clients.[27]

Through a combination of detention, solitary confinement, release and intimidation, the police played off some NLF members against the others. If you make a satisfactory statement, we will release you, the police told detainees. Satisfactory statements were rare, indeed; even when released, people were frequently brought back – a circular chain of indescribable stress. Initially Francke, married with two children and another on the way, recounted that he 'looked up at the public gallery and saw my friends there. I could not give evidence. I just could not.'[28]

Later, though, Francke begged to testify. He was held for twenty-eight days, then released after making a twenty-one-page statement. But once released he became persona non grata in his community. Like the van der Heydens, he had lived in Gleemoor, Athlone, but both families had moved to Lansdowne. Francke tried taking his wife to a cinema outside their area but had to return home while his wife went on alone. 'Everybody knows why the police release a detainee early – because he has made a statement,' he told the Court. 'I had a life of hell outside. My friends pestered me with questions and branded me a traitor. They asked me why I had made a statement to the police and called me a fifth columnist.'[29]

His wife pressured him to testify because not one friend had helped her while he was detained. He had planned to leave the country. But then he heard that Dulcie September had been allowed to see Elizabeth van der Heyden, who told her that she and Neville Alexander had been allowed to confer, that they had both made full statements and instructed others to do so too. Whether this was accurate is not known.[30] But Francke believed it was. Enraged, he considered giving evidence. Then he read in the papers that Dempster was a police spy, and that Dempster's claims contradicted his own earlier statement. So he felt his testimony would not be accepted and, therefore, he would not get immunity. However, he changed his mind, and on 26–27 November he provided details of NLF meetings and discussions. He hurt them badly, describing the NLF as a 'military organization … Nobody disagreed with guerrilla warfare as a method.' Moreover, he added, Coloureds

27 *Torch*, 20, 27 November 1963; *Fascist Terror*, pp. 75–6.

28 'Released detainee,' *Cape Times*, 7 December 1963.

29 *Cape Times*, 7 December 1963; Shadley Fataar to author, 14 July 2024.

30 I have no corroborating sources. Alexander later claimed he initially put everything on the overseas German cell and said he was their only South African link, Matsemela, interview, Alexander, A2.4, p. 19.

who collaborated with the regime were to be dealt with later.[31] His testimony cost him dearly. He was shunned by teachers and students alike when he returned to Livingstone; the Teachers' League dropped him, and art students drew cartoons of him as a rat.[32]

Francke was followed by Landers, who had just completed a diploma in Education and been offered a teaching position in Beaufort West. Like Francke, he did not initially want to cooperate with the police: 'I only admitted as much as they knew.' The police came to his house in early August and said he must accompany them. He made a statement; they let him go. The next week they appeared at his college, told him they were not satisfied with his statement and that he must go to the Caledon Square Police Station, where he made another statement. The next week they fetched him at college and drove him to Caledon Square. Altogether, he made four statements, each more detailed. Finally, he decided to testify for two reasons. First, like Francke, he had heard from September that Elizabeth van der Heyden and Neville Alexander had instructed the others to make statements. Secondly, he believed that the police knew everything.[33]

Landers, too, was a hostile witness, contesting the defence claim that the NLF consisted of study groups: 'this organization had definite aims which it planned to carry out.' The Court interjected: 'You did not consider it to be a study group?' Landers replied: 'No.' The NLF wanted to replace the state '[c]hiefly by means of guerrilla warfare,' he insisted. However, prodded by the Court, he acknowledged that 'weapons weren't really discussed as such.' Advocate Strauss claimed that Landers had lied in his first three statements and now wanted only to exculpate himself. Later Gordon cross-examined Landers. The NLF's aims may have been to replace the government, as Landers claimed, 'but in regard to the method it was no more than a study group which was studying methods?' 'Yes,' replied Landers, 'it was an organization studying methods.'[34]

Teacher Xenophon Pitt from Queenstown agreed to testify for the state. But Frank Musson wrote letters to all those planning to give evidence saying that they would be known across the world for what they had done. The letters were mailed to West Germany and sent back to South Africa in new envelopes with German postmarks. When Pitt received his letter, he asked APDUSA's Alie Fataar to get him out of the country, which he evidently did, aided by Musson.[35] Another Queenstown cell member, machinist William

31 *Cape Times*, 27 November 1963.

32 Wieder, *Teacher and Comrade*, p. 94.

33 *State vs Alexander*, pp. 551–2.

34 *State vs Alexander*, pp. 510, 553–4, 540, 550, 557; *Cape Times*, 29 November 1963.

35 Interview, Musson.

Hoffeldt, testified that they functioned as a study group, acknowledging that Dr Abrahams had visited them.[36]

But not everyone succumbed to police pressure. Kenneth Jordaan had been picked up, made a statement, and upon release went underground and into exile. Even those who remained refused to testify. The trial took a 'tense turn' on Monday 2 December as three witnesses refused to give evidence. These included Cyril Jacobs and Yusuf Lucas, followed by Daniel Swabel, who 'hesitated as the accused watched him intently. Then he too declined.' Police investigator Sergeant D. J. Greeff took the stand, claiming he had found a plastic bomb – a plastic bottle and pipe – and revolver parts at a house in Elsies River in July. The defence was taken by surprise – this was the first time Advocate Gordon had heard this presumably fabricated claim. Court was adjourned so that Gordon could confer with his clients.[37]

The state had intended Gerald Giose to be its chief witness. Unlike his comrades, seemingly paralysed in their homes, in August 1963 Giose approached the Swedish Envoy Dr Eyvind Bratt, who gave him sanctuary but advised him to leave the country. In January 1964 Giose stowed away on a Swedish ship, but he was discovered and arrested at Walvis Bay, South West Africa. Taken to Bellville, the police beat him up but told him they would give him the opportunity to testify against the NLF because his father was a Christian minister. He was dragged into court, so battered he could not walk, but twice refused to testify. Taken to Caledon Square, he was given coffee laced with an unknown drug. He recalled:

> Hardly half an hour afterwards, I began to feel tingling sensations all over my body and my mind became very light. I began to scream uncontrollably. When the ladies were walking down Buitenkant Street, the sound of the stiletto heels on the stone pavement sounded like pistol shots in my head.

He was eventually sent to Valkenberg Psychiatric Hospital – one of many ninety-day detainees sent there – and only released in 1968.[38]

36 *World Outlook*, 1, 14, 27 December 1963, 5; *State vs Alexander*, Heads of Argument for Appellants, para 24.

37 *Cape Times*, 3 December 1963; *State vs Alexander*, pp. 578–9. These were the only allegations about weapons.

38 'Gerald Giose, National Liberation Front/Yu Chi Chan Club – ANC/Umkhonto we Sizwe' (Cape Town, 6 December 1995), in Tor Sellström, ed., *Liberation in Southern Africa – Regional and Swedish Voices: Interviews from Angola, Mozambique, Namibia, South Africa, Zimbabwe, the Frontline and Sweden*, 2nd. ed., Uppsala: Nordiska Afrikainstitutet, 2002, pp. 122–7, 124–6, https://www.diva-portal.org/smash/get/diva2:272726/FULLTEXT01.pdf, accessed 27 March 2023; Interview, Elizabeth

In the meantime, Swabel changed his mind. An optical mechanic, he had met Kenneth Abrahams by chance and, after a few discussions, Abrahams proposed that he form an NLF cell in Maitland. There is no evidence that Swabel had been politically active before then – symptomatic of the NLF's naivety. He was introduced to Dempster the informant, who bragged about his knowledge of guns. Swabel attended several regional meetings, but indicating his lack of interest, declined to attend another because he had 'a good game of dominoes in the afternoon.'[39] Yet he confirmed the study group nature of the Maitland cell, which was formed 'to study and find out.'[40]

The Rivonia prosecutors were concerned with the documents, typewriters and duplicating machines seized at Liliesleaf Farm, but especially with Umkhonto's weapons. The NLF had not used arms, so the NLF prosecutors focused entirely on its literature and the typewriter and Photostat machine used to produce it – tools of the trade for intellectuals. Later that same afternoon, Trotskyist Enver Marney testified that he had borrowed Neville Alexander's typewriter for his niece, who was studying typing. Marney slanted his replies to support Alexander, explaining that his ideas were 'very widespread and very common amongst the youth of his sort.' Marney supported the development of 'a modern labour movement,' opposed black and white nationalism and thought he was convincing Alexander. The next day it was Dorothy Adams' turn. She had been arrested in front of her Pauw Gedenk Primary students and moved from one prison to another every few weeks to break her. But she refused to testify: 'I can't do it. I can't do it,' she cried out, as she was led out of court, tears streaming down her face. She was sentenced to five years house arrest, like the others who refused to testify.[41]

After the typewriter came the Photostat machine, which Dr Abrahams had purchased for his professional use and which the police sought to locate because it had allegedly been used to reproduce pamphlets. Detective-Sergeant van Wyk tried to beat the information out of Marcus Solomon, who did not know where it was. In early September, several days after his return to Cape Town, Solomon made a statement in expectation of being released. He had no reading material, not even a Bible, and worried constantly about his siblings, whom he supported. Not only did the police say they would detain his sister and girlfriend if he did not talk, but 'I was told I would be kept indefinitely under the 90 days. If necessary 90 years,' he told the Court. 'Those were the

---

van der Heyden, Elfindale, Cape Town, 8 June 2018; *Cape Times*, 19 November 1963; *State vs Alexander*, pp. 1010.

39 *State vs Alexander*, pp. 695, 720–1.

40 *State vs Alexander*, p. 725; Heads of Argument for Appellants, para 24.

41 *State vs Alexander*, pp. 593–5; *Cape Times*, 4 December 1963; Joffe, *State vs. Mandela*, p. 181; interview, Adams; Williams, 'Dorothy Williams (nee Adams).'

words used by Det. Sgt. Van Wyk.'[42] On 27 September Solomon was taken to a room in Caledon Square. Van Wyk, a detective and two Special Branch members were present. Solomon was repeatedly asked where the Photostat machine was. Finally, van Wyk took off his jacket and punched Solomon four or five times on his left ear and temple – the left side of his face, in Solomon's words – a hook, in boxing terms. Van Wyk then grabbed him by the shoulders, pulled him in close and kicked him six or seven times in the solar plexus with his knee – a common martial arts move – causing severe pain. The action tore the left shoulder seam of Solomon's shirt. Van Wyk pushed Solomon to the floor face down, crossed his legs and sat on them, demanding to know where the Photostat machine was. Solomon finally told them Lionel Davis had it. Davis was brought in. The police threatened to lock up his mother if he did not reveal the machine's location. But he coolly said nothing. It wasn't that he was contemptuous of the police, he later told the Court: 'I just regard them as being part of the machinery of the State and I am opposed to the State.'[43]

Several days later Solomon laid a charge against the police. Dr Elias Ruttenberg examined Solomon but did not wish to know what had happened. Questioned by Mr Strauss about Solomon's claim, Dr Ruttenberg replied: 'That is possible.' He had examined Solomon for external injuries, acknowledging that there might be internal injuries without external signs.[44] As West German students celebrated Human Rights Day on 10 December with flyers citing the Alexander trial, the judge and prosecutor repeatedly questioned Solomon about what constituted a face and where a face ended. They pressed him about his claim of being repeatedly kicked with a knee, incredulous, despite Solomon's reply that it was a judo move. They grilled him about the location of the swelling he experienced on the side of his head: 'At the time I was so bewildered I didn't take very much notice feeling exactly how high the swelling, or where this feeling of swelling really was,' he stated. The day after the beating he suffered a severe headache and pain in his ear, stomach and back. By the time the doctor examined him the pain had subsided.[45]

Lionel Davis testified that the side of Solomon's face was red and swollen, and his shirt torn. He therefore thought that Solomon 'must have been under some form of ill treatment.'[46] He too was grilled about what constituted a face and whether he had really seen Solomon's shirt – wasn't Solomon wearing a different top? asked the prosecutor. The judge and prosecutor found it 'extraordinary' that Solomon claimed to have been assaulted over

42 *State vs Alexander*, pp. 865–6.

43 *State vs Alexander*, pp. 870–1, 874–5, 880, 917, 920; interview, Davis.

44 *State vs Alexander*, pp. 879, 857–8.

45 *World Outlook*, 2, 3, 17 January 1964; *State vs Alexander*, pp. 887–8, 893–4, 907.

46 *State vs Alexander*, pp. 911–12.

the Photostat machine, when the police had not touched Davis. He had surely laid a charge against the police because he hated them, they suggested. Indeed, the prosecutor claimed Solomon had fabricated the assault.[47]

On 12 December Justice van Heerden heard arguments about handwriting specimens obtained from Marcus Solomon and Elizabeth van der Heyden during their ninety-day detentions. Based on common-law precedent, Gordon contended, such a sample must be given freely and voluntarily, without fear of the person in authority. Elizabeth gave her sample claiming Warrant Officer Botha told her she would be released if she complied; Solomon gave his because he 'was afraid they would beat me up again.' Notwithstanding their solitary confinement and Solomon's fear of further beating, the judge deemed their samples freely given. Indeed, he added, even if van der Heyden had misunderstood the Ninety-Day Act, her sample would still have been 'freely and voluntarily' made. He found van der Heyden to be 'a very unsatisfactory witness': her vague memory meant he could not accept her evidence. By contrast, Warrant Officer Botha impressed him 'as a most reliable witness,' and he found it 'highly improbable and inconceivable' that such an experienced police officer would mislead a witness.[48] The *Cape Times* had run numerous articles over the past few months about solitary confinement's damaging effects on memory. Justice van Heerden had presumably missed them.

Later that day, just before the long Christmas recess, Gordon requested bail for the accused. This had previously been denied because of concern about witness intimidation, but he assured the Court that had been reduced to a minimum. But Nöthling opposed bail. The accused might influence an important witness or leave the country – their organ *Liberation* had advised them to flee should they be arrested and obtain bail. In fact, Nöthling added, Solomon and Bam had been arrested while absconding. Bail was denied.[49]

The prisoners were kept at Roeland Street Gaol, men and women on opposite sides of the building. On 22 December the men were taken by boat to Robben Island Prison. Gordon, Strauss and Richman took the ferry to Robben Island, met with the accused and told them to prepare their instructions. On 12 January Head Warder Venter informed the men they would be going to Cape Town the next day. The next morning, they were assembled and handcuffed. Alexander held a sixty-page file with instructions to counsel. Although the instructions were privileged, Chief Warder Killian nonetheless insisted that the file had to be read before it could be removed from the Island; Alexander became irate. The next day the documents were returned 'piece by piece' and 'in a disorderly state' with sections missing. Looking through the papers the accused saw a memo in Detective-Sergeant van Wyk's writing.

47 *State vs Alexander*, pp. 892, 896, 901; *Cape Times*, 12 December 1963.

48 *State vs Alexander*, pp. 882, 905, 922–23, 925.

49 *State vs Alexander*, pp. 946–8.

Later questioned, van Wyk stated that he had last seen the memo in his office at Caledon Square, the implication being that he had seen the instructions to counsel, despite his denial, even before the prosecution had closed its case.[50]

The defence

The trial resumed on 3 February with the prisoners back at Roeland Street. The prosecution concluded its case, confident that it had demonstrated the group's use of conspiracy to plan armed struggle. Outside the courthouse, white fear was palpable: 'Cuba trains Bantu to fight S. Africa,' the *Cape Argus* had warned less than two weeks before.[51]

The defence began on 5 February. Against the state's charge of conspiracy to foment armed struggle, the defence sought to demonstrate, first, that the NLF consisted of study groups examining different methods of struggle; after all, it was not unusual for extra-parliamentary groups to discuss violence since the country had been experiencing sabotage attacks for several years. Secondly, the NLF was concerned with building a united front. Thirdly, the YCCC's pamphlets and *Liberation*'s articles represented the views of the authors, not the organization. Fourthly, individual members held different views on armed struggle. Fifthly, not all members attended every meeting or activity, so their actions were separate, not joined. Sixthly, the NLF's use of secrecy was typical of extra-parliamentary political groups, which always feared arrest. Finally, the SASBLF was indeed a bursary and loan fund for students hoping to study overseas.[52]

But before Advocate Gordon elaborated the defence, he argued for his clients' rights as detainees. Perhaps he was thinking of Rossouw versus Sachs, discussed in the introduction, and the Cape Provincial Division's decision to uphold certain rights of detainees; this would not be overturned until March. Gordon contended that the removal of accused numbers 1, 2, 3, 5, 6, 7 and 11's instructions to counsel during the Christmas break constituted a breach of privilege that undermined the basis of a fair trial. Indeed, names of persons not yet known by the state were mentioned in the instructions – putting those persons at risk of detention. However, the judge accepted the police and prosecutor's claim that there had been no breach.[53]

50 *State vs Alexander*, pp. 2156–61; *World Outlook*, 2, 20, 15 May 1964, pp. 17–18; Heads of Argument for Appellants, paras 1–9.

51 *Cape Argus*, 23 January 1964.

52 *State vs Alexander*, pp. 543, 550.

53 *Fascist Terror*, p. 77; *State vs Alexander*, p. 2160; Heads of Argument for Appellants, pp. 1–8. Although the judge overlooked the violation of privilege in this trial, the South African judiciary did not evidently have a fixed view on the issue. On 12 May 1976 SWAPO members Aaron Muchimba and Hendrik Shikongo, tried under

The defence also sought to exclude statements made in solitary confinement because they were not freely or voluntarily made.[54] Neville Alexander and several others voiced their belief that they were prejudiced both by the breach of privilege and by statements made during solitary confinement. Indeed, five of the accused – Neville Alexander, Don Davis, Dorothy Alexander, Elizabeth van der Heyden and Lionel Davis – refused to enter the witness stand and be cross-examined, not because it was a white court, but because of the denial of common-law standards of pre-trial procedures. Instead, they made unsworn statements, even though cross-examination under oath carried more legal weight; in the Rivonia Trial, Prosecutor Yutar was shocked when Mandela declined to be cross-examined, although the other accused agreed to be. Nonetheless, Bam, September, Hendricks, Leslie van der Heyden, Doris van der Heyden and Solomon took the stand to be questioned under oath. But the decision of some of them not to enter the witness box had negative consequences for all of them, the defence argued. All the accused would have benefited, it contended, had Neville Alexander's defence evidence been accepted.[55]

In contrast with Umkhonto members, who were generally older and had prior experience with the police, most NLF members thought they had to make statements, Bam recalled.[56] Elizabeth van der Heyden, for one, made several statements during solitary in the understanding that she would be released; the police had repeatedly told her they were only interested in Neville Alexander and Kenneth Abrahams. She did not accept responsibility for her statements nor recall what she had written. 'I do not consider any statements given while in detention to be freely or voluntarily given,' she stated. 'However, this Court, has already ruled that things done while a person is detained under the 90-day clause of the General Laws Amendment Act are admissible. I therefore feel that I cannot give evidence freely and it is for this reason that I have elected rather to make a statement from the dock.'[57]

Dorothy Alexander suffered severe headaches and sleeplessness in prison; she made a statement to get released so that she could resume her prescribed 'nerve pills,' which the prison authorities refused to provide.[58] Don Davis

---

the Terrorism Act, were given death sentences. Gwen Lister, *Comrade Editor: On Life, Journalism and the Birth of Namibia*, Cape Town: Tafelberg, 2021, p. 177, writes: 'After a complaint to the South African Supreme Court about the fact that confidential documents relating to their defence had been leaked to the security police, the matter was taken to the Appeal Court, where both were acquitted and discharged.'

54 *State vs Alexander*, p. 2164.

55 *State vs Alexander*, Heads of Argument for Appellants, pp. 1–8; le Roux and Davis, *Lawfare*, pp. 81–82; Joffe, *State vs. Mandela*, 156–7.

56 Matsemela, interview, Bam.

57 *State vs Alexander*, pp. 1540; 662–72.

58 *State vs Alexander*, pp. 1558–9.

had planned to testify under oath but changed his mind because, first, his instructions to counsel had been confiscated, prejudicing his position and, secondly, in detention he had made a statement, having understood that it would not be mentioned in court. But he now understood that it could be mentioned and hurt him further. Bam made a statement about eight days after his detention. Somehow, he acquired pens and slipped several notes to his comrades explaining the implications of making statements to the police under the Ninety-Day Act and advising that the decision was theirs.[59]

On solitary confinement

South Africa's use of peacetime solitary confinement began after the Defiance Campaign with the passage of the 1953 Public Safety Act. The use escalated in the early 1960s as the government bypassed safeguards against psychological abuse and physical torture of prisoners. Solitary, a 'secret punishment,' observed nineteenth-century British author Charles Dickens, is a 'slow and daily tampering with the mysteries of the brain … its ghastly signs and tokens are not so palpable to the eye and sense of touch as scars upon the flesh … its wounds are not upon the surface … it extorts few cries that human ears can hear.'[60]

A week after the trial opened, Professor Kurt Danziger, head of UCT's Psychology Department, highlighted its perils in the *Cape Times*. More than 500 individuals had been detained in solitary since the Ninety-Day Act came into effect, he observed. Of these, over 150 were later released without charge. Those detained were held in a small cell at least twenty-three hours a day with no diversion, not even reading material. Although the effect of solitary varied depending on the individual's capacity to cope, the impact was always negative. Starved of human contact and companionship, prisoners might say anything, not knowing what was true or false.[61] 'Fear of the unknown' and wondering 'would you be tortured' were Lionel Davis's greatest anxieties in solitary. Marcus Solomon became extremely disoriented; worse than the interrogations was the anxiety about what would happen to those close to him.[62]

59 *State vs Alexander*, pp. 1355–6, 1471, 1497, 1514–15.

60 Quoted in A. S. Mathews and R. C. Albino, 'The Permanence of the Temporary: An Examination of the 90- and 180-day Detention Laws,' *South African Law Journal*, 83, 1, February 1966, pp. 16–43, 25; Johann Louw and Catherine O'Brien, 'The Psychological Effects of Solitary Confinement: An Early Instance of Psychology in South African Courts, *South African Journal of Psychology*, 37, 1, 2007, pp. 96–106, 97.

61 Kurt Danziger, 'How Solitary Confinement Affects Prisoners,' *Cape Times*, 12 November 1963; Louw and O'Brien, 'Psychological Effects,' pp. 97–8; Mathews and Albino, 'The Permanence of the Temporary, pp. 16–43.

62 Interview, Davis; Drew and Ntsebeza, interview with Solomon.

Despite the repeated bans on left-wing newspapers, and the fines, detentions and banning of individual editors, the mainstream press – with its psychedelic combination of bikinis, beaches, cocktail dresses, pet stories and sabotage reports – was still relatively free.[63] Only the assassination of US President John F. Kennedy on 22 November 1963 had pushed South African news off the *Cape Argus*' front page. The press covered criticisms of solitary widely. 'Ban Solitary Confinement: "Inhuman, Unjustifiable" Say Specialists' read the *Cape Times* on 17 December 1963. Sixty leading psychiatrists, psychologists and medical specialists from the Cape and Natal appealed to Minister of Justice John Vorster that acute mental punishment was just as abhorrent as physical torture. It could even cause hallucinations and psychosis.[64] Take the Dennis Brutus case. After fleeing South Africa, he was captured and taken to Johannesburg. Outside Marshall Square Police Station, he fled police custody but was shot in the back. The first ambulance to arrive was for whites only; one for blacks came forty minutes later. Finally imprisoned, Brutus was so exhausted from being trampled on in an overcrowded cell that solitary seemed preferable: 'In fact, however, after a month or two I began to have hallucinations,' he recounted, 'and I attempted suicide, and I had to be hauled out of there.'[65]

To support its contention that statements made during solitary should not be allowed, the defence brought in three mental health experts. First was Dr James McWilliams McGregor, who had qualified in medicine at the University of Edinburgh in 1937, with specialties in neurology and psychiatry and a diploma in psychological medicine. He was a member of the Royal Colleges of Physicians in London and Edinburgh, an honorary Fellow of the Faculty of Physicians in South Africa, and currently acting head of Neurology at UCT. McGregor was followed by Dr Jane Elizabeth Bain. She had obtained her Bachelor of Medicine and Surgery at UCT in 1957, completed a one-year internship in the Department of Neurology and Psychiatry at Groote Schuur Hospital, then obtained a diploma in Psychiatry at McGill University in Montreal in 1963. Since October 1963 she had been at the Groote Schuur Department of Psychiatry engaged in clinical work, consultation and research. Both maintained that persons in solitary would struggle to distinguish between reality and the assumptions and suggestions of their interrogators and thus would make unreliable statements. Those who were repeatedly told they

63 'Timeline of State Action Against the Press in the 1960s,' South African History Online, https://www.sahistory.org.za/article/timeline-state-action-against-press-1960s, accessed 23 November 2024.

64 *Cape Argus*, 23 November 1963; *Cape Times*, 18, 19 November, 17 December 1963.

65 Thompson, 'Dennis Brutus,' p. 73; Beukes, *Long Road*, ch. 2, n. 12.

would be released if they made satisfactory statements would likely alter their statements.[66]

The third expert, Kurt Danziger, born in 1926, had arrived in South Africa aged eleven, fleeing Nazi Germany with his parents. After his UCT degree, he obtained a PhD in experimental psychology from Oxford and served as vice president of the South African Psychological Association from 1961–63. Even before Danziger began studying solitary confinement he realized that laboratory animals could not be taken out of their environmental context: 'The organism apart from its environment was an abstraction that one never encountered in reality ... The unit was not the organism but an organism-environment couple.'[67]

Danziger was compelled to get involved: 'Men who had openly sympathized with Nazi Germany were now in government. Did I as a Nazi victim really have a choice?'[68] Security police and spies floated around campus, especially in the social sciences. Books were banned. 'The powers-that-be considered certain ideas to be a step too far and discussing those ideas could lead to serious repercussions.'[69] He adapted his research techniques since 'the use of a method that depended on the open expression of opinion on sensitive topics [became] more and more questionable.' He allowed the local Congress organization to use a secret room in his department to produce illegal leaflets. He soon realized that the growing use of solitary 'call[ed] for protest on specifically psychological grounds.'[70]

Although Danziger could not examine the accused, he had interviewed other South Africans released from solitary and conducted extensive research on all aspects of solitary confinement, including 'sensory deprivation and so-called brain washing, as well as police literature on interrogation techniques and published first person accounts of political prisoners who had experienced long periods of solitary confinement.'[71] He had also studied the use of isolation by totalitarian regimes: the Soviet Union, Nazi Germany and Korea. 'People had ... been puzzled by the Russian purge trials ... and why people made

66 *World Outlook*, 2, 15, April 10, 1964, pp. 15–17.

67 Kurt Danziger, 'Confessions of a Marginal Psychologist,' unpub. copy, p. 9. My thanks to Adrian C. Brock for sending this to me. Published in Leendert P. Mos, ed., *History of Psychology in Autobiography*, Heidelberg, London and New York: Springer, 2009, pp. 89–130; Joffe, *State vs. Mandela*, pp. 194–5.

68 Danziger, 'Confessions,' p. 11.

69 Adrian C. Brock, 'Rediscovering the History of Psychology: Interview with Kurt Danziger,' *History of Psychology*, 9, 1, March 2006, pp. 1–16, 8.

70 Danziger, 'Confessions,' pp. 14, 19.

71 Danziger, 'Confessions,' p. 19.

these fanciful confessions,' he told the Court. It was later learned that solitary confinement had played 'a major role' in those confessions.[72]

Just as the human body requires nutrients, Danziger explained, so the human brain needed 'a constant flow of numerous and varied experience and information ... Where that is lacking ... you are likely to get intellectual impairment and ... emotional stress occurring.'[73] The intellectual function most impaired by solitary confinement was 'the capacity for reasoning ... the capacity of the person to discriminate between degrees of falsehood and truth ... his capacity for drawing correct inferences.' Those whom he had examined after being in solitary confinement were depressed, anxious and generally drank heavily. Thus, he concluded, isolation constitutes severe stress, and 'a statement obtained from people under these conditions would be tantamount to obtaining it under duress ... It is likely to lead the person into a position where he may draw incorrect inferences from information at his disposal and ... is unlikely to be aware of this impairment [and] therefore particularly vulnerable to suggestion.'[74]

In rebuttal, the prosecution contended that psychology was a young science lacking theoretical unity and scientific status and that Danziger had no direct knowledge of the prisoners' actual conditions. Danziger replied that the study of psychology dated from Aristotle's time; that experimental psychology was at least 100 years old; that in the US there were more papers published in experimental psychology than in physics; that his own experiments were scientifically consistent; and that if the prisoners' testimonies were accurate, they had indeed experienced sensory deprivation, which at the time was seen as scientifically based.[75]

But when Justice van Heerden asked Danziger about the impact of solitary on the recounting of facts, he replied that the ability to recount facts was less likely to be impaired than the ability to reason abstractly. The judge pointed out that he was concerned with the prisoners' abilities to recount facts not to draw inferences, which was the Court's responsibility.[76] Thus, despite the testimony of the three mental health specialists, Justice van Heerden allowed the use of statements made during solitary. By comparison, when Danziger and his colleague R. C. Albino were asked by the Rivonia defence to testify at that

72 *State vs Alexander*, pp. 1203, 1196–7; Mathews and Albino, 'Permanence of the Temporary,' pp. 23, 30.

73 *State vs Alexander*, p. 1206.

74 Quoted Louw and O'Brien, 'Psychological Effects,' pp. 98–9; *Cape Times*, 8, 10 February 1964; *State vs Alexander*, p. 1245.

75 Louw and O'Brien, 'Psychological Effects,' pp. 99–100; Danziger, 'Confessions,' p. 19.

76 *State vs Alexander*, pp. 1235–7.

trial, Mr Justice Quartus de Wet would not allow them.[77] The state defied and disregarded the experts – people who base their views on study and research.

The defence continues

Solitary confinement hurt the accused in many ways, yet during their trial they managed to act rationally. Trying to demonstrate the lack of conspiracy, the defence argued that Kenneth Abrahams – at his own suggestion – was the main proponent of armed struggle, while the others either opposed violence or saw it as premature. The accused maintained these positions consistently in their statements and under cross-examination. Of course, they had been extremely distressed when Abrahams was kidnapped and brought to Cape Town. But by the time the trial began, he was safely out of South Africa. They had also hoped, in Marcus Solomon's recollection, to minimize the roles of Dulcie September, Dorothy Alexander and Doris van der Heyden, so that 'if there was any danger of conviction, they would be less guilty and be discharged.'[78]

As diverse opinionated individuals, their varied perspectives on the use of violence were consistent with the absence of a unified conspiracy. Neville Alexander told the Court he became politically active because of the university apartheid bill, but the Sharpeville massacre made him understand 'that events in South Africa had taken a revolutionary turn … that the masses would soon lose faith in passive methods.' Acknowledging that 'violence as an element of policy in social affairs corrodes the moral fibre of individuals as well as of the state,' he also recognized that sometimes 'violence is essential … For this reason,' he continued, 'I would never accept absolute pacifism as a policy either.' Once sabotage attacks began, all the political organizations began discussing armed struggle. 'We felt that since the Government was doing everything in its power to arm the White population in the form of pistol clubs, police reserves and home guards,' Alexander explained, 'the leadership should acquaint itself thoroughly with the defence measures which would be necessary in the event of a civil war.'[79] Dulcie September's childhood experiences of violence undoubtedly shaped her, but her political consciousness developed from her observations of poverty at Bridgetown Primary. She opposed violence, believing that Parliament could promote change and that 'all methods should be tried first … strikes, boycotts, formation of trade

[77] Louw and O'Brien, 'Psychological Effects,' p. 101; Joffe, *State vs. Mandela*, pp. 194–5.

[78] *State vs Alexander*, pp. 1480, 1567; Solomon to author, 1 May 2019.

[79] *State vs Alexander*, pp. 1667–9, 1657, 1659–60.

unions, demonstrations … if we can prove that those methods won't help us in the struggle, then only will we resort to violence, and only then.'[80]

Although the accused had not theorized the concept of a united front, they were trying to build one, mainly with the Unity Movement affiliates in which most were active, but also with the South West Africa People's Organisation. Bam's study group, which had attended the 18 June Bishop Lavis meeting, included members from a wider array of organizations. The prosecutor grilled Bam as to whether this meeting was an NLF or a united front event. Despite his insistence that it was a united front meeting, the prosecutor claimed it was an NLF gathering.[81] Bam was also probed on his research. He was working on a prize essay on African leadership in Cape Town, Johannesburg and the Transkei. For Cape Town he used the book *Langa* by Monica Wilson and his friend Archie Mafeje, which, coincidentally, had just been serialized in the *Cape Argus* that October–November 1963. For Johannesburg he focused on Alexandra Township, and in the Transkei he interviewed a range of leaders. However, he denied authorship of *Liberation*'s Transkei article, suggesting Ottilie Abrahams – although the piece must surely have reflected his research.[82]

Again seeking to show their diverse views, the accused claimed that in addition to pamphlets two, three and four found by the police, a pamphlet one by Neville Alexander discussed a united front strategy and a pamphlet five titled 'Organisational and Technical Aspects of the Y.C.C.C.: A critique' – purportedly by Bam but actually 'Neville's bright idea' – rebutted pamphlet three's espousal of guerrilla struggle.[83] These claims were made late in the trial, and Justice van Heerden was not convinced; in fact, neither pamphlet had been written. Nonetheless, the various articles in *Liberation* were generally each written by one person and thus reflected the author's views rather than the group's. As Doris van der Heyden pointed out, they may have all read *Liberation*, but they didn't read all the articles. When asked about *Liberation*'s reference to the 'supreme punishment' to be meted out to informers, she took it to be suspension from the group. The prosecutor scoffed. Underground groups generally took a hard line against alleged collaborators or traitors; talking or writing a hard line was easy.[84]

The accused consistently maintained that extra-parliamentary and anti-apartheid groups were concerned with secrecy due to fear of arrest. Indeed,

80 *State vs Alexander*, pp. 1560–1, 1570, 1591, 1596–7; *Cape Argus*, 18 February 1964.

81 *State vs Alexander*, pp. 1420–5.

82 *State vs Alexander*, pp. 1380–6, 1491–2; *Cape Argus*, 26 October, 2, 9, 16 November 1963; Wilson and Mafeje, *Langa*.

83 *State vs Alexander*, pp. 1356, 1811–13; Interview, van der Heyden.

84 *State vs Alexander*, pp. 1892, 1898, 1903.

remarked Alexander pointedly, the *Broederbond* was a secret organization, and although secrecy was its 'modus operandi,' it had never been investigated because of that.[85] The prosecutors made much of several small groups formed by NLF members: the Rover Soccer Club, the Excelsior Table Tennis Club and, especially, the Bursary & Loan Fund. Despite the state's claims that SASBLF funds would be used towards armed struggle, Neville Alexander categorically denied that the fund had any hidden political agenda. He was arranging bursaries for South Africans to study at West German universities, and the fund was to pay for the students' airfare, raising money through individual donations and the organization of social events. He had offered a German class for students wishing to study abroad and mentioned the names of several students who had received bursaries in 1962–63 for overseas study – Franz Lee, Ronnie Esau, Eric Petersen, and Nora and Isabella Schimming. Just before his arrest, the University of Tübingen had informed him of thirty available bursaries for study at West German universities, he told the Court.[86] So sure were the accused that the state would accept the SASBLF's bona fides, that when they learned that the state planned to call Arthur Magerman as a witness concerning the Bursary & Loan Fund, they sent word to Johannesburg through their go-between Edmond Trosée that he should testify rather than flee. Magerman duly told the Court he had met Neville Alexander at the Alexandra home of Martin Mabiletsa. They had discussed art, literature and, after Alexander mentioned that he had studied abroad with help of a bursary, the need for bursary funds for black youth. Likewise, Frederick Hufkie, the principal of Spandau High School in Graaff-Reinet who had met with Solomon, described the Bursary & Loan Fund as 'a laudable effort.' But the prosecution still insisted, without evidence, the fund was an NLF cover.[87]

Conclusion

The prosecution's case relied primarily on the documents and, as in the Rivonia Trial, the lower standard of proof offered by statutory law. While contesting the prosecution's claims, the defence was also concerned with human rights violations and common-law standards for fair trials. However, common law was being continually eroded and superseded by statutes. As the trial dragged on month after month, so did the defendants' incarceration. They were drained and exhausted; the women's periods had stopped. The courtroom thick with tension, Neville Alexander gave evidence on 18 and 19 February. His voice faltering with emotion, he claimed the police had conducted a witch-hunt,

[85] *State vs Alexander*, p. 1699.

[86] Interview, Solomon; *State vs Alexander*, pp. 1580–11, 1761–6.

[87] Phahle, 'Reminiscences,' pp. 10–11; *State vs Alexander*, pp. 187–8, 306–7; Solomon to author, 11 April 2021.

and the state was using him and his co-accused as 'scapegoats.' As he spoke, the accused women began sobbing in the dock, in pain about the past, in apprehension of what was still to come: to walk free, if the charges were dropped; to return to prison, if found guilty. Amazingly, the trial adjourned on the 20th so Bam could write his university Latin exam. The trial resumed the next day, and the defence closed its case on 24 February, once all the accused had spoken.[88]

[88] *Cape Times*, 20 February 1964; *Cape Argus*, 21 February 1964; *World Outlook*, 2, 13, 27 March 1964; interview van der Heyden; Broun, *Saving Nelson Mandela*, pp. 140–2, 149.

Chapter 6

The Verdict

Justice van Heerden gave his judgment on 15 April 1964. The courtroom was packed. The *Cape Argus*' front-page photo showed a crowd on the court's steps, women in dresses and cardigan sweaters, with kerchiefs on their heads, men in jackets and fedora hats. The defendants had been charged with contravening the Sabotage Act and so with conspiring to commit wrongful and wilful acts, Justice van Heerden reminded the court. They were also charged with inciting, instigating, commanding, advising or encouraging others to commit wrongful and wilful acts and with contravening the Suppression of Communism Act. At various meetings they were alleged to have wrongfully and unlawfully conspired so that they would have endangered public safety, law and order and property, and overthrown the government by violent revolution, guerrilla warfare and sabotage, in the process killing, murdering, damaging and destroying property and stealing arms and ammunition. Moreover, it was alleged, each of the accused had identified themselves with the Yu Chi Chan Club (YCCC)'s and the National Liberation Front (NLF)'s aims, and Don Davis had distributed their literature.[1]

The judgment rested on two claims. First, Justice van Heerden equated sabotage and high treason. Under the Sabotage Act, he observed, any person conspiring to commit acts whereby public safety and maintenance of law and order and property would be endangered, damaged or destroyed is guilty of sabotage. A person who conspired to aid or procure the commission of a wrongful act is guilty of sabotage, unless he or she can prove the offence was not calculated, the judge stated. Any hostile intent against the state is high treason.[2]

Secondly, Justice van Heerden turned to conspiracy, defined as an agreement to commit a crime. He noted that in law, any association with an organization that has the agreed aim of committing a crime means such individuals have conspired. Any individual who joins or remains in such an organization after learning of its aims is guilty of conspiracy, which did not depend on the criminal plan's execution, but occurred when individuals agreed with the

1 *State vs Alexander*, pp. 819, 1966–67; *Cape Argus*, 15 April 1964; *Cape Times*, 16 April 1964; Alexander Defense Committee, *Injustice in South Africa*, p. 2.

2 *State vs Alexander*, pp. 820, 1969–72

PART OF THE LARGE CROWD leaves the court at lunch-time to-day after hearing Dr. Neville Alexander and 10 other non-Whites convicted at the sabotage trial at the Criminal Sessions.

Figure 6: Crowd on the steps of Cape Town's Supreme Court after hearing the NLF trial verdict. Source: *Cape Argus*: 15 April 1964.

organization, tacitly or explicitly.[3] Moreover, he continued, the prosecution did not need to establish that individual conspirators were in direct contact with each other. He referred to the trial of the British Queen Victoria versus Charles Parnell, MP, and Others (25 September 1880 to 27 January 1881). That trial concerned Parnell's relationship with the Irish National Land League, a mass organization with links to the underground Fenian movement, which had members in Ireland, Britain and the United States. Britain's Liberal Government had doubted the trial would succeed; indeed, the jury split, and the case was dropped. Nonetheless, Justice van Heerden cited examples from that trial. Because Fenians lived on both sides of the Atlantic, many had never seen each other, yet their actions suggested they sought the same end, he stressed. Thus, the acts of one side became evidence against the other. It was an apt comparison. The British state took control of Ireland after England's initial colonization, and it also laid the foundations from which apartheid emerged.[4]

After summarizing the YCCC and NLF documents, Justice van Heerden noted the defence argument that production of documents did not prove the contents, and that irrespectively, the court would still have to prove conspiracy. The judge rejected this defence claim, citing Criminal Procedure Act 56 of 1955. He argued that Act 56 indicated both that possession of a document was *prima facie* proof of the association, and that evidence ordinarily inadequate to convey proof would afford *prima facie* proof. While the judge agreed with the defence that production of a document was not per se evidence, nonetheless, he concluded, the documents disclosed the type of reading material 'whether or not the events … actually took place or the information supplied is authentic.'[5]

In sum, the court was satisfied that the NLF was the continuation of the YCCC and that its documents were not those of a study group aimed at

3 *State vs Alexander*, pp. 822, 1984; C. R. Snyman, 'The History and Rationale of Criminal Conspiracy,' *Comparative and International Law Journal of Southern Africa*, 17, 1, January 1984, pp. 65–77, 65. Section 112 (1), Criminal Procedure Act 56 of 1955, *Union Gazette Extraordinary*, 1 July 1955, p. 62, distinguished between the conspiracy to commit an act and the actual act, even though both allowed the attorney-general to bypass the jury: 'Whenever an attorney-general decides to indict an accused upon a charge of treason, sedition or public violence, or of an attempt, conspiracy or incitement to commit such an offence, and is of opinion that, if the accused were tried by a jury, the ends of justice are likely to be defeated, he shall state in writing to the Minister such his opinion and the facts upon which it is based and specify the offence for which he proposes to indict the accused.'

4 The judge cited R. vs Meyrick, which discussed The Queen (at the prosecution of The Attorney-General for Ireland) vs Charles Stewart Parnell, M. P., and Others, *State vs Alexander*, pp. 822, 1984–85; David Howell, *A Lost Left: Three Studies in Socialism and Nationalism*, Manchester: Manchester University Press, 1986, p. 86; David Howell to author, 3–4 September 2024.

5 *State vs Alexander*, pp. 823, 1984.

studying politics and forming united fronts, but rather of a paramilitary organization with military and political aims, which 'by means of a combination of political agitation and guerrilla warfare … aimed at the overthrow of the Government.'[6] The defence countered that the documents were selective and that NLF members had diverse rather than unitary views. But Justice van Heerden rejected this, concluding that in establishing the NLF's existence and aims,

> the State has succeeded in showing that if the said acts had been committed the safety of the public and the maintenance of law and order would have been endangered; that property of the State and other persons would have been destroyed and that persons would have been maliciously killed and murdered.[7]

Advocate Gordon argued the Sabotage Act did not apply to treason, but only to specific acts willingly and negligently or accidentally committed. Conspiring to overthrow the state was high treason, which could never be negligent or accidental. Therefore, Parliament did not intend the statute on sabotage to embrace and usurp the greater crime of treason. However, the judge maintained that the Sabotage Act created a new offence of sabotage as a wrongful act resulting in any specific effect. The act was already wrongful, illegal or wilful. If the state failed to prove a wrongful act, then no offence would have been committed. But if the offence were established, the accused must show that it was unintentional.[8] Prosecutor Nöthling contended that 'any wrongful or willful act' was intended to cover 'a wide field of conduct,' and that acts with hostile intent such as militarily possessing towns, occupying public buildings, destroying Government property and disarming the police would be high treason. Of course, none of those remotely related to the NLF's activities. But the judge concurred with the prosecutor that 'the Legislature … has in fact equated sabotage with high treason.' Here, the advocate and the judge were both seemingly concerned with the legislature's intentions, but they approached the problem from different starting points, the advocate from common law, the judge from statutory law. Both Dugard and Le Roux and Davis note that under common law the standards of proof for treason were harder than those for sabotage under the Sabotage Act.[9]

6 *State vs Alexander*, p. 824.

7 *State vs Alexander*, pp. 824, 2006–7.

8 *State vs Alexander*, pp. 820–1, 1968.

9 *State vs Alexander*, pp. 1970, 821; Dugard, *Human Rights*, pp. 230–1; Le Roux and Davis, *Lawfare*, pp. 89–90. Le Roux and Davis, *Lawfare*, p. 89, note that two months later Justice de Wet gave his judgment at the Rivonia Trial. 'The crime of which the accused have been convicted … the crime of conspiracy, is in essence one of

To no avail, Advocate Gordon reminded the court that unlike other sabotage cases, no acts of sabotage had been committed, no arms or bombs had been found and no decision to engage in violence taken. It was 'a tiny weak movement without any possibility of implementing its plans.' And although it was 'a serious case … no serious crime had been committed.'[10] No matter. The accused were found guilty based on hypotheticals.

Then came the sentences, which reflected Justice van Heerden's view of each member's length and degree of involvement. Neville Alexander, Don Davis, Marcus Solomon, Elizabeth van der Heyden and Fikele Bam were each sentenced to ten years; Lionel Davis and Gordon Hendricks to seven years; and Leslie van der Heyden, Dulcie September, Dorothy Alexander and Doris van der Heyden, deemed to be ordinary members of three to four months duration, to five years. However much the accused had tried to steel themselves, emotionally they and their families had hoped for a discharge. The guilty verdicts and the length of the sentences were a shock. The stunned silence as the sentences were pronounced was broken only by Dorothy Alexander's high-pitched wail.[11]

The defence sought leave to appeal, first, that the court had erred in finding beyond a reasonable doubt that the YCCC/NLF had agreed to the state's overthrow by violent revolution, guerilla warfare and sabotage. Secondly, the court had not proved beyond a reasonable doubt that the accused were *ad item* – of a meeting of minds – sufficient to constitute indictable conspiracy to violently overthrow the state. Thirdly, it had not proved beyond reasonable doubt that the alleged conspiracy happened at the meetings alleged in the indictment. Fourthly, it was wrong to find that the state established beyond reasonable doubt that the bursary and loan fund was an NLF cover and that the accused who participated in its activities thought that. Fifthly, it had not proved beyond reasonable doubt that accused numbers five and eleven – Fikile Bam and Gordon Hendricks – were NLF members, which both denied. Sixthly, it had not proved beyond reasonable doubt that Bam was an NLF agent. Finally, the sentences for accused one, two, three, four, five, six and eleven – Neville Alexander, Don Davis, Solomon, Elizabeth van der Heyden, Bam, Lionel Davis and Hendricks – were excessive.

On 27 May 1964 Justice van Heerden refused their application to appeal – he did not see 'any reasonable prospect' of an appeal's success. It was not the court's role to decide whether the country's laws were oppressive to any category of people, the judge stated, although he accepted that the accused, as

---

high treason. The state has decided not to charge the crime in this form.' The judiciary variously thought that sabotage and conspiracy equalled treason and prosecuted them under the Sabotage Act.

10 *Cape Times*, 16 April 1964

11 *Cape Times*, 16 April 1964; interview, van der Heyden; Solomon to author, 1 May 2019.

intellectuals, would see themselves as oppressed. Sidestepping any possibility of mitigation on ethical grounds, he saw his task as evaluating and applying the statutes based solely on Parliament's intentions. Common-law notions would not apply. He was, indeed, to use Dyzenhaus' term, a 'plain fact' judge.[12]

However, Justice van Heerden allowed the defence application to put two special entries on the record and reserve two questions of law. The first special entry concerned the court's refusal to order Police Constable Kotzee to produce and be cross-examined on his notes, which the defence deemed an 'irregularity or illegality.' The second special entry related to Detective-Sergeant van Wyk and other police and prison officials having read the sixty-page privileged document from the accused to their lawyers. On 20 April Neville Alexander, in prison garb, head shaved, was back in court for questioning on this point. Nonetheless, the judge accepted 'without hesitation' van Wyk's word that he had never seen the instructions. He found that members of the prison service were indeed entitled to read prisoners' instructions to counsel to ascertain that the documents were solely for their defence. But it might have been irregular for the head of the prison to delegate this task to subordinates, he conceded.[13]

The first question of law concerned whether it was permissible for a prosecutor to cross-examine an accused person about a written statement made while detained in solitary under the Sabotage Act. Gordon argued that under common law an accused could not incriminate himself unless his evidence was shown to have been freely and voluntarily given – which was impossible under the Sabotage Act. Although the judge had ruled that the Court could determine whether actions were made freely and voluntarily, as in giving handwriting samples, he nonetheless reserved the question. The second question of law concerned whether the judge had erred in telling the accused that evidence from the dock 'may not carry the same weight' as that given under oath from the witness box. Gordon maintained that the judge should have told them that evidence from the dock 'would definitely carry less weight.' However, Justice van Heerden rejected this argument as well. The matters were reviewed and dismissed a year later in March 1965 by Newton Ogilvie Thompson, Wessels and Potgieter. Again, common-law rights would not apply.[14]

[12] *State vs Alexander, Application for Leave to Appeal, Special Entries to be Made and Questions of Law*, Judgment delivered 27 May 1964 (Supreme Court of South Africa, Cape of Good Hope Provincial Division), pp. 2149–51; *Cape Times*, 16 April 1964; David Dyzenhaus, *Hard Cases in Wicked Legal Systems: Pathologies of Legality*, Oxford: Oxford University Press, 2010, pp. 38–9, 48–9; David Dyzenhaus, *Judging the Judges, Judging Ourselves: Truth, Reconciliation and the Apartheid Legal Order*, Oxford: Hart, 1998, pp. 16–19.

[13] *State vs Alexander*, pp. 2151–2, 2156–62, 2169; *World Outlook*, 2, 20, 15 May 1964, pp. 16–18.

[14] *State vs Alexander*, pp. 2164–9; S v Alexander and others (1) 1965 (2) SA 796 (A), 25 March 1965, *South African Law Reports*, June 1965, vol. 2, pp. 797–817; Alexander Defense Committee, *Injustice in South Africa*, p. 3.

***

At the heart of the 1963–64 National Liberation Front trial – *State versus Alexander* – was the contested nature of thinking in apartheid South Africa. The concept that individuals are not punished for their thought dates at least to the Roman Empire.[15] Although this thought crime doctrine has been periodically challenged, we are hopefully a long way from England's 1351 Treason Act, which held a person who 'compasses or imagines the [king's] death' to be guilty of treason.[16]

The thought crime doctrine and the act requirement hold that a person is punished for what one does, not what he or she thinks.[17] Thinking is protected because it is intrinsic to being a distinct human being. It is 'how persons sustain and strengthen themselves, as the particular person that they are,' argues Jordan Wallace-Wolf. The personality develops through thinking and withers without it, so it is crucial for mental health. Thinking as a commitment to understanding the world is also fundamental to freedom. We reach understanding through both correct assessments and mistakes, so reaching an incorrect conclusion is as important as reaching a correct one. As Albert Einstein said: 'Failure is success in progress.'[18]

The process of thinking consists of beliefs and intentions. A belief is what we think is true; an intention is what we think we should do – the answer to the question, 'what is to be done?' Wallace-Wolf points out that an intention continues a belief, but changes it into a new form, providing a bridge between beliefs and actions. But drawing on the thought crime doctrine, only the act should be punishable since antisocial thoughts do not necessarily lead to antisocial acts.[19] The apartheid system, however, was premised on preventing people from considering what was true and what should be done. This is shown by the regime's systematic repression of education at all levels for the black majority, which in turn reflected its quest for acquiescence. In a society ruled by statutes, intimidation and force, the state can hardly allow freedom of thought.

15 *Cogitationis poenam nemo patitur* ['Nobody endures punishment for thought']. Thanks to Jordan Wallace-Wolf for this.

16 Thanks to Gabriel Mendlow for this example.

17 Gabriel Mendlow, 'Why is it Wrong to Punish Thought?' *Yale Law Journal*, 127, 8, 2017–18, pp. 2345–86; Gabriel Mendlow, 'Thoughts, Crimes, and Thought Crimes,' *Michigan Law Review*, 118, 2020, pp. 841–76; Jordan James Wallace-Wolf, 'Mental Privacy,' PhD, University of California, Los Angeles, 2020; Abraham S. Goldstein, 'Conspiracy to Defraud the United States,' *Yale Law Journal*, 68, 1959, pp. 405–63.

18 Wallace-Wolf, 'Mental Privacy,' pp. 11, 21–2, 24–5.

19 Wallace-Wolf, 'Mental Privacy,' pp. 33–4, 47.

Turning thought into a crime flowed directly from apartheid and into the legal system. Not only did the crackdown on black education seek to impede critical thinking and promote acquiescence. During the trial, the disregard for critical thinking about solitary confinement was seen in the judge's rejection of expert opinion, a disregard seen also in the Rivonia Trial. Moreover, apartheid's rule by statute law and the court's increasing disregard for common law reflected the state's arbitrary power, which is antithetical to thought.

Legal discussions of thought crime are framed in terms of the individual, but conspiracy involves more than one person. There are numerous steps between an individual's thoughts – and his or her thought crimes – and conspiracy. The individual thinker must proceed to collective thinking, for starters, exchanging ideas in classrooms, discussion clubs and among friends or comrades. Once a thought is voiced to others, it is transformed into collective thinking, which involves agreement and disagreement and is a necessary part of human society. But there are still crucial steps between collective thinking and conspiracy, namely collective criminal thinking and collective intent. Individuals may harbour thought crimes in their head and voice them to others, who might even agree with the ideas. But this is still not conspiracy, a collective agreement to commit a crime, let alone carry it out.

For criminal behaviour to take place, an individual moves from thinking to holding a belief, to a thought crime, to intention about what should be done, to an aim or purpose, to a decision to act, to preparation for the act and finally to the criminal act. A group moves from collective thinking, to a shared belief, to criminal thinking, to intention, to an aim or purpose, to an agreement to act – conspiracy – then to preparation and finally to the criminal act. Even if a conspiracy can be proven, there is still the matter of activating the agreement to commit a crime. It is difficult to determine when criminal intent is transformed into preparation for action dangerous to a community. In American law, Abraham Goldstein observed, the law of attempts asks, in a linear fashion, at what point criminal intent goes beyond preparatory action to start consummating an act. By contrast, rather than a linear explanation, the law of solicitations – sometimes called incitement – examines the context indicating the probability that an aggressive statement will be transformed into harmful action. But these points are rarely answered with certainty: conspiracy is an extremely elastic concept that allows those applying it to adapt it to their ends.[20]

In *State versus Alexander* Justice van Heerden leapt over the steps of collective thinking, shared beliefs and collective criminal intent, landing directly at conspiracy but without considering preparation and consummation of the act. Statute law did not allow such nuances. NLF members, despite their

20 Goldstein, 'Conspiracy to Defraud,' p. 406.

diverse views, typically had a positive belief in guerrilla struggle and an intent to engage in a future guerrilla war – if necessary. At the time of their arrests, they had written documents and set up groups to study guerrilla struggle. So, they were at the stage of collective thinking about guerrilla struggle and planning study groups, a slow process, as potential group members had to be identified and assembled, literature printed, distributed and read, and discussions to take place. When Neville Alexander returned from Johannesburg in July 1963, for example, he had not made progress on these points. By all accounts, he had discussed only the need for bursary funds to support student travel. There is no evidence that he had even identified prospective NLF members.

If the individual's right to freedom of thought, including thought crime, is generally seen as fundamental, the matter is murkier when we consider groups. States fear collective thinking, even that lacking criminal intent, far more than individual thinking. Thought crime becomes intolerable for states when it moves from the individual to the collective, even when no criminal act has occurred. The 'mystique of numbers' becomes the measure of danger precisely because collective thinking makes collective action possible. In conspiracy doctrine, argued Goldstein, a state of mind becomes the rationale for preventive action against individuals who allegedly threaten society but have not come near executing the threat.[21] Even in Orwell's *1984*, it is only when the two protagonists exchange their views, question Big Brother's power and share their thoughts with a third person that the state moves from surveillance to brutal action. The thought crime doctrine and the act requirement collapse when faced with more than one person.

It is no surprise that Justice van Heerden was so concerned that through their role as intellectuals NLF members could expand their influence: 'Most of you are teachers [and one] a preacher … you were in a position where you could influence others and persuade them to a course of conduct which you had planned and decided on as the most effective … You are not criminals in the sense that we usually have to deal with in these courts.'[22] No, they were thinkers.

[21] Goldstein, 'Conspiracy to Defraud,' p. 406.

[22] *State vs Alexander*, pp. 2026–7.

Conclusion

The white-minority apartheid regime engaged in the intellectual repression of the black majority to promote acquiescence and so maintain itself in power. But black South Africans resisted through various means, including self-education. This book has traced the efforts of the tiny National Liberation Front, part of the transnational New Left movement, to form cells aimed at education about guerrilla struggle. Yet despite its aspirations to form a united front with like-minded groups, the National Liberation Front remained isolated from popular organizations. Nonetheless, the South African state saw its members as threats precisely because their writings challenged people to think critically about overthrowing apartheid.

Of the broad types of political trials outlined in the introduction, the trial of *State versus Neville Alexander and Ten Others* falls into Ronald Christenson's typology of a partisan trial aiming to eliminate dissenting opposition – removing intellectuals from circulation – to further entrench ethnic or racial domination.[1] As the state was intensifying its repression of black South Africans, a tiny group of intellectuals broke from the abstentionist Unity Movement, hoping to promote a political approach combining education and activism.

Trials that criminalize critics of political regimes permeate society by creating ripples spreading far beyond the individuals convicted of anti-regime crimes. The families and close friends of the incarcerated suffer psychological trauma and economic hardship if a breadwinner is imprisoned. These trials hurt countless others, too. Many South Africans were compelled to flee the country because of their association with the NLF and other leftist groups or banned for refusing to testify for the state; some of these would have constituted the New Left generation. The fates of four individuals whose lives intersected with the NLF illustrate apartheid's reach and the varieties of suffering it produced, even for those on the trial's periphery.

German-born Psychology Professor Kurt Danziger testified at the trial. The regime saw his public pronouncements against solitary confinement as a threat, although his high profile provided some protection. '[A]s each turn of the screw of state sponsored racial oppression led to further and more

1 Christenson, 'Political Theory of Political Trials,' p. 555.

desperate acts of resistance,' recalled Danziger, 'the precariousness of the situation became quite palpable.' After the trial he became 'a marked man,' subjected to increasing harassment and intimidation. Castigated in Parliament as an agitator, the detainees he worked with were interrogated about him, his home and car were attacked by vigilantes, and his passport confiscated. Danziger left South Africa in 1965 as a 'prohibited person,' knowing that his return would lead to his arrest.[2]

By contrast, Dutch-born Edmond Trosée, the Cape Town–Johannesburg go-between, lacked a public profile. Followed by the police, arriving home beaten on several occasions, around August 1965 he left Kalk Bay for Johannesburg, 'extremely agitated,' giving his sister Francisca Trosée Hewett his contact book with instructions to burn it if he did not return. Six to eight weeks later, the police contacted Francisca and said her brother had died by suicide – although evidently leaving no note. On 3 October 1965 he fell some twenty feet from a bridge over Harrow Road [now Joe Slovo Drive] near the intersection with Louis Botha Avenue in Yeoville. Witness Mr A. Hausman told the police that while driving on Harrow Road towards the bridge around 3:55 pm, he saw a man fall over the handrail, horizontally, soundlessly, his head pointing downhill on the inclined road, his legs uphill, landing in front of Hausman's car. An elderly grey-haired man wearing a hat and gloves – it was a cold, cloudy day – was on the bridge. 'I couldn't stop him,' he said, then 'mysteriously disappeared.' When Francisca and her husband went to Johannesburg, the mortuary staff allowed her to see her brother's battered and discoloured head, but not his body. The police returned his raincoat, which had a circular blood stain on the back, but did not release his body nor return any other items of clothing. When Francisca questioned this, the police asked her if she loved her children. The couple returned to Kalk Bay; the family held a memorial service without a body.[3]

The Magistrate concluded that Trosée's death was not due to negligence. However, as of 24 November 1965, 'he was not prepared to hold a formal Inquest … but would postpone the hearing sine die,' that is, indefinitely. He must have changed his mind, though, as the family was notified that his report would be read out on 23 December 1965.[4] Almost six decades later, an independent evaluation of the medical report made the following points. One, it was strange that Trosée jumped from a relatively low bridge, as a fall from twenty feet can be survivable. Two, he was alive when he fell and died of head

2 Danziger, 'Confessions,' unpub. copy, pp. 13, 20.

3 Quote, handwritten statement of family member based on discussion with A. Hausman, 3 October 1965; *Rand Daily Mail*, 3, 4 October 1965; Lorette Espi to author, 30 September, 2 October 2022.

4 Baskin & Cohen to Asherson & Asherson, 24 November 1965; Magistrate's Court, Johannesburg, to Mrs Francisca A. Hewitt, Kalk Bay, 13 December 1965.

trauma. Three, he had no injuries on his hands and arms. Usually conscious people throw out their hands when they fall and have extensive injuries of their hands and arms. This raises the possibility that he was unconscious when he fell. Good practice suggests the medical examiner should have taken photographs before and during the autopsy and issued toxicology reports as part of the forensic investigation. If this was done, the family did not receive the material. Although the cause of death was certain, unusually, the medical examiner did not determine the manner of death, whether suicide, homicide or accident.[5] The failure of the police to release Trosée's body keeps alive the possibility that he died at their hands.

Two other individuals, Basil February and Irmgard Bolle, had close emotional ties to one or more of the NLF trialists. Having fled the country, February and his friend James April heard radio reports of the NLF sentences while they were in Lobatse, Bechuanaland. February had planned to continue his studies while abroad, but anger at the harsh sentences compelled him to join Umkhonto we Sizwe. He and April reached Czechoslovakia for military training in June 1965, returned to Zambia in May 1966, then proceeded to Tanzania, waiting to be infiltrated back home. Part of Umkhonto's Luthuli Detachment, they were sent to Wankie, Rhodesia in August 1967 and engaged in battle. Their unit split, with February's group heading towards Lupane, and April's towards South Africa. February was evidently killed by police during a shoot-out on a farm in Figtree, near Bulawayo, dying on 15 August 1967. His family was notified of his death by none other than Spyker van Wyk. On 29 October 2024 February was finally laid to rest in Somerset West, South Africa.[6]

The German student Irmgard Bolle met Neville Alexander while they were students at the University of Tübingen. She worked on African affairs in the Socialist German Students' Union – the SDS. She and Franz Lee formed a tiny

[5] Email from Dr Edward Adelstein, MD, Pathology, Anatomic Pathology & Clinical Pathology, University of Missouri, 9 October 2022 regarding *Report on a medico-legal post-mortem examination, post-mortem serial no. 3016/65*, 26 October 1965, Dr Herrman Lazarus. My emails of 27 November 2022 and 27 July 2024 to the Wits Division of Forensic Medicine and Pathology have gone unanswered.

[6] *Cape Argus*, 28 September, 26 October 1963; Nicole van Driel, 'The life and death of Basil February,' *Politicsweb*, 28 October 2024, https://www.politicsweb.co.za/opinion/basil-february-a-hero-to-friend-and-foe; Dennis Cruywagen, 'At last, Basil February is back in his fatherland,' *Vrye Weekblad*, 1 November 2024, https://www.vryeweekblad.com/en/opinions-and-debate/2024-11-01-at-last-basil-february-is-back-in-his-fatherland; Judith February, 'Freedom fighter Basil February laid to rest in SA at last, more than five decades after his death on foreign soil,' *Daily Maverick*, 1 November 2024, https://www.dailymaverick.co.za/article/2024-11-01-freedom-fighter-basil-february-laid-to-rest-at-last-in-sa-more-than-five-decades-after-his-death-on-foreign-soil; all accessed 3 November 2024; 'James April,' 55–9; van Driel, 'Journey to Wankie,' 27–30.

NLF cell, and after the NLF arrests began, they set up the first Alexander Defence Committee, with Lee as secretary and Bolle as treasurer. Bolle maintained a warm correspondence with Neville's mother, but she had a challenging time. The right-wing *German Student Advertiser* claimed that Alexander was 'a Black racialist who wanted to liquidate all the Whites in South Africa and also the liberal friends of the Blacks,' adding that student contributors to Alexander's defence wanted their money back.[7] While attending Ernst Bloch's seminars at Tübingen, Bolle met fellow student Heide Schlüpmann. Later, they studied together in Frankfurt, becoming close friends, 'discussing topics of our philosophical studies and also our experiences with male dominance in the university,' recalled Schlüpmann. Bolle told Schlüpmann about her love for Neville – she kept his photo on her desk. Perhaps Bolle was suffering from depression or traumatic stress. She left Frankfurt 'in a fairly desperate state,' recalled Schlüpmann, and died not long after, on 25 January 1969, when her car hit a tree along the Cologne–Frankfurt motorway.[8]

Of course, the apartheid regime's physical, intellectual and emotional cruelty is well known. It censored writers, thinkers and artists, while stunting educational opportunities to impede the black majority from considering how to challenge the repressive system. The NLF trial was a stark warning that collective thinking expressed through discussing and writing about such challenges was a crime.

***

Tiny groups are often evaluated in terms of their relationships with large groups or movements. But those relationships are varied and complex. As one example, Tom Lodge argued that the South African Communist Party (SACP)'s significance lay in its ability to influence the ANC, the future dominant party.[9] Whether the SACP influenced the ANC or vice versa or whether they influenced each other remains subject to debate. By comparison, Livingstone Mqotsi contended that members of the minute underground Workers Party merged into the Unity Movement, trying to impose their discipline on the broader organization. But their discipline assumed that political consciousness taught by intellectuals must precede mass action. Those intellectuals emphasized ideas,

7 Archie L. Dick, 'Learning from the Alexander Defence Committee archives,' in Aziz Choudry and Salim Vally, eds, *Reflections on Knowledge, Learning and Social Movements: History's Schools*, Abingdon: Routledge, 2017, 42–54; Archie Dick to author, 24 July 2024; *Cape Times*, 1 August 1964.

8 Heide Schlüpmann to author, 13 September 2022.

9 Lodge, *Red Road*, pp. 336–7.

argued Mqotsi, while neglecting their implementation through mass struggle.[10] Both the ANC's declining fortunes and the Unity Movement's collapse – two very different trajectories – suggest that evaluating small groups solely in terms of their relationships with larger groups is an inadequate measuring stick.

The NLF was not part of a broader organization, but it hoped to build a united front that could support a popular movement. Its young and idealistic members were aware of the limitations of the SACP's Stalinism and the Unity Movement's rigid bureaucracy. In breaking with the Old Left, its members shared characteristics with young people in other parts of world. Its focus on education was both a reaction to Bantu Education and university apartheid and a continuation of the Unity Movement's intellectual orientation, although they tried to transcend the Unity Movement's rigidity through a creative combination of studying, teaching and learning in non-hierarchical cells. Step by step, they formed study groups that might eventually become – but were not yet – guerrilla cells. They promoted a careful approach to political struggle through small group discussions and lectures that included men and women. But talking and writing about armed struggle was anathema to the state, which pre-empted guerrilla struggle by clamping down brutally on the liberation movement. Since the Cape was supposed to be relatively controllable, Elizabeth van der Heyden speculated, perhaps the state feared they were starting a new force. '[V]ery slowly in our trial we could see the way things were going. That they were going to hammer us, this group of intellectuals.'[11]

States often engage in intellectual repression, and Orwell's *1984* offers a sweeping motivation for such repression – to obtain acquiescence to the status quo. Thought crime's essence is constant: states denigrate, disparage and criminalize thinking to intimidate people from using their brains freely and fully. After all, to think is to challenge. Thought crime flourishes both in authoritarian states and in those striving to become authoritarian. However, what states deem to be thought crime varies from one country to the next. Each state's history and characteristics shape its views of what constitutes thought crime. Likewise, what a state sees as thought crime evolves over time as its concerns shift. For the South African state, born from colonial and imperial conquest, thought crime initially concerned what it deemed as efforts to foster hostility between blacks and whites. This was seen in the 1927 Native Administration Act under which communists and other activists had been charged. But this supposed 'hostility' was in fact communication between blacks and whites, which the state saw as a threat to the racial order. In the early apartheid and Cold War era, when fear of communism was pervasive, the 1950 Suppression of Communism Act was cast so broadly

10 L. Mqotsi, 'After Soweto: Another Response,' *Review of African Political Economy*, 6, 14, 1979, pp. 97–106, 100–1.

11 Scanlon, *Representation,* 210; interview, van der Heyden.

that any government critic could be charged. A decade later in the context of ongoing anti-colonial and anti-imperial struggles around the world, thought crime was expanded further through the Sabotage Act to include discussions about guerrilla struggle. While the judiciary might have mediated between political activists and the executive, with the increasing use of statutory law it came down overwhelmingly on the side of the executive and the police.

Orwell's totalitarian state is static: Oceania's struggle is between the inner and outer party which form the state bureaucracy, while the proles are passive. There is no way out of the system. But life is in constant flow and always offers possibilities for change. The importance of South Africa's ephemeral New Left is not only that it illustrates the international reach of the New Left movement and offers us a glimpse of other socialist possibilities. Crucially, its brief history reminds us that alongside all the physical and economic controls over the black majority, limiting thought was central to apartheid – as the Black Consciousness movement understood less than a decade later: 'the most potent weapon in the hands of the oppressor is the mind of the oppressed,' observed Steve Biko.[12] Rejecting the state's claim of black inferiority, the NLF's study groups, however few in number, were a means of resistance and empowerment. But this South African New Left was not only cerebral. It recognized that its predecessor, the Unity Movement, was collapsing due to its failure to accept that ideas come from daily life and struggle as much as from books, and that ideas and activism had to be linked. This significance is even more acute today when our freedom to think, speak and act collectively is under siege.

12 'White Racism and Black Consciousness,' Speech by Steve Biko, Abe Bailey Institute, Cape Town, January 1971, in Thomas G. Karis and Gail M. Gerhart, eds, *From Protest to Challenge: A Documentary History of African Politics in South Africa, 1882–1990*, vol. 5, Bloomington and Indianapolis, Indiana University Press, 1997, pp. 466–74, 471.

BIBLIOGRAPHY

Collected papers and archives

Neville Alexander Papers, University of Cape Town Manuscripts & Archives [hereafter UCTMA], BC1538

Berta Green Langston Papers, Holt Labor Library Digital Collection, HLL_BGL_01_01_015.pdf, Cal State University Dominguez Hills Archives and Special Collections

Nelson Mandela Notebook, Nelson Mandela Centre of Memory, Johannesburg

A. H. Murray Papers, University of Cape Town Manuscripts & Archives [UCTMA], BC1253

Andreas Shipanga Papers, National Archives of Namibia, Windhoek, NAN AACR LS 212

University of Cape Town Centre for Popular Memory [hereafter UCTCPM]

Western Cape Archives, Cape Town

Interviews by author

Kenneth Abrahams, Windhoek, February 1988, Basel Africa Library, PA 153, TPA153_20_A

Kenneth Abrahams, Jr., Windhoek, 16 October 2022

Ottilie Abrahams, Windhoek, 28 February 1988, Basel Africa Library, PA 153, TAA18_9_A, TAA18_9_B

Florence Adams, Woodstock, Cape Town, 22 May 2018

Neville Alexander, Cape Town, 14 March 1988 and c. April 1988, Basel Africa Library, PA 153, TPA153_8_A

Michael Arendse, Rondebosch, Cape Town, May 2018

Harry Boesak, Windhoek, 16 October 2022

Norman Bromberger, Stellenbosch, June 2018

Lionel Davis, Cape Town, 6 May 2019

Lorette Espi, Noordhoek, Cape Town, 1 October 2022

Ursula Fataar, Wynberg, Cape Town, 24 June 2018

Nina Hassim, Cape Town, 10 May 2019

Baruch Hirson, London, April 1987

Kenneth Jordaan, Harare, 14 December 1987

Charles Kauraisa, Windhoek, 20 October 2022

Judge Robin Marais, Cape Town, 21 September 2022

James Marsh, Kenwyn, Cape Town, 30 June 2018

Ismail Mohamed, Johannesburg, May 1988
Frank Musson, Cape Town, 10 August 2022
Seymour Papert, Cambridge, Massachusetts, December 1988
Roseinnes Phahle, Johannesburg, 2, 7 July 2018
John Samuels, Cape Town, 11 February 1988
Marcus Solomon, Rylands, Cape Town, 15 June 2018 (with Lungisile Ntsebeza), 7 May 2019
Elizabeth van der Heyden, Elfindale, Cape Town, 8 June, 9 July 2018
Murray van Heerden, Senior Counsel, Cape Town, 10 August 2022

Interviews by August Matsemela

Kenneth Abrahams, 1988, UCTCPM BC1223, https://ibali.uct.ac.za/s/center-for-popular-memory/item/104408
Ottilie Abrahams, Windhoek, 31 October, 3 November 1988, UCTCPM BC1223, https://ibali.uct.ac.za/s/center-for-popular-memory/item/104407
Neville Alexander, September 1988, UCTMA BC1538 A2.1–2.4
Fikile Bam, UCTCPM, item 104311, https://ibali.uct.ac.za/s/center-for-popular-memory/item/104311
Anonymous, UCTCPM, item 104261, https://ibali.uct.ac.za/s/center-for-popular-memory/item/104261

Interviews by others

Ottilie Abrahams, interview by Tor Sellström, Windhoek, 16 March 1995, https://nai.uu.se/library/resources/liberation-africa/interviews/ottilie-abrahams.html
Fikile Bam, interview by Len Morris, Cape Town, 2 August 1999, www.columbia.edu/cu/lweb/digital/collections/oral_hist/carnegie/pdfs/fikile-bam.pdf
Fikile Bam, interview by University of Cape Town Legal Resource Centre Oral History Project, 29 November 2007
Lionel Davis, interview by Jane Harries, UCTCPM, 13 June 1997, Pin 11.05a, 11.05b
'Gerald Giose, National Liberation Front/Yu Chi Chan Club – ANC/Umkhonto we Sizwe,' interview by Tor Sellström, Cape Town, 6 December 1995 in Tor Sellström, ed., *Liberation in Southern Africa – Regional and Swedish Voices: Interviews from Angola, Mozambique, Namibia, South Africa, Zimbabwe, the Frontline and Sweden*, 2nd. ed., Uppsala: Nordiska Afrikainstitutet, 2002, pp. 122–7, https://www.diva-portal.org/smash/get/diva2:272726/FULLTEXT01.pdf
Gerald Gordon, interview by Eve Horwitz, April 1985, UCT Kaplan Centre for Jewish Studies, mss_bc949_ct_tr_gordon_g
Charles Kauraisa, interview by Tor Sellström, Windhoek, 20 March 1995, https://nai.uu.se/library/resources/liberation-africa/interviews/charles-kauraisa.html
Stephanie Kemp, interview by Julie Frederikse, London, 1986, South African History Archive, http://www.saha.org.za/nonracialism/transcript_of_interview_stephanie_kemp.htm

Legal documents

Criminal Procedure Act 56 of 1955, Section 112 (1), *Union Gazette Extraordinary*, 1 July 1955

General Law Amendment Act no. 76, 1962 [Sabotage Act], *Government Gazette Extraordinary*, 27 June 1962, pp. 57–71

Native Administration Act No 38, 1927, Padraig O'Malley, *The Heart of Hope: South Africa's Transition from Apartheid to Democracy*, https://omalley.nelson-mandela.org/index.php/site/q/03lv01538/04lv01646/05lv01768.htm

Abrahams v Minister of Justice and Others, Cape Provincial Division, 30 August 1963, 1963 (4) SA 542 (C), *South African Law Reports*, 1963, vol. 4 (November), 353, p. 629, http://jutastat.juta.co.za/nxt/gateway.dll/salr/3/24156/24754/24785?f=templates$fn=default.htm

State versus Neville Alexander and Ten Others (Supreme Court of South Africa, Appellate Division)

State versus Neville Alexander and Ten Others, Heads of Argument for Appellants (Supreme Court of South Africa, Appellate Division)

State versus Neville Alexander and Ten Others, The State's Main Heads of Argument (Supreme Court of South Africa, Appellate Division)

State versus Neville Alexander and Ten Others, Application for Leave to Appeal, Special Entries to be Made and Questions of Law, Judgment delivered 27 May 1964 (Supreme Court of South Africa, Cape of Good Hope Provincial Division)

S v Alexander and others (2) 1965 (2) SA818 (C), Cape Provincial Division, Judgment 15 April 1964, *South African Law Reports*, 1965/Volume 2 (June), http://jutastat.juta.co.za/nxt/gateway.dll/salr/3/22834/231113/23146?f=templates$fn=default.htm

S v Alexander and others (1) 1965 (2) SA795 (A), Appellate Division, Judgment 25 March 1965, *South African Law Reports*, 1965/Volume 2 (June), pp. 797–817, http://jutastat.juta.co.za/nxt/gateway.dll/salr/3/22834/231113/23145?f=templates$fn=default.htm

Newspapers, periodicals and web sites

Cape Argus

Cape Times

Liberation

The Namibian

Nature

New Era

South African History Online, https://www.sahistory.org.za

South West Africa

South-West Commentator

South West News

The Soyan

The Student, *Students Primer*, *Students Journal* and *News Bulletin*

Sunday Times

SWAPO Cape Town Branch

The Torch
Windhoek Advertiser
Windhoek Observer
World Outlook

Published works

'1960: Macmillan speaks of "wind of change" in Africa,' http://news.bbc.co.uk/onthisday/hi/dates/stories/february/3/newsid_2714000/2714525.stm.

Abrahams, Peter, 'Lonesome' [1942] in Stephen Gray, ed., *The Penguin Book of Southern African Stories*, London: Penguin, 1985, pp. 121–5.

Abrahams, Peter, *Tell Freedom: Memories of Africa*, London: Faber & Faber, 1954.

Abrahams, Yvette, 'Tribute to "Mother of Education",' *The Namibian*, 4 July 2018, https://www.namibian.com.na/179164/archive-read/Tribute-to-Mother-of-Education, accessed 3 August 2020.

Acker, Joan, 'Hierarchies, Jobs, Bodies: A Theory of Gendered Organizations,' *Gender and Society*, 4, 2, June 1990, pp. 139–58.

Adhikari, Mohamed, *Not White Enough, Not Black Enough: Racial Identity in the South African Coloured Community*, Athens, OH: Ohio University Press, 2005.

Adhikari, Mohamed, ed., *Burdened by Race: Coloured Identities in Southern Africa*, Cape Town: Juta and UCT, 2009, 2013.

Akawa, Martha, *The Gender Politics of the Namibian Liberation Struggle*, Basel: Basler Afrika Bibliographien, 2014.

Albertyn, Catherine, 'The Rivonia Trial: Domination, Resistance and Transformation, in Awol Allo, ed., *The Courtroom as a Space of Resistance: Reflections on the Legacy of the Rivonia Trial*, London and New York; Routledge, 2015, pp. 123–47.

Alexander Defense Committee, *Injustice in South Africa: The Case of Dr. Neville Alexander*, New York, c. 1965, Berta Green Langston Papers, Holt Labor Library Digital Collection, Cal State University Dominguez Hills, Archives and Special Collections.

Alexander, Neville, *Studien zum Stilwandel im dramatischen Werk Gerhart Hauptmann*, Stuttgart: J. B. Metzlersche, 1964.

Alexander, Neville, 'Jakob Marengo and Namibian History,' *Namibian Review Publications*, 1, June 1983, pp. 8–23.

Alexander, Neville, 'The Namibian War of Anticolonial Resistance, 1904–1907,' *Namibian Review Publications*, 1, June 1983, pp. 49–70.

Alexander, Neville, 'Aspects of Non-collaboration in the Western Cape 1943–1963,' *Social Dynamics*, 12, 1, 1986, pp. 1–14.

Alexander, Neville, 'Censorship as Intellectual Terrorism: White Spots in Black South African History, or the Worm Inside the Liberation Struggle,' Second C. Walter and Gerda B. Mortenson Distinguished Lecture, 7 October 1991, University of Illinois Library at Urbana-Champaign, 1991.

Alexander, Peter, 'History, Internationalism and Intellectuals: The Case of Harold Wolpe,' *Transformation*, 62, 2007, pp. 109–26.

All African Convention, 'Minutes of the All African Convention Conference,' Queenstown, December 1954.

All African Convention, 'Presidential Address to the All-African Convention Conference,' Edendale, 14–16 December, 1958, Lady Frere: SOYA.

Alleg, Henri, *La Question*, Paris: Les Editions de Minuit, 1958.

Alleg, Henri, ed., *La Guerre d'Algérie*, vol. 3, Paris: Messidor, 1981.

Allen, Vida and Tanja Kruger, *Malay Camp: A Forgotten Suburb*, Departments of Sport, Arts & Culture and Tourism, Environment & Conservation, Kimberley: McGregor Museum, 2006.

Allo, Awol, 'The Courtroom as a Space of Resistance: Reflections on the Legacy of the Rivonia Trial,' in Awol Allo, ed., *The Courtroom as a Space of Resistance: Reflections on the Legacy of the Rivonia Trial*, London and New York; Routledge, 2015, pp. 1–19.

Allo, Awol, ed., *The Courtroom as a Space of Resistance: Reflections on the Legacy of the Rivonia Trial*, London and New York; Routledge, 2015.

'An Extraordinary Life,' *Sowetan Live*, 2 November 2011, https://www.sowetanlive.co.za/news/2007-11-02-an-extraordinary-life, accessed 15 January 2024.

'Andimba Herman Toivo Ya Toivo,' https://www.sahistory.org.za/people/andimba-herman-toivo-ya-toivo, accessed 22 June 2021.

'Athlone – or Cape Flats, Cape Town,' *South African History Online*, 14 July 2011, https://www.sahistory.org.za/place/athlone-or-cape-flats-cape-town, accessed 15 July 2024.

'"Azikwelwa!" Leaflet on the bus boycott issued by the Alexandra Peoples Transport Action Committee,' n.d., in Thomas Karis and Gail M. Gerhart, eds, *From Protest to Challenge: A Documentary History of African Politics in South Africa, 1882–1990*, vol. 3, Stanford: Hoover Institution, 1977, pp. 394–6.

Bam, June, *Ausi Told Me: Why Cape Herstoriographies Matter*, Cape Town: Jacana, 2002.

Barnes, Teresa, 'The Curious Case of Prof. A. H. Murray in South African Political Trials, 1956–76,' paper presented to the 'Rivonia Trial 50 Years On' conference, University of Pretoria, 18–20 June 2013.

Barrell, Howard, *MK: The ANC's Armed Struggle. London: Penguin*, 1990.

Beale, M A, 'The Evolution of the Policy of University Apartheid,' *Collected Seminar Papers, Institute of Commonwealth Studies*, 1992, pp. 44, 82–98, https://sas-space.sas.ac.uk/4228/1/M_A_Beale_-_The_evolution_of_the_policy_of_university_apartheid.pdf, accessed 27 May 2020.

'Benjamin Magson Kies,' *South African History Online*, https://www.sahistory.org.za/people/benjamin-magson-kies, 2020, accessed 13 August 2024.

Beukes, Hans, *Long Road to Liberation: An Exiled Namibian Activist's Perspective*, CreateSpace Independent Publishing Platform, 2014.

Biko, Steve, 'White Racism and Black Consciousness,' Speech, Abe Bailey Institute, Cape Town, January 1971, in Thomas G. Karis and Gail M. Gerhart, eds, *From Protest to Challenge: A Documentary History of African Politics in South Africa, 1882–1990*, vol. 5, Bloomington and Indianapolis, Indiana University Press, 1997, pp. 466–74.

Bonner, Philip and Noor Nieftagodien, *Alexandra: A History*, Johannesburg: Wits University Press, 2008.

Brazzoduro, Andrea, 'Algeria, Antifascism, and Third Worldism: An Anticolonial Genealogy of the Western European New Left (Algeria, France, Italy,

1957–1975), *Journal of Imperial and Commonwealth History*, 48, 5, 2020, pp. 958–78.

'Brilliant city man accused of sabotage,' *Cape Times*, 28 September 1963.

Brock, Adrian C., 'Rediscovering the History of Psychology: Interview with Kurt Danziger,' *History of Psychology*, 9, 1, March 2006, pp. 1–16.

Broun, Kenneth S., *Saving Nelson Mandela: The Rivonia Trial and the Fate of South Africa*, Oxford: Oxford University Press, 2012.

Bunting, Brian, ed., *South African Communists Speak: Documents from the History of the South African Communist Party 1915–1980*, London: Inkululeko, 1981.

Busch, Brigitta, Lucijan Busch and Karen Press, eds, *Interviews with Neville Alexander: The Power of Languages against the Language of Power*, Scottsville: University of KwaZulu-Natal, 2014.

Carneson, Fred, 'Short History of Betrayal,' *Freedom*, New Series, 1, 5, 1 November 1948, pp. 1–2.

Carr, E. H., *What is History?* 2nd ed., London: Penguin, 1990 [1987].

Carter, Gwendolen M., *The Politics of Inequality: South Africa since 1948*, London: Thames and Hudson, 1958.

Chanock, Martin, *The Making of South African Legal Culture, 1902–1936: Fear, Favour and Prejudice*, Cambridge: Cambridge University Press, 2001.

Chivers, Chris, 'Nancy Gordon,' *Daily Maverick*, 20 November 2023, https://www.dailymaverick.co.za/article/2023-11-20-nancy-gordon-a-literary-life-filled-with-love-laughter-and-the-light-of-still-point, accessed 6 October 2024.

Christenson, Ronald, 'A Political Theory of Political Trials,' *Journal of Criminal Law & Criminology*, 74, 2, 1983, pp. 547–77.

Clingman, Stephen, *Bram Fischer: Afrikaner Revolutionary*, Cape Town: David Philip; Bellville: Mayibuye; Amherst: University of Massachusetts, 1998.

Communist Party of South Africa, *Report of Meeting of the Central Committee of the C.P.S.A., held at Johannesburg, on the 28th, 29th and 30th, December, 1931*, RGASPI 495.64.113, Comintern Archives, Russian State Archive of Socio-Political History, Moscow.

Cruywagen, Dennis, 'At last, Basil February is back in his fatherland,' *Vrye Weekblad*, 1 November 2024, https://www.vryeweekblad.com/en/opinions-and-debate/2024-11-01-at-last-basil-february-is-back-in-his-fatherland, accessed 3 November 2024.

Curry, Dawne Y., *Apartheid on a Black Isle: Removal and Resistance in Alexandra, South Africa*, New York: Palgrave Macmillan, 2012.

Daniels, Eddie, *There & Back: Robben Island, 1964–1979*, Cape Town: Mayibuye Books, 1998.

Danziger, Kurt, 'Confessions of a Marginal Psychologist,' in Leendert P. Mos, ed., *History of Psychology in Autobiography*, Heidelberg, London and New York: Springer, 2009, pp. 89–130.

Danziger, Kurt, 'How Solitary Confinement Affects Prisoners,' *Cape Times*, 12 November 1963.

Davenport, Rodney and Christopher Saunders, *South Africa: A Modern History*, 5th ed., Basingstoke: Macmillan; New York: St Martin's, 2000.

Davis, Lionel, 'Telling My Story: Memories of District Six and Robben Island,' in Mario Pissarra, ed., *Awakenings: The Art of Lionel Davis*, Cape Town: Africa South Art Initiative, 2017, pp. 29–38.

de Jong, Alex, 'The Revolutionary Life and Times of Michel Pablo,' *Jacobin*, 23 March 2024, https://jacobin.com/2024/03/michel-pablo-greece-algeria-revolution, accessed 4 July 2025.

Dick, Archie L., 'Learning from the Alexander Defence Committee Archives,' in Aziz Choudry and Salim Vally, eds, *Reflections on Knowledge, Learning and Social Movements: History's Schools*, Abingdon: Routledge, 2017, pp. 42–54.

Dobell, Lauren, 'Review of Dag Henrichsen, *A Glance at Our Africa*,' *Journal of Southern African Studies*, 24, 4, December 1998, pp. 833–5.

Dobell, Lauren, *Swapo's Struggle for Namibia, 1960–1991: War by Other Means*, Basel Namibia Studies Series, Basel: Basler Afrika Bibliographien, 1998.

'Dorothy Nomzansi Nyembe,' *South African History Online*, https://www.sahistory.org.za/people/dorothy-nomzansi-nyembe, accessed 3 February 2021.

Drew, Allison, *Discordant Comrades: Identities and Loyalties on the South African Left*, Aldershot: Ashgate, 2000.

Drew, Allison, *Between Empire and Revolution: A Life of Sidney Bunting, 1873–1936*, London: Pickering & Chatto, 2007.

Drew, Allison, 'Govan Mbeki's *The Peasants' Revolt*: A Critical Examination,' in Thembela Kepe and Lungisile Ntsebeza, eds, *Rural Resistance in South Africa: The Mpondo Revolts after Fifty Years*, Leiden: Brill; Cape Town: UCT Press, 2012, pp. 67–89.

Drew, Allison, *We are No Longer in France: Communists in Colonial Algeria*, Manchester: Manchester University Press, 2014.

Drew, Allison, 'Visions of Liberation: The Algerian War of Independence and its South African Reverberations,' *Review of African Political Economy*, 42, 143, March 2015, pp. 22–43.

Drew, Allison, 'Roseinnes Daniel Phahle,' August 2018, https://www.sahistory.org.za/archive/roseinnes-daniel-phahle-allison-drew.

Drew, Allison, 'Marcus Solomon,' 13 May 2019, *South African History Online*, https://www.sahistory.org.za/people/marcus-solomon, accessed 30 January 2021.

Drew, Allison, 'Elizabeth van der Heyden,' 21 June 2020, *South African History Online*, https://www.sahistory.org.za/archive/elizabeth-van-der-heyden-allison-drew.

Drew, Allison, 'A Gendered Approach to the Yu Chi Chan Club and National Liberation Front during South Africa's Transition to Armed Struggle,' *International Review of Social History*, 67, 2022, pp. 179–207.

Drew, Allison, ed., *South Africa's Radical Tradition: A Documentary History, vol. 2, 1943–1964*, Cape Town: Buchu, Mayibuye and University of Cape Town Press, 1997.

Dreyer, Ronald, *Namibia and Southern Africa: Regional Dynamics of Decolonization, 1945–1990*, 2nd ed., London and New York: Routledge, 2016 [1994].

Dugard, John, Introductory Note, Convention on the Suppression and Punishment of the Crime of Apartheid, New York, 30 November 1973, Audiovisual Library of International Law, https://legal.un.org/avl/ha/cspca/cspca.html, accessed 15 March 2025.

Dugard, John, *Human Rights and the South African Legal Order*, Princeton, NJ: Princeton University Press, 1978.

Dyzenhaus, David, *Judging the Judges, Judging Ourselves: Truth, Reconciliation and the Apartheid Legal Order*, Oxford: Hart, 1998.

Dyzenhaus, David, *Hard Cases in Wicked Legal Systems: Pathologies of Legality*, Oxford: Oxford University Press, 2010.

Ellis, Stephen, 'The Genesis of the ANC's Armed Struggle in South Africa 1948–1961,' *Journal of Southern African Studies*, 37, 4, December 2011, pp. 657–76.

Ellis, Stephen, *External Mission: The ANC in Exile*. Johannesburg: Jonathan Ball, 2012.

Emmett, Tony, 'Popular Resistance in Namibia, 1920–1925,' African Studies Seminar Paper 150, African Studies Institute, University of the Witwatersrand, June 1984.

Eriksen, Tore Linné, 'The Origins of a Special Relationship: Norway and Southern Africa, 1960–1975,' in Tore Linné Eriksen, ed., *Norway and National Liberation in Southern Africa*, Uppsala: Nordiska Afrikainstitutet, 2000, pp. 9–87.

Fanon, Frantz, *L'An V de la révolution algérienne*, Paris: François Maspero, 1959; trans, as *A Dying Colonialism*, New York: Grove, 1967.

Fataar, Alie, *The Disintegration of the U.M.S.A. Abroad*, July 1974, https://disa.ukzn.ac.za/rep19740700026044000.

February, Judith, 'Freedom fighter Basil February laid to rest in SA at last, more than five decades after his death on foreign soil,' *Daily Maverick*, 1 November 2024, https://www.dailymaverick.co.za/article/2024-11-01-freedom-fighter-basil-february-laid-to-rest-at-last-in-sa-more-than-five-decades-after-his-death-on-foreign-soil, accessed 3 November 2024.

Filatova, Irina and Apollon Davidson, *The Hidden Thread: Russia and South Africa in the Soviet Era*, Roggebaai: Jonathan Ball, 2013.

First, Ruth, *South West Africa*, Harmondsworth: Penguin, 1963.

First, Ruth, *117 Days: An Account of Confinement and Interrogation under the South African 90-Day Detention Law*, London, 2010 [1965].

'Franz J. T. Lee,' New York: Alexander Defense Committee, n.d.

'The Freedom Charter adopted at the Congress of the People at Kliptown, Johannesburg on 25 and 26 June 1955,' in Allison Drew, ed., *South Africa's Radical Tradition: A Documentary History, vol. 2, 1943–1964*, Cape Town: Buchu, Mayibuye and University of Cape Town Press, 1997, pp. 121–4.

Friedman, Gerald and Jeremy Gauntlett, *Bar, Bench & Bullshifters: Cape Tales, 1950–1990*, Cape Town: Siber Ink, 2013.

Friedman, Jeremy, *Ripe for Revolution: Building Socialism in the Third World*, Cambridge, MA: Harvard University Press, 2021.

Fullard, Madeleine, 'State Repression in the 1960s,' in South African Democracy Education Trust, *The Road to Democracy in South Africa, vol. 1 (1960–1970)*, Cape Town: Zebra Press, 2004, pp. 341–90.

Gillespie, Joan, *Algeria: Rebellion and Revolution*, London: Ernest Benn, 1960.

Giose, Vaughan, *The Yu Chi Chan Club* [DVD], Cape Town: Rainbow Circle Films, n.d.

Goldblatt, Israel, *Building Bridges: Namibian Nationalists Clemens Kapuuo, Hosea Kutako, Brendan Simbwaye, Samuel Witbooi*, ed. by Dag Henrichsen and Naomi Jacobson, Basel: Basler Afrika Bibliographien, 2010.

Goldstein, Abraham S., 'Conspiracy to Defraud the United States,' *Yale Law Journal*, 68, 1959, pp. 405–63.

Gool, Jane, 'The International Situation in 1961: An analysis presented at the Ninth National conference of the Non-European Unity Movement,' 3–5 January 1962, Edendale, Pietermaritzburg, 1962.

Gordimer, Nadine *The Late Bourgeois World*, London: Bloomsbury, 2013.

Gordon, Gerald, *Let the Day Perish*, London: Methuen, 1952.

Gordon, Gerald, *Four People*, Cape Town and Johannesburg: David Philip, 1986 [1964].

Guevara, Ernesto Che, *Guerrilla Warfare: A Method*, Peking: Foreign Languages Press, 1964.

Gunther, Magnus, 'The National Committee for Liberation (NCL)/African Resistance Movement (ARM), in South African Democracy Education Trust, *The Road to Democracy in South Africa, vol. 1 (1960–1970)*, Cape Town: Zebra Press, 2004, pp. 209–57.

Halisi, C. R. D., 'From Liberation to Citizenship: Identity and Innovation in Black South African Political Thought,' *Comparative Studies in Society and History*, 39, 1, January 1997, pp. 61–85.

Halisi, C. R. D., *Black Political Thought in the Making of South African Democracy*, Bloomington and Indianapolis: Indiana University, 1999.

Halpern, Jack, *South Africa's Hostages: Basutoland, Bechanualand and Swaziland*, Harmondsworth: Penguin, 1965.

Healy-Clancy, Meghan, 'The Family Politics of the Federation of South African Women: A History of Public Motherhood in Women's Antiracist Activism,' *Signs*, 42, 4, 2017, pp. 843–66.

Helliker, Kirk and Peter Vale, 'Marxisms Past and Present,' *Thesis Eleven*, 115, 1, 2013, pp. 25–42.

Henrichsen, Dag, 'Historiography,' in *A Glance at Our Africa*, compiled by Dag Henrichsen and introduced by Zedekia Ngavirue, Basel: Basler Afrika Bibliographien, 1997, pp. 13–44.

Henrichsen, Dag, compiler, *A Glance at Our Africa*, Basel: Basler Afrika Bibliographien, 1997.

Hill, Robert A. and Gregory A. Pirio, '"Africa for the Africans": the Garvey Movement in South Africa, 1920–1940,' in Shula Marks and Stanley Trapido, eds, *The Politics of Race, Class and Nationalism in Twentieth-Century South Africa*, Harlow: Longman, 1987, pp. 209–53.

Hirson, Baruch, 'A Question of Class: The Writings of Kenneth A. Jordaan,' *Searchlight South Africa*, 1, 2, February 1989, pp. 21–35.

Hirson, Baruch, *Revolutions in my Life*, Johannesburg: Witwatersrand University Press, 1995.

Hiwet, Addis, 'Analysing the Ethiopian Revolution,' *Review of African Political Economy*, 30, September 1984, pp. 32–47.

Hooper, Charles, *Brief Authority*, London: Collins, 1960.

Horn, Gerd-Rainer, 'The New Left as a Global Current since the Late 1950s, in Marcel van der Linden, ed., *The Cambridge History of Socialism*, Cambridge University Press, 2022, pp. 584–614.

Howell, David, *British Workers and the Independent Labour Party, 1886–1906*, Manchester: Manchester University Press, 1983.

Howell, David, *A Lost Left: Three Studies in Socialism and Nationalism*, Manchester: Manchester University Press, 1986.

'In Memoriam Gerald Gordon QC,' *South African Law Journal* 116, 1, 1999, pp. 141–7.

Jackson, Robert H. and Carl G. Rosberg, 'Why Africa's Weak States Persist: The Empirical and Juridical and Statehood,' in Marc Williams, ed., *International Relations in the Twentieth Century: A Reader*, London: Macmillan, 1989, pp. 98–116.

'James April,' in South African Democracy Education Trust, ed., *The Road to Democracy: South Africans Telling their Stories*, vol. 1, Houghton: Mutloatse Arts Heritage Trust; Hollywood, CA: Tsehai, January 2008, pp. 47–59.

'Jane Gool – A Tribute,' *African People's Democratic Union of Southern Africa*, 16 January 2020, http://www.apdusa.org.za/jane-gool-a-tribute, accessed 21 August 2025.

Jenson, Jane and George Ross, '1956: French Communists Turning a Corner,' *French Politics and Society*, 5, 1–2, February 1987, pp. 1–36.

Jervis, Robert, 'Hypotheses on Misperception,' *World Politics*, 20, 3, April 1968, pp. 454–79.

Jervis, Robert, *Perception and Misperception in International Politics*, Princeton, NJ: Princeton University, 1976, new edition, 2017.

Joffe, Joel, *The State vs. Nelson Mandela: The Trial that Changed South Africa*, Oxford: Oneworld, 2007.

Johns, Sheridan, 'Invisible Resurrection: The Recreation of a Communist Party in South Africa in the 1950's [*sic*],' *African Studies Quarterly*, 9, 4, Fall 2007, pp. 7–24.

Johnson, David, *Dreaming of Freedom in South Africa: Literature between Critique and Utopia*, Edinburgh: Edinburgh University Press, 2020.

Johnson, David and Henry Dee, eds, *'I See You': The Industrial and Commercial Workers' Union of Africa, 1919–1930*, Cape Town: HiPSA, 2022.

Jordaan, K. A., 'The T.A.R.C. Debacle,' *Discussion*, 1, 1 [June 1950?], pp. 8–15.

Jordaan, K. A., 'A Critique of Mr. W. P. van Schoor's "The Origin and Development of Segregation in South Africa,"' Discussion, 1, 3, June 1951, in Allison Drew, ed., *South Africa's Radical Tradition: A Documentary History, vol. 2, 1943–1964*, Cape Town: Buchu, Mayibuye and University of Cape Town Press, 1997, pp. 249–62.

Jordaan, K. A., 'The Land Question in South Africa,' *Points of View*, 1, 1, October 1959, in Allison Drew, ed., *South Africa's Radical Tradition: A Documentary History, vol. 2, 1943–1964*, Cape Town: Buchu, Mayibuye and University of Cape Town Press, 1997, pp. 325–39.

Jordan, Phyllis P., *A Life's Mosaic: The Autobiography of Phyllis Ntantala*, Claremont: David Philip and Bellville: Mayibuye, 1992.

Jordan, Z. Pallo, 'Denis Goldberg and the Modern Youth Society,' https://www.sahistory.org.za/sites/default/files/2019-05/5_pallo_jordan_a5_rev.pdf, accessed 22 June 2021.

Jung, Courtney, *Then I was Black: South African Political Identities in Transition*, New Haven, CT and London: Yale, 2000.

Kahn, Ellison, 'Honour for Gerald Gordon QC,' *South African Law Journal*, 113, 3, August 1996, pp. 520–5.

Kanter, Rosabeth Moss, 'The Impact of Hierarchical Structures on the Work Behavior of Women and Men,' *Social Problems*, 23, 4, April 1976, pp. 415–30.

Karis, Thomas G., 'The South African Treason Trial,' *Political Science Quarterly*, 76, 2, June 1961, pp. 217–40.

Karis, Thomas G. and Gail M. Gerhart, 'The Congress Movement,' in Thomas Karis and Gail M. Gerhart, eds, *From Protest to Challenge: A Documentary History of African Politics in South Africa, 1882–1964*, vol. 3, Stanford: Hoover Institution, 1977, pp. 3–98.

Karis, Thomas G. and Gail M. Gerhart, eds, *From Protest to Challenge: A Documentary History of African Politics in South Africa, 1882–1990*, vol. 5, Bloomington and Indianapolis, Indiana University, 1997.

Karpov, Victor P., 'The Soviet Concept of Peaceful Coexistence and its Implications for International Law,' *Law and Contemporary Problems*, Fall 1964, pp. 858–64.

Kayser, Robin and Mohamed Adhikari, 'Land and Liberty! The African People's Democratic Union of Southern Africa during the 1960s,' in South African Democracy Education Trust, ed., *The Road to Democracy in South Africa, vol. 1 (1960–1970)*, Cape Town: Zebra Press, 2004, pp. 319–39.

Kellner, Manuel, 'Fourth International Practical Internationalism: Solidarity in Germany with the Algerian Anti-colonial Liberation Struggle – Interview with Hans Peiffer,' *Europe Solidaire Sans Frontières*, 11 April 2018, http://www.europe-solidaire.org/spip.php?article46818, accessed 28 July 2022.

Kemp, Stephanie, 'My Life: The Making of an Afrikaner Revolutionary in the South African Liberation Struggle,' *South African History Online*, 2018.

'Kenneth Abrahams: A Doctor in the Struggle at Home and in Exile,' in Colin Leys and Susan Brown, eds, *Histories of Namibia: Living through the Liberation Struggle – Life Histories*, London: Merlin: 2005, pp. 139–57.

Kepe, Thembela, 'Memorials and Shifting Meanings of Rural Revolts in South Africa: The Mpondo Rural Revolts and Insurgent Scholarship,' *Review of African Political Economy*, 51, 180, 2024, pp. 274–89.

Kgosana, Philip Ata, *Lest We Forget: An Autobiography*, Johannesburg: Skotaville, 1988.

Kies, B. M., *The Contribution of the Non-European Peoples to World Civilization*, Cape Town: Teachers' League of South Africa, 1953.

Kirkaldy, Alan *Everyday Communists in South Africa's Liberation Struggle: The Lives of Ivan and Lesley Schermbrucker*, Cham: Palgrave Macmillan, 2022.

Klimke, Martin, *The Other Alliance: Student Protest in West Germany and the United States in the Global Sixties*, Princeton, NJ: Princeton University Press, 2010.

Kondlo, Kwandiwe, *In the Twilight of the Revolution: The Pan Africanist Congress of Azania (South Africa) 1959–1994*, Basel: Basler Afrika Bibliographien, 2009.

Kunene, Daniel P., 'Ideas under Arrest: Censorship in South Africa' [1981] *Ufahamu*, 38, 1, 2014, pp. 219–38.

Kuumba, M. Bahati, *Gender and Social Movements*, Walnut Creek, CA: AltaMira, 2001.

Landau, Paul S., 'Gendered Silences in Nelson Mandela's and Ruth First's Struggle Auto/biographies,' *African Studies*, 78, 2, 2019, pp. 290–306.

Landau, Paul S., 'The M-Plan: Mandela's Struggle to Reorient the African National Congress,' *Journal of Southern African Studies*, 45, 6, 2019, pp. 1073–1091.

Landau, Paul S., *Spear: Mandela and the Revolutionaries*, Athens, OH: Ohio University, 2022.

Le Roux, Michelle and Dennis Davis, *Lawfare: Judging Politics in South Africa*, Johannesburg and Cape Town: Jonathan Ball, 2019.

Lee, Christopher Joon-Hai, 'The Uses of the Comparative Imagination: South African History and World History in the Political Consciousness and Strategy of the South African Left, 1943–1959,' *Radical History Review*, 92, 2005, pp. 31–61.

Levinson, Deirdre, *Five Years: An Experience of South Africa*, London: Andre Deutsch, 1966.

Levinson, Ralph, 'In Memoriam: Deirdre Bergson (Levinson) (English, 1951) 1931–2023,' *St Annes College Ship Magazine*, 2023, p. 89.

Lewis, Gavin, *Between the Wire and the Wall: A History of South African 'Coloured' Politics*, Cape Town and Johannesburg: David Philip, 1987.

Lichtenstein, Alex, 'Rick Turner and South Africa's "Sixties",' *Working USA: Journal of Labor & Society*, 19, 4, January 2016, pp. 447–66.

Lipton, Merle, *Liberals, Marxists and Nationalists: Competing Interpretations of South African History*, New York and Basingstoke: Palgrave Macmillan, 2007.

Lissoni, Arianna and Maria Suriano, 'Married to the ANC: Tanzanian Women's Entanglement in South Africa's Liberation Struggle,' *Journal of Southern African Studies*, 40, 1, 2014, pp. 129–50.

Lister, Gwen, *Comrade Editor: On Life, Journalism and the Birth of Namibia*, Cape Town: Tafelberg, 2021.

Lodge, Tom, *Black Politics in South Africa since 1945*, London and New York: Longman, 1983.

Lodge, Tom, 'Charters from the Past: The African National Congress and its Historiographical Traditions,' *Radical History Review*, 46/7, 1990, pp. 161–88.

Lodge, Tom, *Sharpeville: An Apartheid Massacre and its Consequences*, New York: Oxford University Press, 2011.

Lodge, Tom, *Red Road to Freedom, A History of the South African Communist Party 1921–2021*, Johannesburg: Jacana, 2021.

Louw, Johann and Catherine O'Brien, 'The Psychological Effects of Solitary Confinement: An Early Instance of Psychology in South African Courts, *South African Journal of Psychology*, 37, 1, 2007, pp. 96–106.

Lundin, Emma Elinor, '"Now is the Time!" The Importance of International Spaces for Women's Activism within the ANC, 1960–1976,' *Journal of Southern African Studies*, 45, 2, 2019, pp. 323–40.

Mabeko-Tali, Jean-Michel, 'Dreaming Together, Fighting for Freedom Together: African Progressive Nationalism and the Ideology of Unity in Portugal's African Colonies in the 1950s and 1960s,' *Journal of Southern African Studies*, 46, 5, 2020, pp. 829–44.

Macmillan, Harold, 'The Wind of Change,' 3 February 1960, *Great Speeches of the 20th Century*, Guardian News and Media, 2007.

Magubane, Bernard, Philip Bonner, Jabulani Sithole, Peter Delius, Janet Cherry, Pat Gibbs and Thozama April, 'The Turn to Armed Struggle,' in South African Democracy Education Trust, *The Road to Democracy in South Africa, vol. 1 (1960–1970)*, Cape Town: Zebra Press, 2004, pp. 53–145.

Maloka, Eddy Tshidiso, *The South African Communist Party in Exile, 1963–1990*, Pretoria: Africa Institute of South Africa, 2001.

Mamdani, Mahmood, *Citizen and Subject: Contemporary Africa and the Legacy of Late Colonialism*, Princeton, NJ: Princeton University Press, 1996.

Mandela, Nelson, *Long Walk to Freedom: The Autobiography of Nelson Mandela*, London: Little, Brown, 1994.

Mangena, Isaac, 'The bus boycott that forced an apartheid U-turn,' *Mail & Guardian*, 1 November 2007, https://mg.co.za/article/2007-11-01-the-bus-boycott-that-forced-an-apartheid-uturn, accessed 4 November 2024.

Mao Tse-tung, *Mao Tse-tung on Guerrilla Warfare (Yu Chi Chan)* [1937], U.S. Marine Corps Reference Publication, Samuel B. Griffith, translator and introduction, [1961], 1989, https://archive.org/details/yuchichanenglish00unse/mode/2up?view=theater, accessed 28 January 2025.

Marcum, John A. *Education, Race, and Social Change in South Africa*, Berkeley, CA, Los Angeles, CA and London: University of California, 1982.

Marks, Shula and Stanley Trapido, 'The Politics of Race, Class and Nationalism,' in Shula Marks and Stanley Trapido, eds, *The Politics of Race, Class and Nationalism*, pp. 1–70.

Marks, Shula and Stanley Trapido, eds, *The Politics of Race, Class and Nationalism in Twentieth-Century South Africa*, Harlow: Longman, 1987.

Martz, John D., 'Doctrine and Dilemmas of the Latin American "New Left",' *World Politics*, 22, 2, January 1970, pp. 171–96.

Mathews, A. S. and R. C. Albino, 'The Permanence of the Temporary: An Examination of the 90- and 180-day Detention Laws,' *South African Law Journal*, 83, 1, February 1966, pp. 16–43.

Matthews, James, 'Azikwelwa,' in Richard Rive, ed., *Quartet: New Voices from South Africa*, New York: Crown, 1963, pp. 35–44.

Mbatha, N. Z. 'Narratives of Women Detained in the Kroonstad Prison during the Apartheid Era: A Socio-Political Exploration, 1960–1990,' *Journal for Contemporary History*, 43, 1, 2018, pp. 91–110.

Mbeki, Govan, South Africa: *The Peasants' Revolt*, Harmondsworth: Penguin, 1964.

Mda, Zakes, *The Madonna of Excelsior*, Oxford: Oxford University Press, 2002.

Meierhenrich, Jens, *The Legacies of Law: Long-run Consequences of Legal Development in South Africa, 1652–2000*, Cambridge: Cambridge University Press, 2008.

Meierhenrich, Jens and Catherine M. Cole, 'In the Theater of the Rule of Law: Performing the Rivonia Trial in South Africa, 1963–1964,' in Jens Meierhenrich and Devin O. Pendas, eds, *Political Trials in Theory and History*, Cambridge: Cambridge University Press, 2016, pp. 229–62.

Meierhenrich, Jens and Devin O. Pendas, '"The Justice of My Cause is Clear, But There's Politics to Fear": Political Trials in Theory and History,' in Jens

Meierhenrich and Devin O. Pendas, eds, *Political Trials in Theory and History*, Cambridge: Cambridge University Press, 2016, pp. 1–64.

Meiring, Jean, '"Do You Remember Still?" – Some Unknown Juvenilia of Vincent Swart,' *Litnet*, 13 April 2022, https://www.litnet.co.za/do-you-remember-still-some-unknown-juvenilia-of-vincent-swart, accessed 27 December 2022.

Mendlow, Gabriel, 'Why is it Wrong to Punish Thought?' *Yale Law Journal*, 127, 8, 2017–18, pp. 2345–86.

Mendlow, Gabriel, 'Thoughts, Crimes, and Thought Crimes,' *Michigan Law Review*, 118, 2020, pp. 841–76.

Menges, Werner, 'UN petitioners retrace long road to freedom,' *The Namibian*, 24 September 2010, http://www.namibian.com.na/news/full-story/archive/2010/september/article/un-petitioners-retrace-long-road-to-freedom, accessed 19 July 2024.

Mercer, Dennis, *Interviews in Depth – Namibia (SWAPO): Andreas Shipanga*, Richmond, BC: LSM, 1973.

Merrett, Christopher, *A Culture of Censorship: Secrecy and Intellectual Repression in South Africa*, Cape Town: David Philip; Pietermaritzburg: University of Natal; Macon, GA: Mercer University, 1994.

Michels, Robert, *Political Parties: A Sociological Study of the Emergence of Leadership, the Psychology of Power and the Oligarchic Tendencies of Organisation*, trans. Eden and Cedar Paul, 1915, New York: The Free Press, 1962 [in German, 1911].

Middleton, Jean, *Convictions: A Woman Political Prisoner Remembers*, Randburg: Ravan, 1998.

Mokonyane, Dan, *Lessons of Azikwelwa*, 2nd ed., 1994 [1979].

Monteiro, Marcio Lauria, 'The International Trotskyist Movement and the Postwar Revolutions: An Analysis of its Theoretical and Programmatic (Re)interpretations (1944–1963),' *Critique*, 44, 4, 2016, pp. 329–49.

Moorsom, Richard, 'Underdevelopment, Contract Labour and Worker Consciousness in Namibia, 1915–72,' *Journal of Southern African Studies*, 4, 1, October 1977, pp. 52–87.

Morrow, Seán, *The Bams of Grasslands Farm: A Family History*, Auckland Park: Staging Post, 2024.

Mphahlele, Ezekiel, 'Censorship in South Africa,' in Ezekiel Mphahlele, *Voices in the Whirlwind and Other Essays*, London: Palgrave Macmillan, 1972, pp. 199–215.

Mqotsi, L., 'Bantustans, Colouredstans & Indianstans,' Speech delivered at the African People's Democratic Union of South [*sic*] Africa Conference, n.d. [1962], https://disa.ukzn.ac.za/spe19620400026044000.

Mqotsi, L. 'After Soweto: Another Response,' *Review of African Political Economy*, 6, 14, 1979, pp. 97–106.

Müller, Alexander, *'The Inevitable Pipeline into Exile': Botswana's Role in the Namibian Liberation Struggle*, Basel: Basler Afrika Bibliographien, 2012.

Musuva [June Bam], *Peeping through the Reeds: A Story about Living in Apartheid South Africa*, Milton Keynes: AuthorHouse, 2010.

Naidoo, Shanthini, *Women Surviving Apartheid's Prisons*, Washington, DC: Just World Books, 2021.

Nash, Andrew, 'The Moment of Western Marxism in South Africa,' *Comparative Studies of South Asia, Africa and the Middle East*, 19, 1, 1999, pp. 66–82.

Nash, Andrew, 'Clearing a Path to Academia: A Tribute to Lungisile Ntsebeza,' *Review of African Political Economy*, 51, 180, 2024, pp. 191–200.

Ndlovu, Sifiso Mxolisi, 'African Leaders and the National Liberation Struggle in Namibia,' in South African Democracy Education Trust, *The Road to Democracy in South Africa*, vol. 5, part 2, *African Solidarity*, UNISA Press, 2014, pp. 664–727.

Non-European Unity Movement, 'The Ten-Point Programme' [1943], in Allison Drew, ed., *South Africa's Radical Tradition: A Documentary History, vol. 2, 1943–1964*, Cape Town: Buchu, Mayibuye and University of Cape Town Press, 1997, pp. 62–3.

Non-European Unity Movement, *Proceedings of 5th Unity Conference*, 20–21 December, 1946, City Hall, Kimberley.

Non-European Unity Movement, *Ninth National Conference*, Edendale, Maritzburg, 3–5 January 1962.

Ngavirue, Zedekia, 'Introduction,' in *A Glance at Our Africa*, compiled by Dag Henrichsen and introduced by Zedekia Ngavirue, Basel: Basler Afrika Bibliographien, 1997, pp. 7–12.

Ngcukaitobi, Tembeka, 'Legality of Evil: Robert Sobukwe and the Apartheid Legal Order,' *Mail & Guardian*, 4 March 2023. https://mg.co.za/opinion/2023-03-04-legality-of-evil-robert-sobukwe-and-the-apartheid-legal-order, accessed 26 March 2025.

Nghidinwa, Marion Mboono, *Women Journalists in Namibia's Liberation Struggle, 1985–1990*, Basel: Basler Afrika Bibliographien, 2008.

National Liberation Front, 'When, Where, Why was the N.L.F. Formed?' April 1962 [*sic*], UCTMA BC1253.

No Sizwe [Neville Alexander], *One Azania, One Nation: The National Question in South Africa*, London: Zed, 1979.

Ntsebeza, Dumisa, 'They Called Me Dennis – A Journey from Messenger to Justice,' Address given to the Notre Dame Law School, 30 January 2023, https://www.youtube.com/watch?v=iAEbh50CPjg, accessed 22 January 2025.

O'Malley, Padraig, *The Heart of Hope: South Africa's Transition from Apartheid to Democracy*, https://omalley.nelsonmandela.org accessed 1 August 2024.

O'Meara, Dan, *Forty Lost Years: The Apartheid State and the Politics of the National Party, 1948–1994*, Randburg: Ravan; Athens, OH: Ohio University, 1996.

'One of two remaining Maoist Swanu China trained cadres laid to rest,' *Windhoek Observer*, 24 January 2022, https://www.observer24.com.na/one-of-two-remaining-maoist-swanu-china-trained-cadres-laid-to-rest, accessed 24 October 2022.

'Operation Mayibuye,' Document found by the police at Rivonia, 11 July 1963, in Thomas Karis and Gail M. Gerhart, eds, *From Protest to Challenge: A Documentary History of African Politics in South Africa, 1882–1964*, vol. 3, Stanford: Hoover Institution, 1977, pp. 760–68.

Orwell, George, *1984*, ed., intro and notes by John Bowen, Oxford: Oxford University Press, 2021 [1949].

Oshinsky, David M., *A Conspiracy so Immense: The World of Joe McCarthy*, Oxford: Oxford University Press, 2005 [1983].

'Otto Schimming Dies,' *The Namibian*, 8 December 2005, https://www.namibian.com.na/11489/archive-read/Otto-Schimming-dies, accessed 22 June 2021.

Pedersen, Susan, *The Guardians: The League of Nations and the Crisis of Empire*, Oxford: Oxford University Press, 2015.

Phahle, Roseinnes, 'The 1957 Alexandra Bus Boycott and its Unsung Heroes,' *South African History Online*, June 2019, https://www.sahistory.org.za/archive/1957-alexandra-bus-boycott-and-its-unsung-heroes-roseinnes-phahle-june-2019, accessed 14 November 2022.

Phahle, Roseinnes, 'Reminiscences of the Arrest of Fikile Bam & Marcus Solomon in 1963,' *South African History Online*, August 2019, https://www.sahistory.org.za/archive/reminiscences-arrest-fikile-bam-marcus-solomon-1963-roseinnes-phahle-august-2019, accessed 15 November 2022.

Pissarra, Mario, ed., *Awakenings: The Art of Lionel Davis*, Cape Town: Africa South Art Initiative, 2017.

Pogrund, Benjamin, *How Can Man Die Better ... Sobukwe and Apartheid*, London: Peter Halban, 1990.

Posel, Deborah, *The Making of Apartheid, 1948–1961: Conflict and Compromise*, Oxford: Clarendon, 1991.

'Profile of Andreas Shipanga,' *Windhoek Advertiser*, 1 September 1978, p. 8, Andreas Shipanga Papers, National Archives of Namibia, Windhoek, AACR LS 212.

'Putuse Dwyili-Appolus, the Benevolent Meekulu of the Struggle (1930–1986),' 13 March, 2015, https://neweralive.na/posts/putuse-dwyili-appolus-benevolent-meekulu-struggle-1930-1986, accessed 14 August 2021.

Rayner, Mary, 'Law, Politics, and Treason in South Africa,' *Human Rights Quarterly*, 8, 3, August 1986, pp. 471–86.

Reitz, Deneys, *Commando: A Boer Journal of the Boer War*, CreateSpace Independent Publishing Platform, 2016 [1930].

Renaud, Terence, *New Lefts: The Making of a Radical Tradition*, Princeton, NJ: Princeton University Press, 2021.

'Report of the First National Conference of Women held in the Trades Hall, Johannesburg, South Africa, 17 April 1954, in Allison Drew, ed., *South Africa's Radical Tradition*, vol. 2, 1943–1964, Cape Town: Buchu, Mayibuye and University of Cape Town Press, 1997, pp. 115–21.

Rive, Richard, *Emergency*, Cape Town and Johannesburg, David Philip, 1988 [1964].

Rive, Richard, *Buckingham Palace, District Six*, Berlin: Cornelsen Verlag, 2006 [1986].

Robertson, Janet, *Liberalism in South Africa, 1948–1963*, Oxford: Clarendon, 1971.

Roux, Edward, *Time Longer than Rope: The Black Man's Struggle for Freedom in South Africa*, Madison, WI and London: University of Wisconsin, 1978 [1964].

Sachs, Albie, *Stephanie on Trial*, London: Harvill, 1968.

Sanders, Z. [Zena Susser], 'Aspects of the Rural Problem in South Africa,' lecture delivered to the Johannesburg Discussion Club on 1 December 1952, *Viewpoints and Perspectives*, 1, 1, 21 February 1953, in Allison Drew, ed., *South Africa's*

Radical Tradition: A Documentary History, vol. 2, 1943–1964, Cape Town: Buchu, Mayibuye and University of Cape Town Press, 1997, pp. 316–21.

Sandwith, Corinne, *World of Letters: Reading Communities and Cultural Debates in Early Apartheid South Africa*, Pietermaritzburg: University of KwaZulu-Natal, 2014.

Sasman, Catherine, 'Otto Schimming: A self-made man,' *New Era*, 22 October 2012.

Saul, John S. and Stephen Gelb, *The Crisis in South Africa*, New York and London: Monthly Review Press, 1981.

Saunders, Christopher, 'The Creation of Ndabeni,' in Christopher Saunders, ed., *Studies in the History of Cape Town*, vol. 1, Cape Town: History Department, UCT, 1979, pp. 132–66.

Saunders, Christopher, 'From Ndabeni to Langa,' in Christopher Saunders, ed., *Studies in the History of Cape Town*, vol. 1, Cape Town: History Department, UCT, 1979, pp. 167–204.

Saunders, Chris, 'Some Roots of Anti-colonial Writing about Namibia,' *Journal of Namibia Studies*, 3, 2008, pp. 83–93.

Saunders, Chris, 'SWAPO, Namibia's Liberation Struggle and the Organisation of African Unity's Liberation Committee,' *South African Historical Journal*, 70, 1, 2018, pp. 152–167.

Scanlon, Helen, *Representation & Reality: Portraits of Women's Lives in the Western Cape, 1948–1976,* Pretoria: Human Sciences Research Council, 2007.

Scott, Joan Wallach, 'French Feminists and the Rights of "Man": Olympe de Gouges's Declarations,' *History Workshop*, 28, Autumn 1989, pp. 1–21.

Sellström, Tor, ed., *Sweden and National Liberation in Southern Africa*, vol. 1, Uppsala: Nordiska Afrikainstitutet, 1999.

Sellström, Tor, ed., *Liberation in Southern Africa – Regional and Swedish Voices: Interviews from Angola, Mozambique, Namibia, South Africa, Zimbabwe, the Frontline and Sweden*, 2nd. ed., Uppsala: Nordiska Afrikainstitutet, 2002.

Serfontein, J. H. P., *Namibia?* London: Rex Collings, 1976.

Shell, Sandra Rowoldt, 'Bisho Jara,' 27 October 2015, updated 6 November 2020, *South African History Online*, https://www.sahistory.org.za/people/bisho-jarsa, accessed 6 May 2025.

Shipanga, Andreas with Sue Armstrong, *In Search of Freedom: The Andreas Shipanga Story as told to Sue Armstrong*, Gibraltar: Ashanti, 1989.

Sikakane, Joyce, *A Window on Soweto*, London: International Defence and Aid, June 1977.

Silvester, Jeremy, 'Forging the Fifth Province,' *Journal of Southern African Studies*, 41, 3, 2015, pp. 505–18.

Simpson, Thula, 'Mandela's Army: Urban revolt in South Africa, 1960–1964,' *Journal of Southern African Studies*, 45, 6, 2019, pp. 1093–1110.

Simpson, Thula, *History of South Africa: From 1902 to the Present*, Cape Town: Penguin Random House, 2021.

Slobodian, Quinn, *Foreign Front: Third World Politics in Sixties West Germany*, Durham, NC and London: Duke University Press, 2012.

Slovo, Joe, *Slovo: The Unfinished Autobiography*, Randburg: Ravan, 1995–1996.

Smith, Janet, and Beauregard Tromp, *Hani: A Life Too Short*, Johannesburg and Cape Town: Jonathan Ball, 2009.

Smith, Tina, 'Remembering District Six: The Restorative Art of Lionel Davis,' in Mario Pissarra, ed., *Awakenings: The Art of Lionel Davis*, Cape Town: Africa South Art Initiative, 2017, pp. 41–54.

Snyman, C. R., 'The History and Rationale of Criminal Conspiracy,' *Comparative and International Law Journal of Southern Africa*, 17, 1, January 1984, pp. 65–77.

Soudien, Crain, *The Cape Radicals: Intellectual and Political Thought of the New Era Fellowship, 1930s-1960s*, Johannesburg: Wits University Press, 2019.

Soudien, Crain, 'A Re-reading of Ben Kies's "The Contribution of the Non European Peoples to World Civilisation",' *Social Dynamics*, 48, 2, 2022, pp. 191–206.

South African Communist Party, 'A Landmark in South Africa's History: The Sixth National Conference of the South African Communist Party,' International Bulletin, no. 4, December 1962, in Allison Drew, ed., *South Africa's Radical Tradition: A Documentary History, vol. 2, 1943–1964*, Cape Town: Buchu, Mayibuye and University of Cape Town Press, 1997, pp. 358–64.

South African Communist Party, *The Road to South African Freedom: Programme of the South African Communist Party*, London: Inkululeko Publications, 1962.

South African Democracy Education Trust, *The Road to Democracy in South Africa*, vol. *1 (1960–1970)*, Cape Town: Zebra Press, 2004.

South African Democracy Education Trust, ed., *The Road to Democracy: South Africans Telling their Stories*, vol. 1, Houghton: Mutloatse Arts Heritage Trust; Hollywood, CA: Tsehai, January 2008.

South African Democracy Education Trust, *The Road to Democracy in South Africa*, vol. 5, part 2, *African Solidarity*, UNISA Press, 2014.

South African Union for Progressive Judaism, SAUPJ Support, 'A Pioneering School that Survived Against the Odds,' 2 April 2013, https://saupj.org.za/a-pioneering-school-that-survived-against-the-odds, accessed 23 January 2025.

Southall, Roger, *Liberation Movements in Power: Party & State in Southern Africa*, Woodbridge: James Currey; Pietermaritzburg: University of KwaZulu-Natal, 2013.

Society of Young Africa National Executive Committee, 31 May 1959, 'The Maritzburg Conferences and the Tasks of the Immediate Future,' *The Soyan*, Durban, December 1959.

Steinberg, Jonny, *Winnie and Nelson: Portrait of a Marriage*, London: William Collins, 2023.

Stevens, Simon, 'Violence, Political Strategy and the Turn to Guerrilla Warfare by the Congress Movement in South Africa,' *Journal of Southern African Studies*, 47, 6, 2021, pp. 1011–28.

Stites, Richard, *The Women's Liberation Movement in Russia: Feminism, Nihilism, and Bolshevism, 1860–1930*, Princeton, NJ: Princeton University Press, 1978.

SWAPO of Namibia, *To Be Born a Nation: The Liberation Struggle for Namibia*, Luanda: SWAPO of Namibia; London: Zed, 1981.

Swart, Mia, 'The Road to Freedom Passes through Gaol: The Treason Trial and Rivonia Trial as Political Trials,' in Awol Allo, ed., *The Courtroom as a Space of Resistance: Reflections on the Legacy of the Rivonia Trial*, London and New York; Routledge, 2015, pp. 149–70.

Tabata, I. B., *The All African Convention: The Awakening of a People*, Johannesburg: People's Press, 1950.

Tabata, I. B., *The Boycott as a Weapon of Struggle*, June 1952, https://www.sahistory.org.za/sites/default/files/The%20Boycott.pdf, accessed 16 August 2021.

Tabata, I. B., *University Apartheid in South Africa*, April 1957.

Tabata, I. B., *Education for Barbarism*, Cumberwood: Apdusa Views, 1979 [September 1958].

Tabata, I. B., *The Pan-African [*sic*] Congress Venture in Retrospect*, NEUM, September 1960.

Tabata, I. B., 'The National Situation,' Speech to the Non-European Unity Movement Conference, January 1962.

Tabata, I. B., 'Presidential Address', APDUSA, Cape Town, April 1962.

Thomas, Cornelius, 'Disaffection, Identity, Black Consciousness and a New Rector: An Exploratory Take on Student Activism at the University of the Western Cape 1966–1976,' *South African Historical Journal*, 54, 2005, pp. 72–90.

Thomas, Cornelius, 'Finding the Durban Moment in Cape Town: New Directions in Student Activism in the Western Cape, 1972–1976,' n.d., https://www.sahistory.org.za/sites/default/files/Paper_Cornelius_Thomas.pdf, accessed 31 August 2022.

Thompson, E. P., Preface from *The Making of the English Working Class*, August 1962, in Dorothy Thompson, ed., *The Essential E. P. Thompson*, New York: New Press, 2001, pp. 3–8.

Thompson, William E., 'Dennis Brutus: An Interview,' *Ufahamu*, 12, 2, 1983, pp. 69–77, https://escholarship.org/uc/item/6tc554rb, accessed 1 April 2024.

Tötemeyer, Gerhard, *South West Africa/Namibia: Facts, Attitudes, Assessment and Prospects*, Randburg: Fokus Suid, 1977.

Travel and Holiday: A comprehensive guide to the Cape Province of the Union of South Africa for the tourist and holiday-maker, 1954.

Trotsky, Leon, 'On the United Front,' 2 March 1922, in *The First Five Years of the Communist International*, vol. 2, https://www.marxists.org/archive/trotsky/1924/ffyci-2/08.htm, accessed 9 June 2025.

Troup, Freda, *In Face of Fear: Michael Scott's Challenge to South Africa*, London: Faber & Faber, 1950.

Truth and Reconciliation Commission Final Report, https://sabctrc.saha.org.za/reports/volume3/chapter5/subsection8.htm

Tyner, James A., 'Self and Space, Resistance and Discipline: A Foucauldian Reading of George Orwell's *1984*,' *Social & Cultural Geography*, 5, 1, March 2004, pp. 129–49.

United Nations, *Fascist Terror in South Africa: Report of the United Nations Special Committee on Apartheid*, March 23, 1964, pp. 62–97, https://www.sahistory.org.za/sites/default/files/archive-files4/Acn1764.0001.9976.000.017.Apr1964.8.pdf, accessed 28 April 2023.

van der Linden, Marcel, 'The Prehistory of Post-Scarcity Anarchism: Josef Weber

and the Movement for a Democracy of Content (1947–1964),' *Anarchist Studies*, 9, 2001, pp. 127–46.
van Driel, Nicole, 'The life and death of Basil February,' *Politicsweb*, 28 October 2024, https://www.politicsweb.co.za/opinion/basil-february-a-hero-to-friend-and-foe, accessed 3 November 2024.
van Zyl Smit, Dirk and Norma-May Isakow, 'Assessors and Criminal Justice, *South African Journal on Human Rights*, 1, 3, November 1985, pp. 218–35.
Vigne, Randolph, *Liberals against Apartheid: A History of the Liberal Party of South Africa, 1953–68*, Basingstoke: Macmillan, 1997.
Vinson, Robert Trent, '"Sea Kaffirs": "American Negroes" and the Gospel of Garveyism in Early Twentieth-Century Cape Town,' *Journal of African History*, 47, 2, 2006, pp. 281–303.
Walker, Cherryl, *Women and Resistance in South Africa* 2nd ed., Cape Town: New Africa Books, 1991 [1982].
Wallace, Marion with John Kinahan, *A History of Namibia: From the Beginning to 1990*, New York: Columbia, 2011.
Ward, Max, *Thought Crime: Ideology and State Power in Interwar Japan*, Durham, NC: Duke University Press, 2019.
Ward, Max, 'Thinking Like a State: Policing Dangerous Thought in Imperial Japan, 1900–1945,' *positions*, 30, 1, 2022, pp. 35–60.
Western, John, *Outcast Cape Town*, Cape Town, Pretoria and Johannesburg: Human & Rousseau, 1981.
Whittaker, Shaun, 'Namibian Moments in the Life of a Socialist Educator,' *Education as Change*, 17, 2, 2013, pp. 261–73.
Wieder, Alan, *Teacher and Comrade: Richard Dudley and the Fight for Democracy in South Africa*, Albany, NY: SUNY Press, 2008.
Wieder, Alan, *Ruth First and Joe Slovo in the War against Apartheid*, New York: Monthly Review Press, 2013.
Wilson, Monica and Archie Mafeje, *Langa: A Study of Social Groups in an African Township*, Cape Town and London: Oxford University Press, 1963.
Wood, Ellen Meiksins, 'A Chronology of the New Left and its Successors, or: Who's Old-Fashioned Now?' *Socialist Register*, 31, 1995, pp. 22–49.
Wulfsohn, Gisèle, 'Malibongwe: Let us Praise the Women,' Apartheid Museum, 2006, https://www.apartheidmuseum.org/uploads/files/Malibongwe_-Let-us-praise-the-women.pdf, accessed 10 December 2024.
Yu Chi Chan Club [Neville Alexander], *Pamphlet no. II: The Conquest of Power in South Africa* [1962].
Yu Chi Chan Club [Kenneth Abrahams], *Pamphlet no. III: Technical and Organisational Aspects of the Yu Chi Chan Club* [1962].
Yu Chi Chan Club [Elizabeth van der Heyden], *Pamphlet no. IV: Secret Communications* [1962].
Zeleke, Elleni Centime, *Ethiopia in Theory: Revolution and Knowledge Production, 1964–2016*, Leiden: Brill; Chicago, IL: Haymarket, 2020.
Zewde, Bahru, *The Quest for Socialist Utopia: The Ethiopian Student Movement c. 1960–1974*, Addis Ababa: Addis Ababa University Press; Woodbridge: James Currey, 2017.

Unpublished papers, theses and dissertations

Akoshile, Aisha, 'An Age-Old Tug of War: Understanding the intergenerational conflicts of Southern African nationalist groups,' BA, History, Columbia, 2021.

[Arendse, Michael?], 'Dulcie September Biography,' n.d.

Banda, Simon, 'My Senior Certificate Years (Standards 8, 9 and 10) of the Early Sixties,' n.d.

Dollie, Na-iem, 'Dialogical Narratives: Reading Neville Alexander's writings,' DLitt et Phil, History, University of South Africa, 2015.

Drew, Allison 'Social Mobilization and Racial Capitalism in South Africa, 1928–1960,' PhD, University of California, Los Angeles, 1991.

Drew, Allison, 'Neville Alexander and South Africa's New Left, c. 1957–1964,' *Rethinking Africa Series Occasional Paper*, no. 6, UCT Centre for African Studies, February 2023.

du Toit, Andries, 'The National Committee for Liberation ("ARM"), 1960–1964: Sabotage and the question of the ideological subject,' MA, University of Cape Town, 1991.

Gamedze, Asher, 'Ensemble Study and Struggle: A history of the Yu Chi Chan Club and the National Liberation Front,' PhD, University of the Witwatersrand, 2024.

Hogan, Michael R. '"Remov[e] Us From the Bondage of South Africa": Transnational resistance strategies and subnational concessions in Namibia's Police Zone, 1919–1962,' PhD, West Virginia University, 2021.

Kondlo, Kwandiwe Merriman, 'In the Twilight of the Azanian Revolution: The exile history of the Pan Africanist Congress of Azania South Africa, 1960–1990,' DPhil, Rand Afrikaans University, 2004.

Lissoni, Arianna, 'The South African Liberation Movements in Exile, c.1945–1970,' PhD, SOAS, University of London, 2008.

Lodge, Tom, 'The Paarl Insurrection,' Paper presented to the Wits University African Studies Seminar, October 1979.

Lodge, Tom, 'Insurrectionism in South Africa: The Pan-Africanist Congress and the Poqo movement, 1959–1965,' PhD, University of York, 1984.

Macqueen, Ian Martin, 'Re-imagining South Africa: Black Consciousness, radical Christianity and the New Left, 1967–1977,' PhD, University of Sussex, 2011.

Ngavirue, Zedekia, 'Political Parties and Interest Groups in South West Africa: A study of a plural society,' DPhil, University of Oxford, 1972.

Nyoka, Bongani, 'Archie Mafeje: An intellectual biography,' DLitt et Phil, University of South Africa, 2017.

Rassool, Ciraj Shahid, 'The Individual, Auto/biography and History in South Africa,' PhD, University of the Western Cape, 2004.

Samson, Marika Giles, 'Rethinking Judicial Responsibility: The case of judicial persecution,' DCL, McGill University, 2019.

Solomons, Curtley, 'Reading the Voices of a Fractured Coloured Elite: Coloured intellectuals and newspapers in the Cape, c. 1959–1966,' MA, University of Stellenbosch, 2022.

Strauss, H. 'South Africa 1960–66: Underground African politics,' Collected Seminar Papers, London: Institute of Commonwealth Studies, 1973.

van Driel, Nicole, 'The Journey to Wankie: A biography of James April,' BA Hons, University of the Western Cape, 1990.
van Laun, Bianca Paigè, 'In the Shadows of the Archive: Investigating the Paarl march of November 22nd 1962,' MA, University of the Western Cape, 2012.
Wallace-Wolf, Jordan James, 'Mental Privacy,' PhD, University of California, Los Angeles, 2020.
Williams, Clifford, 'Dorothy Williams (née Adams) 1928–2011,' 2011.
Woeber, Catherine Anne, '"A Good Education Sets up a Divine Discontent": The contribution of St Peter's School to black South African autobiography,' DPhil, University of the Witwatersrand, 2000.

INDEX

Page numbers in *italic* type refer to illustrations and their captions

Printed and bound by CPI Group (UK) Ltd, Croydon, CR0 4YY

13/09/2026

14961005-0003